KEITH A. SELAND

The Humaniverse Guide ® - We Are Them, They Are Us: Our Ancestors, Us and ET

*Keith A. Seland*

First published by THG Authors Inc. 2025

Copyright © 2025 by Keith A. Seland

All rights reserved. No part of this publication may be reproduced, stored or transmitted in any form or by any means, electronic, mechanical, photocopying, recording, scanning, or otherwise without written permission from the publisher. It is illegal to copy this book, post it to a website, or distribute it by any other means without permission.

Keith A. Seland asserts the moral right to be identified as the author of this work.

First edition

ISBN: 979-8-9938187-1-9

This book was professionally typeset on Reedsy.
Find out more at reedsy.com

*This work is dedicated
to those curious or interested,
and who wish to discover who they are,
what may await them,
and to navigate toward better lives for all.*

To learn about our ancestors
is to learn about ourselves.

Keith A. Seland

# Contents

*Preface*   ii
*Acknowledgments*   iii
INTRODUCTION: A STORY   1
Act I: AWARENESS!   25
THE MIND   47
Act II: REVOLUTIONS   72
SYMBOLISM   99
RITUAL   129
ARCHAEOASTRONOMY   159
Act III: UNIVERSALS   206
EXTRATERRESTRIAL   226
*About the Author*   261

# Preface

Step into the mysterious world of Nam and Muh, where ancient secrets of 'us' are uncovered and unite with modern knowledge to demystify what it means to be 'you'. This deep survey will enlighten and raise your consciousness to an inquiry about "where you came from, where you are, and where you could be going". Nam and Muh demystify this metaphysical and spiritual journey by showing what it was like for them growing up, growing old, and passing on their wisdom to the next generation of homo sapien sapiens, and serves as a deep survey of how 'you' became 'you'.

The Humaniverse Guide ® - We Are Them, They Are Us: Our Ancestors, Us, and ET, introduce Nam and Muh as captains of your ship, known as Biosphere I (the Earth). Nam and Muh will navigate a constructive route for finding our place in this world, and usher us into a discretionary fate that will include unexpected cooperative relationships with other life forms both on Earth and on other worlds.

Meeting up with these new cooperative relationships will be a most fantastic learning experience our species will ever undertake. Because Biosphere I is yours, our human nature and human condition have a vested interest in being and becoming curious, making inquiries, observing, discovering, and concluding about this Great Chain of Life we know, and, through our new discoveries, will come to know. The Humaniverse Guide- We Are Them, They Are Us: Our Ancestors, Us and ET offers you an opportunity to take a first look at what the future holds for us.

# Acknowledgments

I hold much appreciation for our ancestors, as represented in this discussion by Nam and Mew as protagonists, engaging in multiple roles to enlighten both you, the audience and myself. Their work must be acknowledged and applauded by all of us, as members of the human species. They made us what we are today! We have and can learn a lot from them as we navigate into our most exciting future and relationships with us and all other life forms.

I also would like to thank Karen Szudzik for her editing and pre-production expertise, as well as Shari Berg for her design expertise in cover art for this project.

# INTRODUCTION: A STORY

*True wisdom comes to each of us when we realize how little we understand about life, ourselves, and the world around us.*

-Socrates

*Key words: Generalized intelligence, specialized intelligence, semiotics, agrios, Great Chain of Being, situational cultural bias.*

The story so far to our world…

…opens finding Nam and Muh, a fictional couple living on Earth, tasked with many stresses and hopes on their minds. These include a never-ending roller coaster of travail, tension, and optimism in the search for food, adapting to this rapidly changing ancient eco-world, and experiencing a new mindset of social urbanization.

The ecological world is different in some geographies of this global theatre production. The pace of climate change and its effects on communal living in the Levant of Asia Minor, the coastal Mediterranean, and equatorial Africa occurred faster here than in the Australian, South American and North American land masses, even though each place is itself undergoing unique metamorphic changes. For you see, it has been many millennia since Nam's and Muh's kind, modern-day humans, woke to a new awareness of self, all along the way learning, building and molding both intellectual cognition and confidence in the grand master plan of life engagements with their environments and themselves. They are masons of change building the framework for the modern version of "us" to be allowed to thrive in our lives.

The time of Nam and Muh is the trailing and leading bookends of the Paleolithic and Neolithic period of the Revolutions when the Earth emerged into an era of special accelerated change both geologically and ecologically. These changes, in turn, promoted consequential alterations to humankind's chapels of intelligence. This evolutionary cocktail transformed culture, worldview, philosophy and purpose into the one in which we live today. Let's explore some of these exciting details by looking into a day in the life of Nam and Muh. We are them and they are us!

The satisfaction in Nam's mind, as his *generalized intelligence* correctly predicted the appearance of the livestock herd at the glade on this precise day of migration, would have been applauded by even a modern-day observer. Examples to the cyclical rhythm of natural phenomena on Earth like this abound, and Nam's mind has recognized another one. The hunt for food has been made easier due to the release of nature's icy ecological stranglehold on the bounty of life and the growing mental capacities taking place within. The minds of Nam's people were genetically the same as they were the bricklayers for this mental awareness and cognition just as Nam does for us today.

Muh meanwhile, practices her own mindful awareness and critical thinking regimen. With the identical cognitive process, she acknowledges that this day is when new plant foods are now ready for cultivation. A month prior would have been too early for a month from now the animals would have harvested this field themselves and departed on their continual migratory food journey. She has learned, both from her parents and from observational intelligence, the process for harvesting and preparing foodstuff for long-term storage in the cold season ahead.

These technological advances and labor efficiencies were developed in a piecemeal course throughout millennia to create a positive marginal economic benefit so the family community will thrive better in the future. This also means that Muh, her children and other family members have more

## INTRODUCTION: A STORY

available daytime now to help construct a permanent residence structure, itself an additional technological and cultural advancement of urbanization.

Recognition of nature's cycles of time, climate, and pattern phenomena help Nam and Muh plan for collecting and storing foodstuffs in preparation for the new, colder season to come. Muh also is often culturally tasked with tending to the sick in their family community. On this day one of her children suffers from lethargy and a colicky cough. Not to worry though. She fetches a certain plant leaf and stem for treatment of this malady. Muh stokes the cooking device, steeps a water-based medicine with the leaves as the active ingredient and watches as her child drinks. Not many hours later her child is back to her normal self. This is just another of many roles Muh plays as doctor and parent/guardian, just as is practiced today.

As this part of domestic life courses through its day, other family and community roles are taken on by Nam. Another most important role for him is that of a cosmologist. While it is understood that his environment operates in a cyclical nature, the many patterns that make up this tapestry are also themselves perceived to be fluid, dualistic and unpredictable in their nature. Nam understands this as he watches the sun rise and set, replaced a short time later by a darkness in the sky (the light of the sun is now gone) and by many dots of light and sometimes a bright "night light" (the moon) that grows larger and brightens and then grows smaller and less bright alternately. He sees this pattern recur every day. Nam recognizes this as indicative to the cyclical nature of his environment.

The duality of this example is illustrated by the light of the sun in competition with the dark of the night. Our consciousness perceives that light is good and dark is not so good in a utilitarian sense. The pattern of the stars, though proceeding only slowly enough in their rotation cycles around the sky so as not to be immediately recognized as predictable, nevertheless were and will become predictable to Nam's lineage. Together with other learning lessons, he develops the critical thinking mass of knowledge that life itself and universal phenomena are naturally cyclical as a developing cosmological worldview. Thus, this new awareness of mind gives birth to the first two study disciplines we call the sciences of medicine and astronomy.

Nam and Muh continue to learn that these traits of nature are omnipresent patterns that existentially influence their lives. They cannot ignore these patterns and hope to survive. Nam and Muh's growing learning capacity show continual and rapid development of awareness and understanding of the world around them that far exceed the demonstration of instinctual behavior. This includes another duality, one of man and woman, and the unique features both bring to the evolution table. Dualities, because they contain a "me versus you" or "us versus them" thought process, will evolve our human condition into an ideology where competitive means will determine possession outcomes. Prevalent within this ideology will be absorption of a "good vs. bad" duality.

Worldwide observational environments contain the land, earth, and sky above and eventually other people. These easels of nature are a catalyst showing Nam and Muh a way to coexist and thrive. This mental construct will advance the *generalized intelligence* Homo sapien sapiens' needs to survive both Earth's ecological changes and competition from other species as that which played out during the last 100,000 years before the Neolithic Revolutions of the Holocene period; the one in which we live today.

As part of this grand plan Nam's and Muh's ancestors learned that many of nature's features and traits recur as patterns. For many dozens of millennia existence on most of the major earthen land masses felt as frigid as one would in our arctic regions today. 'Inclement' is an understated description; harsh' embodies a more accurate bite to that reality. Even in those cold Ice Age landscapes, cycles and patterns of recursive nature abounded in the universe. These cycles produced enough food, water, and oxygen for life to survive and evolve. Cycles and patterns are necessary, then, for life itself and for us, to anthropically perceive them.

* * *

Before we can perceive anything, we must make **observations.** Our

## INTRODUCTION: A STORY

biological sensory apparatus must gain awareness and be able to process the stimuli. **Perception**, then, is a second step in the grander process of thought, **cognition**, and knowledge. Woven into nature's tapestry are the cryptographic cycles and patterns they learned to decode. This new knowledge was passed down to us, and this cycle continues as we are doing the same for our descendants in the future as purposeful pursuit of new knowledge.

The nature of cycles and observation are only two reasons for life to exist anywhere in the universe. Another reason, uncovered from the known archaeological and anthropological record, the "hierarchy of life forms" was scripted for our purposes like this.

Picture two weight scales and title them **'Power and Control.'** The purpose of each scale is to measure one of two relationships; the first between humans and his environment and the second between the animal kingdom and humankind in a food acquisition competition. Story development of both scales depict humankind as subservient to the forces of the other competitor in the earlier Paleolithic times. Humankind then acquired a critical mass of *specialized intelligence* to develop strategies with which wrestle control of both principles away from their adversaries, when the final grips of the Ice Age were relinquished about 12,000 or so years ago. Advancement of the human condition only acquired any real measure of environmental power and control during this time. When these are taken in total, the *highlighted terminology* in this chapter becomes a basis of rationale and proof of concept to my proposal that our ancestral kin are a valid, reliable and credible proxy of study as our future life compass. These concepts will be a major focus of your investigation and my discussions. We are them and they are us.

The animal and human creatures consume many of the same flora for their survival as herbivores. Some animals are carnivorous and consume the same fauna as humans. Humans, meanwhile, need a separate classification term; we became known as omnivores, needing both flora and fauna to maintain our biological homeostasis. Along life's way many events of overlapping competition for resources are best visualized as a Venn diagram of food resource competition.

Power and control are major tools of strategy for short and long-term survival in many dimensions. Early Homo ancestors, before Nam and Muh's time, became aware of recognizing this first as an instinctual brain operative. The brain then grew to be part of a network of neurology that embodies perception, cognition, and memory. This then allowed us to develop first specialized intelligence; the art of tool making for specific purposes and uses, then generalized intelligence; the aptitude for multitasking. These adaptations allowed us to out compete other species for world dominance as, anthropocentrically speaking, the dominant terrestrial species.

We competed with the animal kingdom, Denisovan and Neanderthal man, among others of 100,000 years ago in that challenging Ice Age world to obtain power and control for our survival. It was around that period when the scale tipped ever so slowly to show a change in dominance. The earliest known cave inscriptions of this time illustrate the animals as still environmentally dominant within regions; the holders of power and control. No humans were conceptually included in these scenes. The balance of power, through the eyes of early humankind, was imbalanced favorably toward the animal kingdom and would remain so until only the last 10,000 years or so.

Then, for reasons Nam and Muh's brethren only incrementally began to comprehend and utilize as motivation for future endeavors, human lives begin to change, mostly for the better. Consequently, power and control over nature's homeostasis changed. Humans themselves, that is their brains, literally woke up. Recognition of their place in nature began to offer new advantages and disadvantages simultaneously. Knowledge and application exponentially led to new knowledge and application. Nam and Muh are progeny of this ongoing process. This evolution was not caused by a "eureka one-off" type of cataclysmic event, as is often misaligned and misused in such debates and explanations. They also learned the need and discovered the mechanisms with which to teach each other, namely their offspring, the knowledge they amassed during their lives.

Hunter gatherers and early Neolithic instinctively, then intellectually

## INTRODUCTION: A STORY

discovered, learned, and memorized many pattern and cyclic designs in the natural universe. Food and water being existential for survival, Nam and Muh learned that lives of the animal kingdom and food crops existed in a nature of recurring cyclical behavioral patterns. The day and night, and life itself were also in cyclical synchronicity. The appearance of the sky, both day and night, constantly changed but their respective depictions always reappeared in their original imagery. When compared with today's science methodology system of study, our ancestors like Nam and Muh utilized essential elements of this practice in their own daily lives. They thought the same way we do today on many levels because they possessed the same neurology and anatomy.

Nam and Muh survived and perpetuated this lifestyle happily and holistically in an egalitarian society within an authority of a "one-for-all and all-for-one." They became aware that they were afforded the implements of life. While they had to work, often with patient effort, to obtain food and water those opportunities nevertheless were presented to them. Questioning 'where and by whom these opportunities come from' came later. For now, in Epipaleolithic times obtaining enough food to survive was the only prerogative.

Where and how did Nam and Muh acquire/develop the mind to lead successful and productive lives? An entry point may lie in the form of inspecting the known record of clues left for us dozens of millennia ago by their Neanderthal ancestors. Today we know that the human brain, specifically the younger features of the hippocampus and neo frontal cortex regions, are rather special, if not unique, to some life forms on Earth. Evidence that Neanderthals of millennia ago held profound emotional meaning to their brethren has been uncovered showing funerary ritual and burial cultures. The prospects are encouraging that the future will uncover many more such discoveries.

Many animal species today demonstrate some of these same awareness characteristics. The *hippocampus* contributes to the activities of the limbic behavioral control center. The human *neo cortex* separates advanced brain potential from that of our animal kingdom species. Specifically, our cognition allows for awareness of environmental stimuli, perception, compartmentalization, pattern awareness, analysis, conclusion, and memory storage for future use. Together these features help Homo sapien sapiens to feel and think more expansively and acutely than other life forms. Our **attitudes and behaviors** are driven this way. So was the experience for Nam and Muh.

Their thought processes operate like ours today. Their **cognitive pathway** works to utilize our **observational skills and awareness** to perceive, retrieve, compartmentalize, and store memory information just like we do today. Undoubtedly, their knowledge library was not as large as ours is today, though their memory centers possessed the capacity to do so. A significant feature in this dynamic is that Nam and Muh's cognitive systems are hard-wired into their anatomy, as is ours.

For example, some of these constructs, such as programming for instinctive behaviors, evolved into ancient humankind's nature hundreds of thousands to millions of years ago. Another feature is our brain's capacity to multitask through assignments to which it is tasked. I call this **multitasking cognitive utilization.** We should thank them for developing this dynamic for our use and advantage.

Our prehistoric ancestors also possessed the anatomical capacity to use speech. Our lack of a dynamic vestigial air sac, a biology present in other primates, is the feature which allows humankind to use speech at all, especially the use of language. This vestigial air sac is a two-edged sword. The sac allows our primate species and others to broadcast the powerful jungle sounds they use as their linguistics, but its presence prevents their adapting to and anatomically utilizing linguistic speech like us. This is because use of language places too many demands on organisms with this sac due to the many instantaneous changes in sound frequencies speaking requires. Due to the absence of these sacs, we can possess the faculties of linguistics and spoken language.

Certainly, in the Paleolithic (lower, middle, upper), Epipaleolithic (Mesolithic) and Neolithic eras our anatomy was like it is today. Our ancestors also possessed the anatomical capacity for language and speech.

## INTRODUCTION: A STORY

This is because their brain's cognitive frontal neocortex and hippocampus systems and the functional absence of the vestigial air sac enabled this function. So, our Epipaleolithic and Neolithic brethren possessed the anatomy that could utilize our familiar sounding speech production. However, it remains unclear whether they who existed during those time periods used speech to assign names to other people.

The last Ice Age cycle was ending as the Dryas climate periods took stage. Revolutions of thought, ecology, and biology shook the essences of humankind. The mechanisms of awareness and the mind were in full advancement at their respective accelerated velocities. Power and control over their environments and the animal kingdoms shared these accelerated tendencies.

Nam and Muh showed new purpose and meaning in expressing their symbolic forms of communication. The media for this semiotics expanded to now include pottery implements, personal adornments such as tattoos, makeup and cranial deformation relics, trinkets, building cultures and expansive reflections of the world around them, including the land, earth below, the sky above and those life forms which were contained in these environments. They were now making many more profound statements about such expansive intellectual pursuits as emotions, cosmology, and storytelling as teaching and learning strategies.

It is obvious that Nam and Muh were carrying on these symbolic traditions as descendants of practices that humankind invented millennia before. Through many successive generations these intellectual and technological advancements were refined and accelerated and continued to influence successful adaptations to people's new and changing environments. Nam and Muh are just one example of success in this evolution.

Natural selection is a historical factor that defines the long-term survival of Homo sapien sapiens within the species. People today live longer with a lower risk of contracting many major diseases and a higher incidence of cure rates, because of genetic mutations that are characteristic of natural selection. Knowledge is another principal factor as Nam and Muh could not directly see or understand, only know by intuition, inference, observation or perhaps being shown the symptomatic nature of these diseases.

Nam and Muh's social structures were broadly egalitarian, as noted. Sweat equity required cooperation among hunter gatherers. The marginal cost-of-food acquisition, in an intuitive sense, compelled early humankind to adopt small groups in this quest. These attitudes and behaviors were observed from the same behaviors of animal packs in their similar activities.

Extensions of this learned behavior pattern compelled Nam and Muh to create a division-of-labor among the daily tasks required for their preservation. Using cognitive reasoning, intuition, observation analysis, and trial-and-error, Epipaleolithic and early Neolithic people segmented labor activities according to talent, productivity, design, and an early form of engineering. Along the way, they also discovered that a type of gender specialization existed to where males were more talented and productive at certain activities and females likewise. A labor culture was formed this way to produce the most efficient and productive outcomes and not because of any gender bias. Examples of such gender divisions exist in both directions in early recorded history. Survival was the most important motivation. Because of this labor structure, the social culture was decidedly equal among all tribe members.

This labor structure served our ancestors well in maintaining a holistic approach to life in the early Neolithic/Holocene. This holistic awareness helped Nam and Muh to perpetuate a culture where a solid family structure, sharing, harmony, perpetuating the family tree, appreciating their environment, and structuring a life compass and worldview according to nature's cyclical processes were the important matters of existence.

The Tree of Life concept was universally created by all cultures. This was cognitively derived from Nam and Muh's observations of the tree in nature. The tree grew for many years beyond the lifetime of a single or many generations of humans. This means that Nam's children's children could see the same tree, both physically and metaphorically, and visualize its full meaning years later. But they remembered that it was much larger than when Nam knew of the same tree. The tree grew many branch networks and observed that all the branches were connected to the trunk. Many trees also lose their leaves in the autumn every year in a natural cyclical recurring process. Nam and Muh's people saw and learned this as a transformational process in their lives in adoption of moral life codes and as additional recognition to the harmony and equilibrium of nature.

\* \* \*

The Revolutions created new ways of perceiving their world that extended the conscious entanglement of man during the Holocene beyond the individual self. Among these creations was the intellectual discipline of *semiotics*. Symbolic representations are tools adopted to facilitate knowledge about something to others. In addition to forming a moralistic culture from this analytical cognitive methodology, Nam and Muh use these tools to make their contributions to a tribal system of symbolic representation, including use of metaphorical representations and proto language.

A characteristic of human attitude and behavior today, passed on to us by them, is one that we communicate about what we see (observe), the 'input' for discovery of new knowledge. The 'throughput' process describes our perception and cognition of information plus storage into our memory for later use. The 'output' is the dissemination of that information, and any new knowledge others could create from this activity. Because our observational theatres consist of a defined environment, or what we see around us, we learn and construct new knowledge from what we literally see in our three-dimensional universe. This pathway becomes the source of new information and knowledge that comes from what Nam and Muh saw of the animal kingdom attitudes and behaviors, the landscapes, the ground, the water below us and the skyscape above.

The days of the Nam and Muh family community were active, the role playing was dynamic, the tasks were many, and the stress and fear was abundant and recursive as part of human nature. In addition to satisfying their physiological needs of food and drink, the emerging urbanization way of existence compelled Nam and Muh to bear new responsibilities and stresses in the symbolic sense. Nam spent much time tasking with Muh to build their living residence. The raw material resources they used included mud and clay bricks, stone walls and roofing sub-structures. Inherent in their design, layout and architecture are metaphorical symbolic attributions, often consisting of highly sophisticated geometrical layouts from shapes they observed in nature. Their mindful engineering included purposeful construction on the leeward side of the hill, close enough to the top to prevent both damaging wind and draining erosion to affect their home when the prevailing winds, rains and snows were captured by the ever-present effects of gravity.

The blueprints for village-sized communities, then later large cities, embodied similar critical thought, planning and purpose. These included grid layouts corresponding to cosmic sky patterns, known by us today as star constellations. This fantastic manifestation of the Neolithic mind illustrates this representation both within a single and among many buildings. As these buildings were now made to be permanent structures, symbolic representations were built-in as mnemonic teaching strategies for the current and descendant generations.

Nam and Muh's generation were adolescents to a growing way of communicating and teaching via symbols and external material linguistics. They took turns scribing their stories: Nam illustrated successful hunting adventures and ritual pastimes, while Muh described daily life scenes and some of her observations of nature and landscape scenes. Frequently, accounts of this media/scope were told firsthand. The division-of-labor typically depicted men as hunters or community priests, while women were assigned roles as cultivators, processors of food and medicine, and caretakers of child development and domestic affairs. This isn't a ubiquitous division among ancient civilizations but the one that best served its respective utilitarian purposes given their cultural custom, talent, and worldview factors and considerations. Some of the symbolic records were created by males and others female, with no safe harbor for bias as is omnipresent today. Survival is the prime directive for this division of labor among our

# INTRODUCTION: A STORY

Neolithic ancestor's cognition.

A significant characteristic of symbolic representation culture was that the scribes recorded what they observed. A recurring theme that crosses geological time boundaries was that Nam and Muh depicted stories of significant life events. These were related to food acquisition, dispute settlement, navigation, family and community life, and were, most especially, spiritual/cosmic by nature. Available media recording materials were not unlimited; Nam, due to the amount of travel inherent in his job, usually found useful writing media while Muh secured the raw materials and processed them into usable writing implements.

Nam and Muh reasoned they were not only sharing their knowledge but also taking in the responsibility of preserving and showcasing it for the benefit of future generations. Not only was knowledge represented in rock writings but also by folklore, biology, social bonding and ritual practices, in addition to their pottery, tapestry, and fabric material cultures, and building architectures.

Their culture curated stories that were used to teach their young. The ritual and social bonding activities are recreations that serve the same purpose. It is reasonable to conclude that body feature schemes were used as social status structures, job responsibilities and the like. These features were demonstrated in forms of tattoos, body painting, and items worn on the body. such as amulets, charms, totems, or talisman, noted earlier.

As Nam and Muh deepened their comfort zone into an urban lifestyle, other life activity such as pottery, clothing, fabric, and tapestry manufacture came to occupy significant parts of their days. The labor allocation of talent and skills drove the activity set of who was to do what for family upbringing.

This new labor industry extended into the building trades, as part of a new social Revolution that we practice to this day. Building things added to our generalized as well as our specialized intelligence. Ceremonial centers of feasting, then later trade, ritual social bonding temples, residential and food storage architectures filled the new urban landscape. With these new social advances came new sources of stress, tension and continued fears of daily living. A new social strategy of leadership came to dominate tribes and nations worldwide as some of the major aspects of egalitarianism were forgotten and replaced by communal cultures with a more totalitarian flavor of governance, a new form of power and control that would lead to development of new competitive principles. Not only did humankind tip the scale of control away from the animals in the *agrios,* or the wild outside environment, but their socialization inadvertently presented a new dimension to them.

Not all the fears, stresses, and tensions of daily life were eliminated in the Revolutions. While biological sustenance improved, many aspects of life remained mysterious, far-reaching and difficult to reconcile, and external material cultures were transformed. Their spiritual, eschatological, and cosmic fears, stresses, and tensions of early Holocene humankind grew even more entangled. The most significant constant to Homo's mindful awareness of the Universe remained compartmentalized as the below-world, the living world, and the above-world. In their holistic, synchronous cognitive nature, all three remained the most important aspects of both life and the afterlife. Coupled with the four cardinal directions of terrestrial direction, these cyclical patterns became illustrative of the new way of thinking. This ethos came with them as stored baggage into modern times and were also exploited as tool strategies to manipulate social behavior in the new urban environment.

Even though the human species exhibit similar characteristic traits over time, the current and past social homeostasis was affected by many heterogeneous characteristics. Support for this is strong when, as far back as the Paleolithic, cultural differences abounded worldwide even though our genetic makeup is theorized to have been interchangeable and universal. The historical record shows varying degrees of geographic lifestyle advancements as causation to this state of reality.

For example, urbanization came to the Levant, the present-day Asia Minor, before its potential and reality was experienced by many other world regions. Consequently, social internets, technological proliferation and worldview ideologies did not evolve at the same velocity at the same time on Earth. Inspecting the current societal state-of-affairs will show that we

## INTRODUCTION: A STORY

may not have advanced much in global awareness and recognition of the human species as one large civilization even though people worldwide share the ability to take part in lifesaving and advancing medical interventions. Most of these differences are contained in the mindset and ideologies of the various human social communities. A homogeneous outcome on any of these dimensions may require a translation 'bridge' that initially recognizes these differences and then reconciles the divergences between heterogeneous and homogeneous community existences.

How has life affected us and where will it go? You will come to realize that all life forms on Earth were and continue to be linked in a *Great Chain of Being*, that hierarchical theory of how all living matter harmonizes to maintain its overall homeostatic existence, as proposed by Aristotle and Plato in Western philosophy. Empirically, this theory is supported by the truth that, first, trees and foliage convert chemical matter (carbon dioxide and other compounds) into the oxygen that all life needs to exist via the process called 'photosynthesis'. This truth then permitted formation of increasingly complex life forms whose quantity through time expanded exponentially into ever more complex forms that culminated on our planet with the evolution of all animals and human beings. Finally, the laws of natural homeostasis defined the parameters of food sustenance requirements for all life on Earth utilizing all these forms. The human mind developed an intuition that Earth was a gigantic, closed life system, which included required participation of all these forms in the Great Chain of Being to perpetuate their life.

Humankind only very recently acquired a level of consciousness about the function of some empirical laws in our universe. We do not know much about the implications of anthropic matters that govern life within this set of laws, and an omnipresent understanding of these laws is very far off in the future. Still, human intuition created a fantastic blueprint for this Great Chain of Being thousands of years ago. An empirical understanding of the Great Chain of Being came later but this intuition was completely accurate and predictive.

The cognitive intelligence of intuition continues today as a predominant mechanism for motivation, inquiry, proof, and advancement of new knowledge. Intuition <u>suspects</u>, the methodologies of motivation and inquiry <u>inspect</u>; and proof and advancement are <u>circumspective and retrospective</u> (ideally). An analogous argument can be made that, as our ancestors wondered about and experienced other manifestations of phenomena that affected their minds, perceptions and lives, their intuitions could not enable an empirical process for some of them.

For example, their intuitions developed knowledge about a non-material soul that linked an individual's terrestrial life in the living world with a cognition of transcendence of that soul into an eternal existence. This 'place' became heaven (or hell) and was known as the above world of the celestial skyscape. Consequently, their minds constructed a workable cosmic interface in which humans, and all other types of organic and inorganic matter participated. An ordered structure such as this worked because the human brain is wired to detect patterns and a cyclic nature to environmental phenomena.

When our ancestors witnessed incidents whose circumstances and features broke this type of observation, to allow their minds to accommodate these perceptions, a religiosity of gods, deities, and 'the others' was created. Beings appearing from the skyscape, some of which demonstrated acts of a fantastic or otherwise impossible nature for our reasoning powers, was such a circumstance. Their empirical knowledge was insufficient to reconcile what was happening within their ordered brain structure. The power these beings demonstrated was beyond human control, so the concept of super powerful deification was mindfully assigned. This mindset applied regardless of whether these super powers were chemically contrived, reached from a trans dimensional transport, or real in-the-moment physical visits.

Who are you? Where did you come from? Did you have help in becoming you? As we look at the anthropic nature of extraterrestrial life or as ET would look at us, can The Great Chain of Being accommodate life forms outside of planet Earth? Given the complexity that we perceive the current iteration of The Great Chain of Being to contain, and our knowledge of

## INTRODUCTION: A STORY

many examples of where the conditions for the existence of other life exist, such as other planetary bodies with potentially requisite life ingredients of oxygen, heat, pressure, water, etc. - it is entirely reasonable to predict this. With this body of knowledge, intuition, and focus, some believe we are alone in the Universe, at least publicly for whatever reasons. Minds are shaped by anatomy, neurology, life experience, and training. These attitudes and behaviors uniquely define us. They drive the acceptance or rejection of conclusions within our mindful compartmental box. How large that box is and whether the box is closed defines a closed-minded or open-minded approach to perception and cognition. It is omnipresent, however, that none of us can consider every possible perspective when inspecting the efficacy of any theory as expansive as this. Maybe the question of "are we alone?" in the Universe, in a thought experiment, could be posed to an artificial intelligence to see what conclusions it can derive.

\* \* \*

I have introduced you to the many dynamics inherent in learning about 'you.' The characters, Nam and Muh, are where you and I came from. The fabric of their lives is a product of these dynamics interwoven as they enable a unique journey for succeeding generations down to us and beyond. How they became us in this uniqueness is the result of cause and effect: anatomy, natural selection, reproductive development, geology and geography, ecology, climate, cosmic forces, life forms and intrusions.

In experiencing how nature operates and then applying its instruction set, Nam and Muh learned and adopted into their ethical and life purpose its many patterns and cycles. These patterns touched all aspects of their lives, from cosmic and spiritual to the everyday social and ritual roles the Neolithic human of our Age, the Holocene, had to undertake to survive and evolve. Their applications evolved through numerous modifications continuously improving their lives. Along the way, they encountered many existential "great filters", as described by social scientist and economist Robin Hanson in his 1996 paper, *The Great Filter: Are We Almost Past It?*

Our lives today are ubiquitously touched by all these dynamics, even as we come face-to-face with more existential "great filters" today and will continue to encounter in our future. Learning the ways and knowledge left to us by our human teachers is only a premise to the main production, the title of which I have selected as *The Humaniverse Guide ® - We Are Them, They Are Us: Our Ancestors, Us and ET*.

Nam and Muh are cast as protagonists in Act I of our human performance. They would be about 12,000 years old if alive today, or they could be 70,000. Nam and Muh acted out their lives in much the same way whether they were 12,000 or 70,000 years old, because they were the same beings - and as they are with us in many ways. The rest of what is known about them and their kind will be revealed in the following pages.

My scope of investigation is compartmentalized into a time frame consisting of only the last 70,000 or so years, though I will reference findings dated to more than 100,000 years ago. This is because more is known about our ancestral kin of recent times than in older periods. I suggest that a point of logical empiricism in the reality of history is that the more recent the period under study, the more data is available. This suggests that availability of data samples at any time drives the reliability of knowledgeable inference.

As we chart our course through the present and into the future, a future that will show us the many ways and varieties of life that exist, we will encounter more of these experiential threats to our existence in Act II. Hopefully, by studying our ancient knowledge, we can raise awareness of the reality that humans are purposed and provided with the tools necessary to successfully navigate our way through its rough waters to a more enlightened existence. Act III will be our coming out party in learning how far and wide The Great Chain of Being is remembered or not.

*We are them and they are Us…* is a deep inspection of the fate and destiny of our species' present and future through studying our past. Much of the text will explore what I call a "Mathematical Algorithm of Humankind. There are three components, denoted as: $T_1$ = we were, $T_2$ = we are, and $T_3$ = we

## INTRODUCTION: A STORY

could be. The addends for each are collectively summed as "who+when +where+what+how+why." See below for their curation.

English Franciscan Sir William of Ockham, the fourteenth century philosopher, curated the ideology known as Occam's Razor. His thesis selects the simplest path and form of theory construction and evaluation which is often the correct solution to a question. Currently, there is only one formative body of accessible evidence that can allow us to investigate the questions I discuss. "What can we learn from our ancestral brethren, Homo sapien sapiens, that will help in the search for understanding ourselves today?"

When the question involves us in ancient times and places, we must be on guard against a phenomenon faced by all researchers. This challenge arises from fallacious and inverted logic manifested by *situational cultural bias*. This is where the researcher insinuates his culturally influenced modern mindset, knowledge and critical thinking as the definitive and unquestioned mindset our ancestors used; a kind of temporal fallacy that causes the former and latter errors. In the former a premise is fallaciously manifested as conclusive, such as, "Our ancestors did something this exact way, so it is always right for us to do so in that way." In the latter, they start with a form of the question, "What can we discover about ourselves today that can help in learning about our ancestors?" We are humans; therefore, despite our training, these challenges persist, and awareness must be part of the practice.

This question is, of course, a different one from mine. My question, "What we can learn from our ancestors that can help in learning about ourselves?" takes an entirely different approach to insight and discovery by using an analog whose dataset is, admittedly, sometimes argumentative but constantly growing in substance and direction.

A summary of my research methodology, which provides insight into some of these questions and aims to offer you the best experience with the material to be presented in this investigation, is as follows. I begin with a body of observations, ask questions regarding the presence and behavior parameters of the observed data, generate inquiries about the phenomena that remain unexplained and lack current answers, analyze the material record, integrate existing knowledge and information into the experiment, make inferences about the experimental results, and then adjust for any incomplete or insufficient results by cycling another experimental pass through the process or using the results as input for another investigation. The dataset for this investigation is influenced by normative and descriptive dimensions, a logic focused on the people it aims to benefit.

Thus, my discussions are multidisciplinary by their nature, drawing from sources and methodologies in the anthropological, archaeological, archaeoastronomy, and the natural science disciplines. To efficaciously obtain knowledge about humans requires studying them from this comprehensive blend of perspectives. Humans have been and are a social life form. Their external records offer valuable insights into all aspects of human life and are of equal importance for study.

I prefer this methodology to discuss and propose guidance in our current and future quest for destiny, relationships and living in a world that will include knowledge of and interaction with new life, new understandings about ourselves and thus further erode the anthropocentric tendencies in our culture. Logic fits the circumstances because our quest for knowledge and self-understanding would be existentially hindered without use of what ancient information was left to us. The best source for empirical information in this realm came from people who were just like us. Without their acquired knowledge we would, undeniably, not exist as we do today. But except for the research communities that have debated these issues with their specialized circles in their confined communities, our society knows little about this knowledge of who we are and where we are headed. These premises will serve as the rudders guiding my narrative.

My work will contain a metaphorical flavor of data, navigation and multidisciplinary thinking, as it deeply explores both the evolution (the gradual long-term assimilation of knowledge, advancement and change into cultures) and revolution (an out-of-place, short-term, exponentially transformative advancement of knowledge and change) of our species - an essential analysis methodology omitted by practitioners in many research communities. Epochs of Pleistocene prehistory and Holocene recorded history have shaped the existence of our ancestral kin on the stage of planet Earth.

The motivations for this performance consist of (which is ongoing) emerging manifestations of the Homo sapien sapiens life form, the theatre production's protagonist. These manifestations include *Awareness, Mind, Revolution, Symbolism and Ritual*; the subjects of Chapters 2 through 6. The props called upon in this performance include various factors that shaped the script: genealogy, instinct, social culture, developmental culture, biology, environment, geography and geology, ecology, and life experience. I will sometimes present situational examples using these factors in an adversarial manner, to be known as antagonists to the Homo sapien sapiens. The unique situational blend of these theatre motifs will be performed as Act I, also known as '$T_1$' in my Mathematical Algorithm of Humankind, directed, produced and driven by the attitude and behavior process.

Act II, like Act I, explores my "Mathematical Algorithm of Humankind" but from a different perspective. Act I will analyze the dataset addends of the 5-w's and 1-h's to find the sum of who "we were." Act II references the same dataset addends of the "we are" reality. Act III projects a view of the same addends to the proposal of "we could be." Thus, $T_1$ = we were. $T_2$ = we are. $T_3$ = we could be. "T" represents the Greek letter Tau, meaning 'life and resurrection'.

Attitude and behavior were, are and will be formatively omnipresent, dynamic, and fluid in all Homo sapien sapiens understudy. The salience of this bio logistic interfaces with all aspects of the human life form. They drive our instincts, (basic biological urges) social cultures, (our relations with other people), environment (our relations with other life forms and the physical world around us) and operate (live) within our universe in this way. Our sensory environment observes a phenomenon or event, attitudinal cues are activated and processed, the attitudes themselves and concluding behaviors are shaped from an analysis of those cues. This realm has not been subject to much comprehensive investigation in the research literature. It is my hope that new roads of knowledge can be paved from recognition to the prevalence, pervasiveness and efficacy of these concepts on the human condition.

I have hinted at a future that will, show us the many ways and varieties of life that exist. Our ancients also gave us knowledge of their learning achievements through contacts with other life forms, both terrestrial and non-terrestrial. It is not about who is or being right or wrong in any individual mind's belief - it's about what is real and adapting to changes that make our civilization better.

I will utilize a few recurring themes and thought points throughout to help you understand and appreciate how difficult it was and is for humankind to survive. Reading this passage, you will gain more valuable insight from being introduced to them now.

You will also benefit by remembering that the logistics of geological time will be encountered throughout. The Homo genus lineage has existed for over a million years. Some of the concepts I discuss are processes that performed over hundreds of thousands of years to their maturity. Embedded within this concept is the inference that almost all the revolutions that occurred to guide our evolutionary track were not caused by single "eureka" events. At the very least, any revolution consisted of an entire series of events, each with far-reaching effects. Dates of reference are frequently included in data descriptions. I have tried to eliminate, as much as possible, vacillating between absolute and theological dating. This means that I will use the convention of absolute dating and only offer a theological dating reference when its use will enrich your understanding. For example, 12,000 years ago is the equivalent of 10,000 BCE from a theology calendar perspective.

The last over-arching framework I would like for you to keep in your thoughts are the life force factors that our ancestors endured to survive, evolve, and that continue to thrive today. Our human nature and our human condition by extension, were shaped by the forces of nature and nurture. These are compartmentalized as Earth's geology, geography, climate and weather, ecological, cosmological forces, biological, genetic, social, cultural, and reproductive developmental. No scorecard exists to where each factor can be ranked in any way; they were and will continue to be, all influential and entangled. It is no leap of faith to presume, or argue, that these forces will continue to shape our present and future theatre, no matter what that future theatre becomes.

One additional dynamic of what I call "the X-factor" is a protagonist in this production. This X-factor is what I titled 'the human mind'. We are a special species who live on Terra firma and have known this for our recorded history. Our selection for mindful consciousness and capacity for advanced intellect is what currently differentiate us from all other life forms on Earth. Where the mind takes our intelligence is an essence of the story. Intelligence is one thing; it is but a tool. How our nature directs the mind to use its intelligence is the overseer; the governor of us. It remains in power and control.

We may have already found or will come to reason that the future human mind will be populated with knowledge of "the others"; those life forms with minds comparable or more advanced than ours, or those possessing only a more basic instinctive intelligence evolved primarily for physical survival within their home environment and little else. Inherent within the definition of the term, *anthropocentrism* which contains an innate consciousness of fear that has persisted through recorded history. Our fear of "the others" was illustrated first by our ancestors against the animal kingdom and its environment, the agrios, and became hard-wired into our instinctive being. Then our more recent ancestors created a supernatural culture, however defined, to deal with another version of "the others". The body of knowledge we have acquired today has shaped our consciousness to deflect some of the subservient attitude-behavior present back then.

We may find, though, that fear persists. This may be due to the part of our hard-wired instinctive consciousness trained to be this way, or of an isolated innate fear of the unknown, or both. If fear is an instinctive behavior, it often seems to override the intelligent mind's attitude-behavior mechanism. Our mind is directed in this way when "the others" are introduced.

What may be required is a new connectivity of awareness and understanding between our instinctive fears and our advanced intellect. Our mind has expanded a working methodology that can accommodate a new rational perspective of "the others." Its protocol is quite illustrative of the steps in the evolutionary development story of humankind, as you will discover. A final thinking point I would like to share is this: To recall a 20$^{th}$-century popular culture axiom that may be underutilized but is full of existential direction, "the mind is a terrible thing to waste."

# Act I: AWARENESS!

*We can only ever understand the present by knowing the past.*

-Steven Mithen, *The Prehistory of The Mind*

*Keywords: Temporal nature, anatomically modern humans (AMH), attitude and behavior apparatus, attitude cues, basal brain core, multitasking cognitive utilization, Honeycomb Model of The Mind, observational awareness, observational skills, patterns and cycles, agrios.*

We are them and they are starting to become us…

*How did we become aware?*

Humankind's achievement of a self-aware mind was not directly caused by a single "eureka" event. Many discoveries in nature that involve the human species behavioral life are mistakenly argued from the perspective of a "one time" causal event. These events, consequently, are then frequently portrayed within such parameters by research literature. The underlying arguments in those situations quickly become empirically flawed due to the argument's *temporal nature* involving long yearly time frames sometimes approaching millennia and eras within the scope of the investigation. I, therefore, assert that insight into the questions within the investigations that follow will be most correctly found from the perspective of a dynamic process that lasts a long time and could realistically contain many related consequential events.

We are our ancestors; they are us in this domain; both are known as *anatomically modern humans* (AMH). These evolutions happened within the last 100,000 years, though by way of a most correct introduction, our compatible natures on many dimensions can be asserted to have existed as far back as the Denisovans of about 300,000 years. Other equivalent AMH's of this period include the Jebel Irhoud of Morocco (320,000), the Khoisan of South Africa (300,000), Florisbad of South Africa (250,000) and the Omo-Kibish I of Ethiopia (230,000). Note that, except for some Denisovan discoveries, these AMHs, also known as *early modern humans* (EMH) lived in a geography to what is known today as sub-tropical and tropical regions.

Due to the geologic time frame required for nature to enable climatic, ecological, and geographical changes to their landscapes, it is reasonable to corroborate that they favored an efficacious anatomically modern human life sustenance for both man and animal that was like the experience within our temporal geographical climates today. Main reasons for this dominion include the suspected influence of numerous Ice Age cycles, and nature's responses to such disruptions to, the ecological homeostasis existing in those times.

The breaths of the Ice Age cycles dynamically enabled temporal episodes of a temperate eco environment followed by abysmal ones. Life finds it easier to survive in temporal rather than equatorial climates due to the influences of temperature on all aspects of life in that environment, including but not limited to the availability of food and water. Therefore, they chose those locations and moved in a nomadic fashion as needed. As I will explain in detail, food and water sustenance, architecture cultures, and social cultures inherently negotiate our instinctual and mindful decisions as the most basic of life forces.

To summarize, climate was one of the most significant drivers of ancestral behavioral lifestyle patterns. These considerations manifested themselves in the overall dictation by nature to remain nomadic. The alternative was extinction. Consider the remains of the Skhul and Qafzeh peoples found in Israel in the 1930s. They were analyzed to be, instead of hominid species, more advanced Homo sapien AMHs, dated to as early as 120,000 years ago. This trail of discovery disappeared about 80,000 years ago. Also found in the area were numerous Neanderthal remains dated to about 60,000 years ago. The time gap between the disappearance of the AMHs and the return of the Neanderthals are theorized to have been caused by a geologic cooling and drying of the region at the time the Skhul and Qafzeh disappeared (Trinkaus 1993). Climate changes then favored a return of the Neanderthal. This is anomalous because there is no known evidence of contact or intermingling between the AMHs and the Neanderthal indigenous of those periods.

Our ancestors were the same people as we are today to the largest extent possible without being identical in all aspects of existence. Their skills in most areas grew and were shaped into our adoption, adaptation, and continued practice of the following features of culture and human condition as an accurate statement. Archaeological evidence suggests that biologically equivalent human species worldwide, such as the Neanderthal, potentially the Denisovans and others, shared many compatible features of being human. These similarities included funerary and burial mindsets, artifact cultures, body ornaments, symbolic representations with discerning use of color, and abstract and determinative forms of cave art from over 70,000 years ago (McGill 2015, 69). Ornamental beads, inscriptions of geometric figures, and heat-treated spear tips have been discovered in Blombos Cave, South Africa dated to over 71,000 years ago (Henshilwood 2002, 1279). The current controversy over seeking knowledge through these discoveries portends a dynamic course showing that we will learn more in the future.

\* \* \*

*The Function of Awareness:*

The *attitude and behavior apparatus* were, are, and will be omnipresent, dynamic, and fluid in all Homo sapien sapiens within this narrative. It is one of a handful of recurring themes that I will rigorously explore. The salience of this bio logistic interfaces with all aspects of the human life form. Mindful decisions are driven using our instincts (basic biological urges), social cultures (our relations with other people), environment (our relations with other life forms and the physical world around us), and operate (live) within our universe in this way. Our sensory environment observes a phenomenon which gains our attention. Then our perceptions activate and process *attitude cues* specific to the behavior under consideration. The attitudes and subsequent behavior responses are shaped from an analysis of those cues. Behavior responses in humans define the event reality path in our minds. This entire process is manufactured by our brain chemistry and can be performed instantaneously or may take some time and is dependent upon how much the mind's cognitive systems may need to drive output potential solutions.

This realm has not been subject to as much investigation of both breadth and depth in the research literature as needed to promote better insight into "who we were" and "who we are." It is my hope that new roads of knowledge can be paved from recognition to the prevalence, pervasiveness and efficacy of these concepts on the human condition. A more rigorous treatment of the many features defined within the attitude and behavior apparatus will be discussed in later chapters. But, upon reflection, I feel that you will be better served if I detail a few concepts upon which other themes will be built.

As I begin, an attitude and behavior process defines and shapes every decision all humans make throughout our lives. Some have studied this phenomenon, known in literature under the title 'cognitive intelligence'. Our bodies are stimulated to observe and perceive an event from our sensory environment. The brain processes this input, compares it with associated knowledge of similar stimuli from memory recall, and navigates our feelings and response as to what is happening at that moment. All information is categorized and molded into adoption of an attitude about the event. This process of observation, data collection, analysis/perception, knowledge comparison and attitude adoption drives toward a conclusion to answer the underlying hypothesized question and is manifested as the ultimate behavior response. Data from this episode is also routed to a memory storage system.

This elegant process happens within the magnificent biological apparatus which is our brain; a creation that is universal in nature among all known life forms that contain a sentience. Our AMH ancestors, for purposes of answering the question 'how did we become aware', behaved the same way as we do today as "actors in the drama of their lives" did in their time. This is evidenced by the artifacts and symbolic representations left for us to study and interpret.

Let me briefly introduce the characteristic factors that drive attitude and behavior episodes in humans, and many animal species, along with some of their inherent functional features as follows:

- Instinctual
- Neurological/genealogical
- Life Experiences (always unique but share common attributes among individuals)
- Social Cultures (a subset of Life Experiences salient enough to be considered separately)
- Environmental
- Emotional (the Limbic System Neurology subset that often interferes with rational thinking and decision-making)

'Instinctual' cognitive characteristics, as noted, are those which became hard-wired into the brains of our genus lineages millions of years ago. Discoveries made from the archaeological fossil and tool kit records found throughout the world repeatedly infer this. Examples of these characteristics include the will or drive to survive and procreate. Attitudes that proliferated in the sense that strategies to secure food sustenance, to overcome dangers, and passing on their being to offspring were obviously omnipresent, recurring, and resulted in the species' proliferation down the lineage trend line to Homo sapien sapiens - us.

The architecture that was created for this became known as our instinctive *basal brain core*; the deepest spatial brain region in eukaryotes that contain such a functional system. The autonomic nature of behaviors thought to be derived from this neurological pathway drive through this network. This cognitive nature was conjectured to be present in all animals from over 50 million years ago and speculated to also be present much earlier than that, as far back as the dinosaur era that ended about 65 million years ago. We know this core to be the oldest functioning region as all other younger brain regions that operate much more of our mental capacities are spatially situated peripherally around the basal brain stem. It is the presence of these newer regions that sets higher order animals apart. It is here where the attitude-behavior protocol began its functionality. We recognize it today when comparing brain architectures and resulting observational attitudes and behavior patterns of various animal types.

'Neurological and genealogically' based factors evolve as tasked to the mind's neural anatomy through time. They are a de facto contributor to all and serve as a foundation with which other factors become cohorts in all attitude-behavior responses.

'Life experiences' are always unique in their totality to an individual, but which help shape a frame of mind. The mind's memory library recalls past experiences with congruent characteristic elements for synthesis by the brain's cognitive pathways to drive an attitude viewpoint.

'Social cultures' were a major reason for the evolution of awareness in a person. Some have argued that human beings have been social animals since the beginning of their genealogical existence. Everyone today interacts with other people every day of their lives. This was also the case when nomadic hunter-gatherers roamed the Earth in kinship tribes. Many behaviors are a manifestation of the attitudinal viewpoints developed from direct interaction with others.

'Environmental' factors have also been part of the attitude-behavior apparatus of Homo sapien sapiens since creation. A decision to either do something or behave in a certain way is dependent on the circumstances. Presence of this factor supports a causation that was influenced by Earth's Ice Age cycles and the larger framework of the dynamics of the Earth's ecosystems over eons worth of time.

'Emotional' factors, on the other hand, relate to the critical thinking interface the mind often conducts with inputs from the brain's limbic system. This psychology has been studied extensively and from investigation of our ancient external material semiotics, supports the conclusion that they behaved like we do today.

One can infer from an inspection of the attitude-behavior science that data contained within the brain centers for all six of these factors are consulted and many are active during an episode. Their existence is necessary for the framework of the mind to successfully evolve. This includes the discovery, creation and development of awareness. Again, I propose that the attitude-behavior phenomenon came from development of awareness of self, others, and from the person's living environments. I will show many examples supporting the connections between us and ancestral man by driving the point, "it is as it was".

An introduction to this evolutionary provenance is illustrated here. The discovery of self-awareness was like a person seeing a reflection of himself in a pool of water. We visualize this today when we observe our pet expressing the same behavior. Awareness of "the other" was discovered by our ancestors when the person saw both himself and the environment, including the presence of others, around him in the same pool of water. Discovery of the person's environment came to his awareness by the movements of nature around him. The development of self and cultural awareness beyond instinctiveness was necessary to allow the mind to initiate deployment of cognitive intelligence.

Here I utilize a more all-encompassing term by calling this a *multitasking cognitive utilization*. It describes more precisely how the brain's neuro pathway drives information through the cognitive critical thinking analysis process by processing information in a multitasking environment. The most critical additional feature of this is that, like the fastest computer routines, stacks and sub-routines existing and yet to be invented, multiple brain processing centers can simultaneously interact to compare information within a multitasking cognitive pathway. This topic will be discussed in detail in the chapter titled *The Mind*. For now, think of multitasking cognitive utilization as an advancement to cultural awareness where now attitude cues can be formed and analyzed within such a multitasking event to navigate behavior outcomes.

An overview of these attitude-behavior characteristics appears below. I will introduce the framework of a design titled, *'The Honeycomb Model of The Mind'* then explain other important concepts that support my theory that "we are them and they are us". The six dimensions of the attitude-behavior apparatus are illustrated here as a reference building block throughout the remainder of this book.

Just in case you do not recognize the strategic significance embedded in its portrayal, I am utilizing the same process of symbolic representation to describe this ideology that our ancients utilized since the Paleolithic. I have taken a robustly popular geometric pattern from nature (a honeycomb) to describe the model to demonstrate an empirical cognitive pathway process that encourages awareness and understanding of this concept. Symbolic representations are the main subject of my chapter titled *Symbolism*. Our ancestors did not create a symbolic cultural environment in a eureka event, but my model is illustrated as a building block toward a processual endpoint. Initially they had to discover and develop the awareness tool to better equip them for the marathon journey that led them to join us in the promised land of mindful kindred brotherhood.

A primary objective in showing the Honeycomb Model of The Mind is to suggest that all six factors were needed for the proliferation of the evolved mind in a gradual but continuous process of deployment and development of attitudes and behavior responses that lead to new knowledge. The honeycomb geometry allows for the greatest accumulation of something within a given surface area for any geometric shape that occurs in nature. In nature, the honeybee creates the honeycomb from a geometric circle to store the most honey within its confines. This model is intuitively appealing because it too can store the greatest amount of cognitive information with the same parametric elements as the honeybee version. Additionally, the model illustrates the process whereby the cognitive mind drives a salient process of multitasking when an attitude-behavior episode takes place and will be explored more deeply in the next chapter, *The Mind*.

*Diagram of*
*The Honeycomb Model of The Mind*

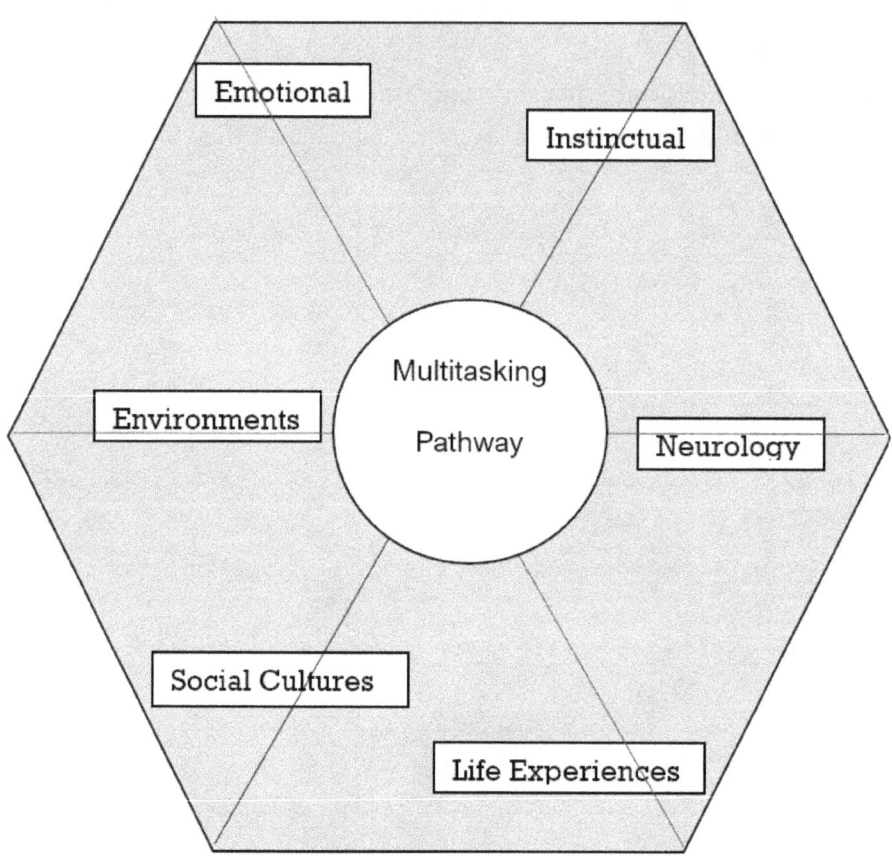

Our lives, and those of our phenotypically compatible ancestors, are biologically governed to process information make decisions, which then shape our attitudes and behaviors in interpreting meaning to the events of our lives. Those affected by the behavior responses are the protagonists and antagonists, and our environments and attitude cues are the props.

Awareness can be defined as the sentient understanding that something in the environment has stimulated our thought process to begin a data collection, perception and analysis procedure leading to an attitude-behavior action. The individual is stimulated by these cues, takes notice of the situation, develops a perception and cognition of the events, and the episode culminates in the development of his attitude-behavior response.

Attitudes and behaviors are present in all dimensions of human life experience. Connections between behavior development show a strong correlation from the mnemonic recall accessibility of stored attitudes and their stability over time, from their experience with the attitudes, and related behavior outcomes (Glasman and Albarracin 2006).

Some are instinctively automatic behavioral responses commonly referred to as the subconscious hard-wired brain apparatus. One example of this is the attitude "feeling" of hunger or thirst and the autonomic behavior endpoint to "seek food or water" to alleviate that hunger or thirst as the conclusion to this process. Hunger and thirst mechanisms are instinct biologics and were genetically favored to humans and all life forms existing on Earth. A second example is the attitude/feeling embodied in the threat of danger to one's safety and its own instinctual subconscious psychology to behave in a certain way.

A third example embodies the existence of attitudes of instinctual reproduction and the automatic behavior response mechanisms. Reproductive behaviors have been obvious by their sheer existence and availability for study, and to include all sentient life forms and their instinctual attitudes and behavior histories. Fossil records of many sentient life forms prove this reality. The dating of these fossils suggests that those instinctual characteristics of life forms existed for many millions of years.

But these are examples of attitude-behavior episodes that are autonomic instinctive basal brain urges and thereby autonomic by nature. Of interest at this juncture are those which transformed humans' awareness of themselves, others and their environments beyond the instinctive and into the higher levels of intelligence; the specialized and general levels that will be a recurring theme of my narrative.

A divergent course of investigation must be undertaken when an attitude-behavior process is attempted that moves beyond satisfying basic autonomic needs and urges for food, water, safety, reproduction, and the like. It is moving beyond "why" these needs exist to address the "when, where and how" of those needs. In this domain there exists a conscious decision tree of behaviors that serve as endpoints in the attitude-behavior demonstrations, derived from analyzing the factors that construct the variety of attitude cues that, in turn, drive those behavior responses. I am framing a discussion as to when, where and how the creation of self-awareness attitudes took place that enabled humans to assign meaningful awareness to the observations they made.

*Observational awareness* can be defined as the use of our biological senses to receive stimulus information data from the surrounding environment in an enlightened manner to which meaning can be derived. It is part of the larger concept of *observational skills*, also referred to as "mindfulness". Observational skills make use of our perceptions of stimulus data and our brain's cognitive, analytical and memory information pathways which drive understanding and an assignment of meaning to what is being observed.

A person must have the capacity to cognitively process and record observations to enable awareness. Our biological sensory network allows for efficacy of this mechanism. Because our considered ancestors had the same biological sensory genealogy as we do, the same network was used to achieve an equivalent result. Their brains did not possess the same knowledge library of memory information as we have today, but they contained the capacity to achieve this functionality. This is important in an extended and unrelated analysis. However, if genealogy was the same, then the same basic awareness achievements are reasonable to deduce, and from the archaeological record, are proven to have been achieved. I will later discuss many examples of such artifacts, symbolic representations, and enlightened knowledge left by our ancients in support of this statement.

The genealogical, anatomical, and biological characteristic traits of our kindred people were similar in functionality, if not the same. Our special advantage - this enlightened additional knowledge - had its provenance from our ancestors. Let's thank them for this! We are them; they are us.

## ACT I: AWARENESS!

*\*\*\**

*To What Did They Become Aware?*
*The Objects of Awareness*

- Visually observable objects in their surrounding natural environment, including other life, features of the living world, the below world and the sky world above
- The *patterns and cycles* embodied in all these Objects. These are the Laws of Nature; physical laws, mathematics, socially constructed patterns among humans and animals
- Themselves
- People like them and other life forms

An attitude is developed from processing an awareness of the situation at hand. For example, let's continue with examples of food sustenance, and others, to illustrate this mechanism, but now apply it to how our primal ancestors would have encountered and processed the objects of awareness.

Here are examples demonstrating this primal awareness of self and of other objects of awareness. Food sustenance was more immediate to our ancients' survival and more labor intensive the further back in time. Therefore, the daily attention allocated to this activity was more frequent and occupied more of man's brain activity. Upper Paleolithic and Neolithic humankind developed better hunting strategies temporally by learning of animal migration patterns and cycles, and later, in proto-agrarian times, of similar planting and cultivation schemes.

Numerous examples of this phenomenon were ubiquitously recorded in ancient cultural records. It was the same example Nam and Muh would have experienced fundamentally in their learning of nature's weather and climate cycles that drove their search for food sustenance. Their contemporaries soon became both instinctively and intelligently aware of nature's patterns as the spring and summer seasons cycled into the days of autumn and winter for each yearly cycle.

A cave painting of a bovine creature found in Cáceres, Spain has been dated, by uranium-thorium dating, to have been created 64,000 years ago. It embodies a symbolic representation (SR) to the awareness of the thinking mind humankind had attained on a "first level" dimension of cognitive intelligence. The panel shows just the bovine in its literal form as an Object of Awareness. There were no additional inherent, implied, or metaphorical second-level or tripartite meanings or story lines present in the painting's symbols.

More basically, the panel does not tell a story; no other symbols or figures are contained within the scene. But the critical thinking mind who created this message was consciously aware and motivated enough to communicate the existence of this creature at this location to others. Perhaps it was scripted as a marker identifying this as the location of a food source for other nomadic groups, a place for food processing, an instruction set, or maybe for aesthetic enjoyment. Any of these possibilities define the inherent nature of a knowledge transfer which the creator meant to be communicated to others. Cáceres also portrays a consciousness of mind; an awareness of self and of others who found meaning and purpose in the SR. Presence of this example suggests that the anatomical cognitive apparatus in humans was present then to allow for the growth of the attitude-behavior apparatus that gave Homo sapien sapiens the capability to practice and evolve SR and a communication of knowledge to others.

An early known literal symbolic representation of patterns in nature was found on the South Coast of South Africa at the Blombos Cave site. The Blombos drawing contains a series of geometric figures (hashtags as we know them today and other meaningful symbols) and animal reliefs dated 71,000 years ago. The panels illustrate suspected hidden metaphorical and maybe tripartite making of meaning as if the creators of these Objects of Awareness were trying to tell its readers one or more messages beyond a literal illustration.

Another example is taken from the Neolithic site of Çatalhöyük in Anatolia (Turkey), located in what is known as the Levant region. Numerous uncovered hunting stories dated to 7,000 BCE show dozens of tribesmen, depicted as very small in composition, stalking a wild bull predatory animal, depicted to be much larger in comparison. All the Objects of Awareness are present here, in addition to other symbolic meaning making, which includes statements about the indigenous cultures' ritual and social traditions.

I give special attention here to introduce another ideological characteristic of early humankind from the Çatalhöyük example and derived from the attitude-behavior mechanism that will be discussed later. This is the concept of power and control over one's environment and of others. The early Neolithic peoples of the Levant region of Asia Minor were only starting then to develop enough psychological confidence to enact competition strategies that would ultimately tip the scale of power and control from the animals and their *agrios* environment toward humans.

The power, control and competition dimensions, and how they were storied in the ancestral semiotics are of recursive importance to learning about us and will be discussed at length throughout this book. The Çatalhöyük panels, the pillars of nearby Gobekli Tepe, further back in time at Kimberely, Australia, Cueva de las Manos in Patagonia, Apollo 11 Cave, Africa and as far back as Blombos Cave offer just a few examples as to where the awareness to power, control, and competition were illustrated. The agrios held more power than humans for all time until the Neolithic/Holocene. Animals were overwhelmingly depicted as wild, violent and much larger on the panels in composition because of this perception and cognition reality. Only when we developed multiple symbolic representations at the time of the Revolutions of the Neolithic did the story of the battle for power, control, and competition transform in favor of the human authority. Global representations illustrate this repeatedly throughout the ancient world.

The reality of these examples demonstrates many things. First, it is suggested that the objects of awareness mindset; of self, of others, their surrounding observational environment, and the patterns and cycles inherent in nature, were present and utilized in fundamental ways. This generalized intelligence was considered important enough for their authors to divert time away from food survival activities to communicate with others about this knowledge. The authors were aware of themselves and others, demonstrated the feeling and need for 'something to say' and communicated their ideas. Ecological and climatic changes also favored more discovery and contact among these "others," as the disparate tribes of Homo sapien sapiens and other Homo species, including Neanderthal and Denisovan, among others. This created the need for meaningful communication.

Second, when humans had enough practice with the objects of awareness to fully adapt to a new expanded version of modern cognitive intelligence, they discovered that better methods of food sustenance and more efficient labor practices created better life conditions in general. This also allowed for more efficient time management and entry into other expanded life activities. To use the Maslow Theory of Needs Hierarchy, created by psychiatrist Abraham Maslow in the 1940s, the pursuit of human needs evolved up the pyramid toward permanent architectural building cultures, urbanized social cultures, and more spiritual, religious, philosophical and empirical pursuits of intrinsic life purposes.

The mind's agency to become consciously aware of such highly sophisticated concepts as control over and competition within his external material environments has a known provenance suggested to about 44,000 years ago. The discovery of a cave painting at the Lubang Jeriji Saléh site in Borneo, Indonesia depicts an early hunting scene introducing human anthropomorphs. Whereas the Cáceres painting is entirely descriptive in form, the Indonesia painting is an enriched meaning-making story with both descriptive and emotive storytelling motifs, that is prototypical of a second-level metaphorical form of SR.

Because the evolution of SR was influenced by the evolution of generalized intelligence, the heightened consciousness of changing attitudinal cues created by the stimulus-response cognitive mind and influenced by the dynamic informational inputs of his sensory environments, manufactured the perception and cognition and associated attitudes and behaviors. This episodic active-static process is individualized for every person in his or her reproductive development to what Zeder (2009) called a 'habituation process' of human growth and learning development. Symbolically representative cultures are driven to where, "the potential for directed change in cultural systems is greatly, perhaps even exponentially, enhanced over that found in biological systems by the human ability to evaluate behavior outcomes and to abandon, adjust, or perpetuate behavior responses based on this evaluation" (Zeder 2009).

Throughout the Upper Mesolithic era, dynamics of natural selection, ecology, geology, geography, and reproduction development unique, habituation cults regulated the maturation of SR on Earth to which archaeological and anthropological research is still in the adolescence of inquiry and discovery. This gave the hunter-gatherer an entire era's worth of time to adopt and apply this expanding cognitive awareness of power and control over his environment. Through growth of his ability to adapt, inventing better tools of weaponry, and utilizing his cognitive multitasking, this allowed Homo sapien sapiens to endure, while other related species faced extinction.

Remains in Upper Mesolithic Middle Europe still show manifestations of these highly advanced concepts such as urban living and funerary ceremonies dating back 35,000 years ago. The end of the last Ice Age, about 12,000 years ago, became the delineation point to the origins of the Holocene era and the Neolithic period. From the time of this geological/ecological transformation into the Younger Dryas periods, the human mind developed a selected attitude-behavior modification to extend its growing sense of self-image and awareness to a relationship with the conscious world in what Jacques Cauvin called "psycho-cultural changes" (Cauvin 2000).

Dated discoveries include the uncovering of multivariate interpretative 'art' forms of the mind with dual, metaphorical, and even tripartite meaning, in conjunction with a nurtured concept of urbanized existence. This cognition of duality and multivariate meaning was repetitive and played a seminal role in later growth of an ethos of life for the human species; and many dualistic principles in the worldview of moral philosophy. The maturity of the semiotic language of communication shows that simple cave 'art' was replaced by more sophisticated formats, including trinkets, seals, ornaments, amulets, pottery, relief carvings, monoliths, totems, and architecture in Middle Europe and Southwest Asia. These expressions were new recursive symbolic forms of "external symbolic storage" (Donald 1998, 184) and that appears in external material cultures worldwide (Coward and Gamble 2008).

\* \* \*

I have been discussing "to what did they become aware?" using a framework of normative behavior principles supported by descriptive data and analysis. Most of this discussion has been aligning with the "how" and "what" dimensions of my Great Mathematical Algorithm of Humankind; the $T_1$ variable that shows "who we were". They all witnessed the same behavioral experiences in their world as we do today, as inferred from the artifacts, if one supports the conclusion that their anatomy was the same as ours. By witnessing, I mean those things that were processed by any or all their senses. From a close inspection of the archaeological records, they held sight as the primary observational tool that allowed a successful evolutionary track for humankind. The archaeological records uphold the notion that, since before the Paleolithic Era, the visual and sensory capabilities of Homo sapien sapiens were the equivalent of ours today. Remember also that ancient man's resultant behavioral responses to these observations were vastly different from our behavior responses given the same event, because we possess more empirical knowledge with which to interpret those observations. What is most important here is to recognize that they created the framework with which we observe, think, interpret, and behave today.

So, what did our ancient brethren see? The terrestrial environment, or the living world, provided similar landscape characteristics to drive a life existence for all save for any local ecological or climatic differences that caused different landscape environments. These localized differences were powerful in shaping the pace of advancement of cultural landscapes at a particular period. This recurring characteristic will be recognized throughout my narrative. A lot of fauna and flora life forms, as tangible real objects and matter, were present then and now, as another tie that binds this analysis with them and us. The circumstances of the 'below world', that land or water under our feet, were also similar. They both descriptively saw these things and were aware that these features had meaning to them that could be explored and from which reason and understanding could be derived. Nature showed them that these environments were full of cyclic patterns with which they could interact and reconcile their life views and existence. They could also touch them in the real physical sense. Touching created the requisite intelligent meaning-making that shows up in all ancient cultures, semiotics, and social behaviors.

Pattern perception is a hard-wired element of our brain and anatomy. The brain's neurology and cognition are afforded the ability to perceive patterns in nature and our environment. Additional perimetric support for this theory lies in the reality that a blind person, and many animals, can still maneuver around his environment successfully without imminent fear of injury because his other sensory systems compensate for the lack of visual acuity. The blind person's brain clearly illustrates the objects within his environment from input provided by the other senses with heightened sensitivity. His brain can define and illustrate the patterns of objects. The physicality of objects, matter, and life forms in both the living and below worlds would retain the same basic meaning for us today as back then. A rock was and remains a rock; a tree was and remains a tree; a mountain, a grazing animal, a fish, etc. All these objects and life forms were physically accessible by our ancestral kin and, therefore, more tangibly meaningful. What these material objects, matter and life forms meant in their minds as a matter of cognitive abstraction were significantly influenced by their physical accessibility or lack thereof.

More tangibly meaningful than what? Here is where the power of the human brain and its capacity for abstract analysis and behavior deals with things or material objects that we cannot physically touch. When our ancestors looked up into the sky, they saw a most mysterious domain. They were aware that the light by which the earth's surface and land below could be seen and materially felt came from above, and of the powerful dominance it had on life. In nature's ritualistic display they saw the cycles of light each day and the tiny specks of light that each night filled the sky as Earth's daily rotation permitted.

They quickly developed awareness that these specks of nightly starlight, as well as the position of the daily sun and our moon, moved around the sky as larger cycles themselves except, for one; the North Star. This is a very important point I will discuss later. All the stars moved in this way, and some of them disappeared altogether for a while before reappearing again in the next yearly cycle as the Earth orbits around our Sun. Further awareness arose when they saw, with the discovery by their descendants, that those same specks of starlight not only moved around and sometimes disappeared, but that groups of them would come to occupy a different segment of the night sky grid, and a different star would seem to stop motionless for a while as the Precession of the Equinoxes allowed for even a new North Star, the one that supposedly never moved, every couple thousand years. They were aware of the sky and its timely patterns and cycles but were prevented from touching the material sky world themselves.

Ancient man was also overwhelmed by the mindset that he was observing this dimension of the natural universe that was awe-inspiring, magnificent, unexplainable, and entirely unreachable except in their minds. This intersection, to where empiricism and imagination diverge is their point of interpretive departure from our modern minds. Without the ability to apply any sensory framework except to see and reason, they were left with interpreting the sky world through their eyes and minds.

These are just some of the features that defined the sky world as the most salient contributor to their human condition, as more aligned to his awareness of self, to others, the environment and to his primal cognitive thinking. Our senses today dictate the same mindset of attitude-behaviors and associated emotions as lived by our ancestral kin, with our bonus of new knowledge. The *Archaeoastronomy* and *Universals* chapters will offer insight on these elements of the human condition as they relate to the sky world.

To reconcile life, purpose and their soul's existence through a fashioned eternity, their imagination intellect had to replace the inability to touch, feel, and be with that world. All these features are a big part of what differentiate humans; them and us, from other terrestrial life forms. Awareness is one part of the apparatus that is the human mind. Let's explore more of what made Nam and Muh tick, and how we can study and learn about that mind to better explore, help and shape ours, and ultimately our future.


*References*

Cauvin, Jacques. 2000. *The Birth of the Gods and the Origins of Agriculture:* Translated by Trevor Watkins, Cambridge University Press.

Coward, Fiona, and Clive Gamble. 2008. "Big brains, Small Worlds: Material Culture and the Evolution of the Mind." *Philosophical Transactions of the Royal Society B: Biological Sciences* 363, no. 1499: 1969-1979.

Donald, Merlin. 1991. *Origins of The Modern Mind: Three Stages in the Evolution of Culture and Cognition.* Cambridge, MA: Harvard University Press.

Glasman, L. R., and D. Albarracín, 2006. "Forming Attitudes that Predict Future Behavior: A Meta-analysis of the Attitude-behavior Relation." *Psychological Bulletin,* 132 (5): 778–822.

Henshilwood, C. S. 2002. "Emergence of Modern Human Behavior: Middle Stone Age Engravings from South Africa." *Science* 295 (5558): 1278–80. https://doi.org/10.1126/science.1067575

McGill, Liam 2015. "Neanderthal Behavioral Modernity and Symbolic Capabilities," Field Notes: A Journal of Collegiate Anthropology: Vol. 7, Article 5. Available at: https://dc.uwm.edu/fieldnotes/vol7/iss1/5

Trinkaus, E. 1993. Femoral Neck-shaft Angles of the Qafzeh-Skhul Early Modern Humans, and Activity Levels Among Immature Near Eastern

Middle Paleolithic Hominids. *Journal of Human Evolution.* 25 (5).

Zeder, Melinda A. 2009. "The Neolithic Macro-(R)evolution: Macroevolutionary Theory and the Study of Culture Change." *Journal of Archaeological Research,* 17, (1) 1–63.

# THE MIND

*A mind is a terrible thing to waste.*

-Frederick D. Patterson-Founder:
United Negro College Fund 1945

Keywords: *Primers, cues, basal brain core, external material cultures, observational skills, observational awareness, multitasking cognitive utilization, perception, cognition, power and control, agrios, competition, Mathematical Algorithm of Humankind.*

We are them and they are becoming us…

Every time our ancestors looked up into the sky, they witnessed a most extraordinary complex and confusing domain. They understood that the light by which the Earth's surface and land below could be seen came from above and were aware of the powerful dominance it had on life itself. In nature's ritualistic display they saw the cycles of light each day and the tiny specks of light that each night filled the sky as Earth's daily celestial rotation permitted. In addition, they quickly developed awareness that these specks of nightly starlight, as well as the daily sun and moon objects, moved around the sky as larger cycles themselves. A further awareness emerged when they learned and passed down to their descendants that those same specks of starlight not only moved around and sometimes disappeared, but also that groups of them would come to occupy a different segment of the night sky grid, and a different star would seem to stop motionless for a while.

Ancient man was driven by the mindset that he was observing this dimension of the natural universe that was awe-inspiring, magnificent, overwhelming, unexplainable, and entirely unreachable except in his mind. This intersection where empiricism and imagination diverge, is the point of interpretive departure from our modern minds. Without the ability to apply any sensory framework except to see and reason, they were left with interpreting the sky world through their eyes and minds.

Our senses today dictate the same mindset of attitude-behaviors and associated emotions as lived by our ancestral kin, with the bonus that new knowledge helps us create new meaning and perspective. To reconcile life, its purpose and their soul's existence through a fashioned eternity, their imagination intellect had to replace the inability to touch, feel, and be with that upper world in the moment. All these features are a big part of what differentiates humans; them and us, from other terrestrial life forms. Awareness is one part of the apparatus that is the human mind.

Nam and Muh, our fictional characters, had many generations to hone their awareness skills. This repetitive knowledge building expanded their generalized and specialized intellectual skills. When they had to use their minds to infer knowledge in abstract forms, as from the skyscape, they drew upon life's pathway to cognitive knowledge processing to create meaning. These factors of neurology, instinct, emotions, eco-environment, life experiences, and social input factors motivated and influenced their attitudes and behaviors toward this meaning creation.

The attitude and behavior mechanism was, is, and will be entangled within the fabric of the human mind for the foreseeable future. This pathway diagram is laid out in my Honeycomb Model of The Mind. The salience of this biologistic interfaces with all aspects of the human life form. The mechanism drives our human condition, instincts (basic biological urges), social cultures (our relations with other people), eco-environmental (our relations with other life forms and the physical world around us), and operate (live) within our universe in these ways.

The catalyst for ancient humankind to develop these new cognitive perceptions and capacities notably came from learning to tap into the previously underutilized potential of the brain. The conditions of underused potential continue today as over 90 percent, according to popular research opinion, of the human brain capacity is diagnosed as untapped potential. What our future ancestors will uncover about us in this regard will reside within the same framework of discovery, analysis and reasoning conclusion that we are imposing today upon our ancestral brethren. That is, humans will continue to evolve, developing new awareness, knowledge, and more basic anatomical features, while eliminating some others.

Modern attempts to obtain and dissect knowledge to capture and promote a better understanding of this complex organ in the biological universe have been more marginally incremental than abundant and expedient. A multidisciplinary approach to recent discovery contains contributions from cognitive scientist and philosopher Jerry Fodor. He introduced a model titled "the architecture of the mind" as being functionally modular, consisting of an instinct-driven central core and two peripheral modules: perception and linguistics. This dual horizontal and vertical interface functionality allows the perception module to process sensory stimuli, while the linguistic module facilitates external interactions with others (Fodor 1978). His follow-up work introduced a subdivision of the linguistics module into the model to allow for the formation and interface of an individual's attitudes. These were derived as internal memory attitude *primers* and *cues* obtained from the external environment as the basis for attitude-influencing (Fodor 1983). Support and integration of this framework into the larger mind architecture model is still advocated today.

Fodor's work allowed for additional detail and context into the larger comprehensive attitude-behavior mechanism and how it was practiced by early man. Some situations require the individual to draw on his natural instincts for resolution as proposed by Fodor's central core module, which I will refer to as the *basal brain core*. These include basic food sustenance and danger avoidance attitude-behaviors directed by our central core pathway and not necessarily by social or linguistic attitude primers and cues. Examples of these experiences include collecting vegetables from your garden to consume upon feeling hungry or obtaining a Band-Aid to apply to an open wound. In quotes, this statement appears as: "I am hungry; I will now find food to consume," or "I am hurt; I must find treatment for healing".

These non-socially driven episodes interface with the outside environment but focus solely on information from the individual's mindful experience memory and does not include or minimize the circumstances of the present physical environment and its unique context in relation to the immediate cause of the attitude-behavior, which is to "find food" or to "find treatment for my wound".

A shortcoming to the inspection of Fodor's model is that only the attitude element has been considered by his research methodology. Other situations involve social perceptions and linguistics by their nature because they often involve an individual's interactions with the external world while simultaneously within the presence and/or influence of other people. Together all three of these instinctual, perception, and linguistic interfaces lack consideration of the larger behavioral element.

Concurrently to the introduction of Fodor's work, psychologist Howard Gardner proposed his Theory of Seven Intelligences. His subcategory classifications of the mind include; linguistic, musical, logical, kinesthetic, spatial, and two personal intelligences: one where we become adept at looking inward to our own mind and one to look outward at other people's minds (Gardner 1983). In 1992, psychologists Leda Cosmides and John Tooby compiled data from multiple research studies to conclude that the modern human brain came to work like a Swiss Army knife with many specialized tools that in totality comprised the entire brain function (Cosmides and Tooby 1992).

An example of this technical mind can be observed in the archaeological record. This portrays a revolution in tool making technology to where weapon tips obtained simply from chipping flakes from a larger stone by hominids advanced to multi-step blade manufacturing and refining. Another achievement occurred in Middle Paleolithic times when fire was adopted in this tool making process. Larger weapon blades slowly replaced more clumsy axe tools which allowed for hunting of larger food game in the same period and through the Upper Paleolithic.

In his 1996 work, *The Prehistory of The Mind: The Cognitive Origins of Art, Religion and Science,* archaeologist Steven Mithen created a model of modern man's mental evolution into a series of gradual naturally selected, and environmentally influenced progressions that built upon the active framework of the instinctive brain core. His "intelligences" of the social, general, natural history, and technical mind evolved through tens of millions of years. Indigenous animals of the time possessed this earliest instinctive mind architecture. Through evolution this became known as our instinctive basal stem core; the deepest brain region in eukaryotes that contain such an organ system. The autonomic nature of behaviors thought to be derived from this neurological pathway are processed here. We know the brain stem core is the oldest functioning region as all other younger cerebral sections which control so much of our mental repertoire are spatially situated peripheral to the basal stem. It is the existence of these newer environs that sets higher order animals apart. Even younger specialized regions are the reason our mind is considered far advanced from the rest of the animal world.

According to Mithen, the early mind of about 20 million years ago was influenced by a process in which human intelligence was in its early development and driven by "thinking about social transactions and animals as a natural history intelligence" (1996). Moving farther up his timeline the modularized instinctive intelligence of our oldest hominid lineage evolved various compartmentalized technical intelligences and finally a linguistic phylogeny only a few hundred thousand years ago. It is at this point in his timeline where our current level of cognitive fluidity gains its provenance (Mithen 1996, 211).

The modern human mind of the proto-urbanization revolutions transformed these specialized brain mechanisms into a more generalized and cognitively fluid one that, according to Mithen, included "the animals now making social transactions" (1996, 198). According to Mithen, the generalized mind and the compartmentalized specialized minds, oscillated in importance as the primary mechanism of the mind since the Homo erectus era of over 1.6 million years ago (1996, 145, 195-197). Mithen further refined his ideas into a schematic titled, *The mind as a Cathedral,* showing the latest historical progression of the mind from the earliest general, then the specialized, and finally to the advanced hunter-gatherer cathedral mind architecture (my Honeycomb Model).

This serves as support for my Honeycomb Model of The Mind. The metaphorical schematic begins by transforming the first 'chapel' of generalized intelligence and adding value to each stage by first inserting new specialized node architecture, defined as the chapels of social, technical, natural history, and linguistic intelligence that, according to Mithen, however, could not interface with each other at first. These new chapel nodes functioned like the specialized tools contained in a Swiss Army knife. Mithen's theory thus builds upon Cosmides and Tooby's Swiss Army knife model in describing the evolution of the human mind from the times of the hominid ancestors. More recent chapels were outlined by Mithen to signify creation of new specialized and generalized chapels. This was how the mind developed until roughly 100,000 years ago (Mithen 1996).

This interface constraint is overcome through the evolutionary time periods of the Paleolithic Era by a slow morphological tapping into our brain's underutilized cognitive capacity. This process continued into the Early Neolithic and became the complete transformation to the modern human mind akin to ours today (Mithen 1996, 65-72).

I suggest that the general physical environment also played a significant role in shaping the mindful evolution of our ancestors and continues today. This is shown in the Honeycomb Model diagram. When investigating the questions of who we are and examining our roots, all dimensions of this attitude-behavior pathway must be considered within the entire mechanism, whether the episode involves other people or just the individual.

When considering Fodor's architectural model of core central, perception and linguistics, what arises are insights into a kind of naturally selective chronological pecking order. Humankind's instinctual biology and neurology arrived first which may be why our current knowledge of the brain's architecture explains that the instinct centers are spatially located within the brain's basal stem region.

Later in time, we became aware of self and others in aspects of life, existence, purpose, specialized, and generalized intelligence due to the emergence of perception neurology. This was made possible only because our brain expanded both in intellect and morphology. Our cognitive advancement was shaped by the growth of new brain functional centers. The brain became physically larger and these new functional centers, the cerebral and neo-frontal cortex regions, grew spatially around the core brain stem.

This sequence could be illustrated by the procedure of functioning a computer core memory hard drive then installing additional specialized modules to enable new expanded brain archetypes. These would include the perception, linguistic and limbic behavioral regions that Fodor started to explore, among others.

Still more recently, ancient people obtained many forms of linguistic, social and *external material cultures* only in more modern times. Here I mean that these modern cultures developed in the urban Revolutions of the Early Neolithic didn't exist within a recognizable framework during the Middle Paleolithic up to 100,000 years ago or certainly not back in the time of hominids. The overall attitude-behavior protocol continued to operate, from a perspective of geologic time, from a combination of trial-and-error, maturation of *observational awareness,* development of *observational skills,* and new knowledge that, in a positive feedback loop mechanism, produced more intelligence through time.

Next, I define a few terms and introduce a relationship between two important tools of human development, linguistics and symbolism. Both are generally agreed to be indispensable factors to our successful evolution as a species. Merriam-Webster defines linguistics as, "the study of human speech including the units, nature, structure, and development of language, languages, or a language" (2024). They define symbolism as, "the art or practice of using symbols especially by investing things with a symbolic meaning or by expressing the invisible or intangible by means of visible or sensuous representations" ("Symbolism" 2024). Whereas linguistics exists only within a domain of verbal communication, and because we have no record of any conversations from ancient history, there exists no empirical proof of what information was spoken; therefore, I will not provide a detailed analysis of this still vital instrument of human development. I suggest that linguistics is a major category, but only a category of the broader symbolic communication concept. I will provide a detailed analysis of humankind's semiotics Revolution in the *Symbolism* chapter.

For now, let me focus on introducing this relationship. Fodor suggests that the forming of attitudes, as interfaced with the peripheral linguistic sub-module of his *Modularity of Mind* must be defined to allow for both an individual's mental interpretation of symbolic representations and the attitudinal cues and primers transacted by the other people to the interaction. Both are indispensable elements to our cognition and resulting understanding of existence in our universe. Identified here are two sources of attitude influence; symbolism and other people's actions and behaviors. Here 'symbolism' was suggested in purely socially abstract contexts and then only within linguistic parameters.

Certainly, social symbolism is a major driving force for attitude development. However, other forms of symbolism can be and were derived from natural sources in the environment. The empirical context with which nature operates in this mindset must be included in any conversation where development of the mind of ancient humankind is considered. Moreover, using a current cultural definition of 'linguistics' appears to be too narrow an interpretation when it only suggests alignment with language-as-speech and, consequently, has only been studied as such.

As I will demonstrate later, many forms of symbolism or symbolic representations exist, including that our ancestors utilized to communicate knowledge, information, ideas, or ideologies. I introduce the notion only to make the point of a continually refined aptitude for and practice of observational awareness and skills that included developing attitudes, trial-and-error, mimicry and other strategies and environmental/ecological natural factors, that was needed for our ancestors to succeed in achieving the existential advancements they left for our enjoyment and evolutionary advancement.

\* \* \*

In these last 100,000 years we begin to uncover tangible and symbolic historic evidence transformative to the human mindset; his perception and cognition, to an entirely revelational world and life view.

Both Mithen's (1996) and Cosmides and Tooby's (1992) research, encompassing the development of self and cultural awareness beyond instinctiveness, was necessary to allow the mind to initiate deployment of what I call *multitasking cognitive utilization.* This is where many packets of information, the environmental stimuli that are the datasets which enter our neuro network pathway, are processed simultaneously to become our *perceptions* and *cognition.* These perceptions are combined with our brains' attitude primers and cues as drawn from other people in the social environment, the spatial physical environment, as well as from our brain's memory banks, then driven through the cognitive analysis process. The most critical feature of this process is that, like the fastest computer routines, stacks and subroutines yet to be invented, our brain processing centers still run this multitasking mechanism faster than them and can simultaneously compute information within a multitasking framework.

An example of this procedure is one that drivers use every day; the task of simultaneously activating a turn signal while operating all the other functions of the moving vehicle, such as having the foot on the gas pedal, steering, observing other traffic or objects in or near the road surface. Another common example is where your mind is tasked in remembering to retrieve your cell phone or other paraphernalia from the gym locker while your attention is diverted by a stimulus from a friend or other person who starts a conversation with you.

More generally, operating the controls on a device while operating another device and/or while holding a conversation with another person is a more general multitasking cognitive utilization example. Multitasking cognitive utilization is a feature of the modern mind as a "gift" from our ancestors. This is practiced everyday by everyone.

As the Paleolithic Era progressed, Homo sapien sapiens grew his instinctive, technical, and social intellectual perceptions and capacities. A continuous influence of genealogical, psycho-social, reproductive developmental habituative, environmental, geological, geographical, and ecological factors progressed a growth model of the mind. Knowledge perception and knowledge capacity expanded gradually in a positive feedback recursion loop. This can be perceived through the diagram of my Honeycomb Model of The Mind.

## *Diagram of*

## *The Honeycomb Model of The Mind*

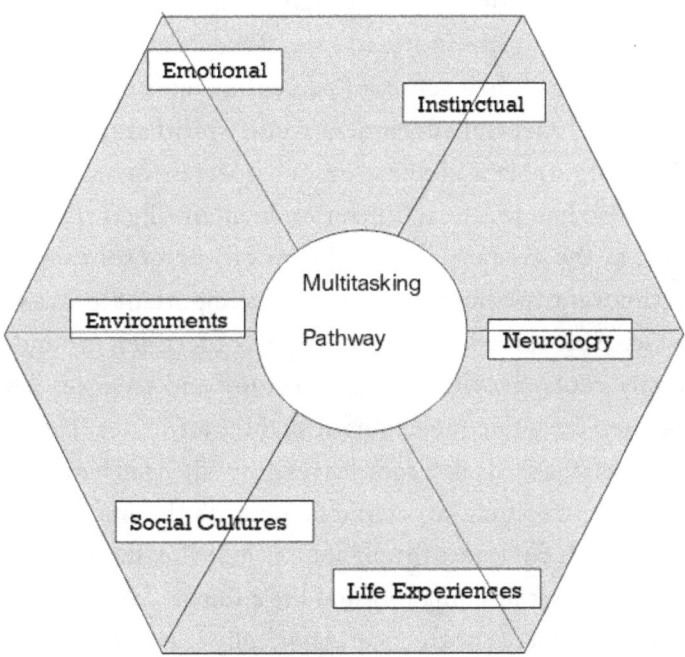

Our mind's functional framework can be illustrated metaphorically in a portrayal of an object from nature; the honeycomb. Human evolution can be aligned from considering this portrayal with that of another object in nature; a tree adorned with said honeycombs.

The tree has been repeatedly relied upon for meaning and purpose throughout human's existence. First and foremost, I express amazement to our ancestral cultures for choosing the tree as such an important symbol. While they probably did not empirically know that the tree was the major source of the oxygen that they breathed, there was much other room for its inclusion into all aspects of their existence. I now suggest to you that, how often have you thought of this function of a tree in your lives?

In all ancestral traditions, the tree was an indispensable link in the Great Chain of Being. The tree was known as the first universal "great spirit" of ancient traditions. This is probably due to its unique structure in nature, intuitive geometrical form, and the many analogies it shares with the patterns and cycles of life and existence. Our ancestors observed trees for as long as they had their senses of perception and cognition.

The tree was a universal adornment to the spirituality and cosmology of virtually every ancient civilization and species for millions of years. The tree has also had practical utilization in all pre-historical eras. It has been known as the Tree of Life, or Flower of Life in some cultures, as a symbolic ethnocentric compass to everything important to an existence in the Universe. This includes being a symbol of fertility, grounded moral values, family roots, growth, peace, harmony and balance, rebirth and immortality, and the interconnections of all these attributes. The life cycle of a tree starts when the seed takes root, leaves grow, then fall with the changing seasons only to grow anew larger and better with the emergence of a new seasonal cycle. This continues throughout its long life. In summary, the tree was a most important teaching tool and life compass for our ancestors.

The stem and roots of the tree metaphorically correspond with the honeycomb's instinctual segment that is our brain's basal stem infrastructure; the core part of our brain to where much of our instinctual behavior is derived. Both represent a trunk whose purpose and function make their respective lives possible. The roots and trunk stem are the empirical core of each one's existence. The form and function of both is in harmony and whose operation is in equilibrium in their minds.

Now let's put on our metaphorical analysis thinking caps. The tree's branch system is a visually appealing representation of our brain's superstructure. Built peripherally upon the brain's basal core system as an evolutionary achievement, thinking about the superstructure in this way is congruous to Mithen's technical, natural history, social and linguistic chapels of intelligence or the Seven Intelligence centers of Gardner's theory. This includes the linguistic, musical, logical, kinesthetic, spatial and the two personal inward and outward inspection centers of our individual self and the external others, respectively, as noted earlier. One can imagine this branch superstructure labeled as a series of descriptive brain centers that we know of today as the cerebellum, caudate nucleus, Broca area, frontal pole, and the three cortex sectors: primary visual, prefrontal and anterior. The physiological purposes, functionality, and work requirements of the respective tree branch and our brain's superstructures, however, are existentially different.

The circuitry of the human brain exists in such a way that allows for the accumulation and amalgamation of a lifetime's worth of attitude and behavior activities to affect a meaningful purpose to our course of life. The honeycomb mnemonic portrays the segments of neurology, instinct, emotion, environment, social culture, and life experience of the individual as necessary inputs, or 'food' that the organism. the brain or the tree respectively, need to operate. The multitasking pathway is that part of the thinking process, or the branch of the tree, that governs thoughts, behaviors, meaning and knowledge, and attached to such are the leaves and honeycombs in the tree. The collection of honeycombs can be situated emblematically around the branch system's three-dimensional space, analogous to our brain's superstructure. This superstructure contains an almost innumerable amount of processing paths with which sensory neurological impulses can travel through to create a thought process. Each node is illustrated as a honeycomb.

Multitasking cognitive utilization was an advancement to this new awareness of self and the many surrounding environments as is illustrated in the diagram. Re conceptualizing and building upon earlier works, it is now known today that the biological architecture of the ancient mind was equivalent to ours in every way and that some of these intellectual activities were already in use even as far back as the time of Homo erectus.

Therefore, I assert that the development of more complex attitude cues, and the multitasking pathway interfacing activities of the cognitive mind system nodes had already long been in use.

This biology was comprised of numerous specialized cognitive systems that can be visualized akin to what generally constitutes the functionality of a computer program. The instruction code for a program uses generic versions of routines, stacks, and sub-routines to help process information. These subsets of the main program possess multitasking capabilities. When scaled up, multiple programs can use the same multitasking mechanism to process even more information and data. This illustration makes much intuitive sense in that the creators of computer systems and their associated programming use the human mind as the overarching design template.

Using Mithen's thesis of the 'mind as a cathedral' (1996, 67), I expand upon his model by reshaping the general/specialized chapel architecture into a descriptive model that integrates the many activities the brain's systems undertake when the thought process occurs. My Honeycomb Model of The Mind allows for all forms of specialized and generalized thinking by following an attitude-behavior protocol that allows for multitasking of the associative brain architectural systems (sensory, cognitive/executive, memory, limbic/behavioral) and processing of the attitude primers and cues into resulting behavioral outcomes. The principle of attitude and behavior is so universal, a morphology of our species as a core essential to how our minds were developed, that I will expand upon what is going on in this protocol.

Attitude cues are inspired and created from observations made in a person's sensory environment and incorporate data from his memory relevant to the situation. A primer is a stimulus that influences the perception, cognitive process, attitude, and potentially a decision behavior of a person. These cues and primers are the instrumentality for what motivates us to act in a certain way.

Our sensory environment observes a phenomenon or event, attitudinal cues are activated and processed, and the attitudes themselves and concluding decisions that translated into behaviors are shaped from an analysis of those cues. This realm has not been subject to much comprehensive investigation in the research literature. It is my hope that new roads of knowledge can be paved from recognition to the prevalence, pervasiveness and efficacy of these concepts on the human condition.

Recalling my definition of *observational awareness* from the *Awareness* chapter, that is defined as the use of our biological senses to receive stimulus data from the surrounding environment in an enlightened manner to which meaning can be derived. It is part of the larger concept of *observational skills*, also referred to as 'mindfulness'. Observational skills make use of our perceptions of stimulus data and our brain's cognitive, analytical and memory information pathways which drive understanding and an assignment of meaning to what is being observed. I will discuss this in more detail in the *Mind* chapter.

Observational awareness can be defined as the perception step in an observational skills exercise that uses our biological senses to receive stimulus information data from the surrounding environment in an enlightened manner for analysis and to which meaning can be derived. The capacity for the brain to accept, process and store observations are the foundation for its ability to create knowledge, memory and intellect.

Observational skills are the abilities of a person's cognitive mechanism to perceive, understand and save environmental stimuli and cues. Observational skills make use of our perceptions of the stimulus data and our brain's memory information library pathway to derive understanding and an assignment of meaning to what is being observed.

Together, these observational skills and awareness are made possible by recently discovered neurological processes enabled in the brain of humans. Two related sub cortical brain nuclei systems, the basil ganglia and the caudate, the latter of which is connected to another significant enabler, the putamen, are all linked by 'bridges' of grey matter pathways. These regions influence both motor and executive brain functions, including learning, memory, motivation, and reward. Both pathways themselves interact with the limbic system to also influence behavior and emotions. These pathways are where perceptions about the environment and the event under consideration are caused, or cued to develop attitudes which, in turn, drive toward a behavior pattern.

* * *

I began with the development of an awareness argument as initiating the mindful transformation of our Paleolithic ancestors into a more modern version of us; still not quite able to navigate through our kind of life with the existential ability of their Neolithic heirs.

It is generally conjectured that during the Middle Paleolithic, humans became operant conditioned to behave in social constructs. A reasonable inference as to the origin of these evolutionary characteristics can be made from inspecting the archaeological weaponry tool record. As time progressed, the tips used for game hunting gradually became larger. These resultant advancements enabled opportunity for group hunting of larger prey.

However, by around 100,000 BCE there occurred an explosion in growth of the hunting tool kit design, materials resource utilization, and construction techniques. This revolution was further influenced by both geographical and period adoption differences among civilizations and humanoid species. Resources such as bone, ivory, antler, and a new variety of stone materials became ingredients of a tool kit inventory that now included tipped projectiles, hooks and other sharp implements that could be utilized to disable their larger prey.

This corresponds with Steven Mithen's general, social, technological (specialized), history and linguistic Intelligences model to where each of the respective "chapels" were grown more recent in time than the preceding (Mithen 1996, 67). These advancements, examples of specialized intelligence growth, were concomitant with social developments, which themselves required development of a specialized social intelligence to work.

Implicit within this argument is the operative requirement that new social cooperation needed to happen for such a record of these artifacts to have been deposited for our discovery. This expansion of hunting cults accorded a corresponding expansion in social cooperation seemingly as a survival mechanism. Here was proof that humankind now possessed the technology, mind and cooperation to hunt wild game food creatures much larger than the individual. Later, when more elaborate food and shelter industries were needed in society, these mindful ways were adopted and adapted to the changing environmental, ecological, and biological conditions, including those of the mind.

A way for you to perceive this progression of the mind and its effects on humans is to visualize the Maslow Needs Hierarchy pyramid, as the 1943 creation of psychologist Abraham Maslow. This pyramidal illustration contains five platform levels of needs goals. The most basic one; the foundation level, was reasoned by Maslow to signify the physiological needs fulfillment challenge. This includes the <u>biological</u> needs of breathing, food and water, along with sleep, sex, and homeostasis of the overall body organism (Maslow 1943). Note that these are all elements of the instinctual basal brain and regulated by those spatially situated environs around the core of the brain. These operative regions are significant and include, but not entirely limited to, the brain stem, cerebellum, hypothalamus, medulla and elements of the limbic system. These sections are peripherally situated and, through the natural selection process and other factors, were created and developed later in humankind's evolution.

Maslow titled his next higher needs challenge the 'Safety and Security' level. Our morphology grew the need for this security level which allowed for the eventual creation of other higher needs levels. This platform included the needs mission of obtaining bodily security, social cultures, health and later material resources, property and labor industries. Note that all these elements contain an inherent significant social element. The platform could be reasonably retitled Social Cultures. Natural selection of this second level was agreed to have occurred around the later Middle Paleolithic (Donald 1991; Mithen 1996; Cauvin 2000). You are now up to speed with an illustrative categorization of what our ancestral kin achieved in the areas of technical and social intelligence.

Note that Mithen's Intelligences model includes a "history intelligence" in his argument. Until about one hundred-thousand years ago there was still no evidence (yet discovered) of in scripted symbolism or any other technique that demonstrates possession of detailed thought within a historical intelligence context. Maslow compartmentalized these features in other levels of his overall Needs Hierarchy model. Also note that, upon a close inspection, you observe (as I have) that there is considerable intuitive overlap amongst an element of need and its potential to be meaningful on multiple levels. For example, the "sex" and "sexual intimacy" features in the 'physiological' and 'love/belonging' dimensions, or the "family" feature that Maslow includes in the 'safety' and 'love/belonging' dimensions could have more than a superficial meaning in both.

The human, as a social creature, was born into being when his mind developed the awareness that, to survive, humans must cooperate with each other for food and shelter sustenance, as well as all other needs challenges. For other creatures, such as those in the large undomesticated feline mammal genus, this characteristic trait is not as dependent. Their "sociability" needs challenges are observed to be dominated by only those associated with reproductive urges for most species, and family activities of the lion (the 'pride', etc.), as one notable exception to this principle. (Crowell-Davis, Curtis, and Knowles 2016; Bradshaw 2016). Even the domesticated cat exhibits regular behaviors we regard as unsocial; i.e. characterized by their need/want for extended periods of isolation from social activities and, when forced into these socialization activities, often show their displeasure by various antisocial behavior responses like hissing, tail-thumping, etc. However, from my observations, domesticated felines do seem to know when to turn on the "social charm" when they are hungry or thirsty. Purr!

*Power and control* cultures existed throughout the Paleolithic Era but were bi dimensional in nature. The subcategories consisted only of the competitive dualities between man and the animal environment and between man and his ecological environment. The ecology of the era is defined here to include the animal world, and the geophysical environment for climate and weather, geography and geology. I will use the ancient Greek term *agrios* to broadly define this concept throughout my narrative. The agrios is a recurring salient theme that you will come to recognize.

Hunting and gathering was the governing food sustenance strategy throughout this era. Most of the hunting and gathering communities comprised only small extended biologically related families. Therefore, no more broadly bonded social communities were known to have existed. This social subcategory of the larger power and control principle was a product of the urbanization Revolution, and its evolution became an academic boundary defining element of the Neolithic Era.

The power and control principle became a behavioral characteristic framework of human psychology with an embedded enduring context of *competition*. The two duality subcategories of power and control, along with competition that existed throughout the Paleolithic were between early man and the animal, and of the eco-environments. Only later in the Paleolithic did inter species competitiveness occur when the known representatives of the Homo sapien-sapiens, Denisovan, and Neanderthal commingled. These dualities were predominately driven originally by Homo sapien-sapiens' instinctive mind. Only later in the Paleolithic did his technical and generalized intelligence (advanced weaponry, sheltering, social behaviors, and a maturing mnemonic of nature's ecological environment) progress sufficiently to acquire a larger and more diverse set of attitude-behavior cognitive mechanisms in dealing with these dualities in a power and control context in the agrios. More recently, in the Neolithic revolution, when he became familiar with and experienced life in an urbanized environment, humankind's social intelligence further developed to then address the new competitive natures of social power and control.

\* \* \*

Humans today learn from the psychological characteristics of repetition, imitation, and mimicry. Did ancestral traditions develop the cosmic manifestations of their existentialism: sun, moon, Milky Way, constellations and gods/deities from repeated mimetic episodes of perceiving and mindful abstract then relating the shapes, forms, styles, substances, and attributes of both the sky and terrestrial environments to each other? Did they create symbolic representations as a product of this process? Did they perceive the patterns in both realms and merge this to create the critical thinking patterns and modeling assignment(s) of cognitive meaning and final assignment of attributes?

Imitation features a mindful process early humans used extensively to adapt, manipulate and modify their environments in some way. For example, the early Neolithic was the time that saw the origins of permanent architecture. In the Levant of the Middle East, we see depictions of construction engineering where the concept of a lintel, a proto conception of a roof structure, was in its early usage. An otherwise heavy object, stone, tree trunk, etc., was placed horizontally atop two vertical pillars. This architectural engineering has many practical applications, and its concept is still used today.

The provenance of the lintel probably came from indigenous observational awareness and skills of seeing tree trunks or boulders stretched across two similarly placed natural "studs" or vertically rising pieces that served as such. Often, they were built tall enough so people could walk underneath them or traverse across the lintel top piece. They certainly watched animals perform the same behaviors in nature. Their intuitive and instinctual minds perceived and adapted what they observed in the natural setting for use in the new application. This type of mimicry was innumerably repeated by Homo sapien-sapiens to establish their dominion over many inventions and achievements that kept them alive and maturing.

Mimicry allowed for establishing long-term memory learning. Small-group social cultures (hunter-gatherer ones-their extended families) established symbolism and mythology as a pedagogical routine after repeated (mimicked) episodic events of the same phenomena. Symbolism and language were later created as efficient means of communication between small-group social cultures and allowed for adoption of an agrarian and urban existence.

Humans derive meaning by comparing the options and alternatives under consideration. We also use analogy to compare two or more things under consideration. Humans also predict, analyze and make decisions on something about future events on a basis of historical evidence, events and critical thinking. Ancients learned and, due to expanded brain functions, remembered and recalled this learning when faced with a new situation. An example of this includes hunting a particular animal, cultivating a vegetable or staying away from a poisonous one.

Archaeologist Ian Hodder supports these statements about the mind and the structures of thought, "Thought could therefore be described as the making of linkages between or the making of patterns within past events including past thoughts". Furthermore, his thought on *meaning* is, "The giving of meaning to the world is no more than a particular reading of it. Meaning involves making a relationship between things" (Hodder 1990, 274).

Social, community and cultural structures are shaped and modified by reinterpretations of existing social, community and cultural structures. A continual methodology akin to the scientific method whereby observations are made, a hypothesis is stated, data collected and analyzed, and conclusions made as to modifying the existing domain or maintaining the status quo until another iteration of this methodology occurs.

Large monumental structures were conceived by leaders, those who possessed a psychological constitution of power and control, to facilitate increasing governance of the social group size. Hodder adds, "This cultural exaggeration and the extension of monuments to incorporate the wider landscape are certainly understandable in view of the desire to increase social group size and domination through the Domus-Foris concept" (1990, 277). This is an example of a thought structure affected by local authoritative, geographical and cultural influences to produce the unique structure, but can produce meaningfully different structures with a different influence set.

For me, thought can be extended into the mind's creation of ideas with reference to or motivated by the future and the present. Therefore, past-present-future are all within the domain of thought. Our human species is hard-wired into this process of creating meaning. The same process of meaning is driven whether today we look for patterns in the clouds and derive meaning, however different from rational, or compare the objects we see in those clouds to others in our mind's memory banks, making a snap judgement on the severity of an accident scene we either witnessed or became involved in, or reading this chapter.

This 'meaning' will often be different for individuals as dependent upon many factors. These include the individual's life experiences, environment, both ecological and geographical, education and learning, the person's worldview and the social groups to which he belongs or has belonged. This last factor is a vital takeaway point in a better understanding of the human species known as Homo sapien-sapiens. Humans are also hard-wired to be social animals. You will gain insight that this biological trait existed in prehistoric man and was birthed out of the most basic need to survive. Humans, like many other species that we can readily study today, had a need for social cooperation to obtain enough food, water and shelter to survive. Natural selection then became a 'governor' to which the most enduring and advantageous of ancient humans, or any other species, were adapted to survive.

* * *

You may get the impression that the process of how the mind works is extremely complex. So, it is and was for our ancestors. They had to grow complexity to pass it down to us. To prevent you from getting needlessly bogged down with analysis and interpretation of overly nuanced detail, I will invoke an underlying principle of 'Occam's Razor' to simplify explanations and inferences from this narrative. Simply put, the human brain is the most complex structure in all known biology and in the anthropic nature of us in the Universe. Its form and function have defied all our attempts at comprehensive understanding. Its style and substance align with this lack of understanding, though we are making very slow progress in both areas. This slow progress is inherently congruent with the evolutionary timescale of the human mind's development.

As you have become aware, the road that allowed the transformation of the mind from pure instinct through awareness to a higher order intellectual environment in my Honeycomb Model of The Mind and the multitasking cognitive utilization, was not short in duration; it took millions of years and a morphology from one anatomical genus (hominid) to another (Homo sapien and onto Homo sapien-sapiens).

Our ancestors neurologically processed information stimuli the same way we do today (the cognitive pathway is the equivalent) but their perceptions differed because they had a different knowledge archive with which to draw from. We have the advantage today of possessing both their archive and the one that has been continually added to since then.

By now attitude cues and behaviors selected for the creation of a new multitasking cognition regime that navigated behavior decision outcomes. The *Mathematical Algorithm of Humankind* was still being shaped by the $T_1$ variable of "who we were," and whose dominance by evolving the "how" and "what" dimensions was preparatory for the transformation into the more complex $T_2$ variable of "who we are". What was left now for Nam and Muh was only to become comfortable with the transformation from a focused open nomadic life to a domesticated and urbanized but boundary-laden one and the accumulation of practice time using the historical, social, and associative intelligences that came from the trials and errors of living life for those tens of millennia. They will soon learn to adapt to sea changes to their egalitarian "one for all and all for one" ethnicity, adopt new forms of symbolic meaning and sociality, and coordinate all of them into a new human ethos within a framework that includes not only the four cardinal directions of terrestrial life but the three vertical ones of the underworld, the terrestrial and the sky world.

In a scene that would have pleased the late Frederick D. Patterson, Nam and Muh did not waste their minds. They are on the precipice of many Revolutions of thought, transformation and success. Let's follow their footprint into the creation of 'us' in Act II.

*References*

Bradshaw, John W.S. 2016. "Sociality in Cats: A Comparative Review." *Journal of Veterinary Behavior* 11 (January): 113–24. https://doi.org/10.101 6/j.jveb.2015.09.004.

Cauvin, Jacques. 2000. *The Birth of the Gods and the Origins of Agriculture*, translated by Trevor Watkins, Cambridge: Cambridge University Press.

Cosmides, L. and J. Tooby. 1992. Cognitive Adaptations for Social Exchange. In *The Adapted Mind*, edited by J.H. BarKow, L. Cosmides and J. Tooby, 163-228. New York: Oxford University Press.

Crowell-Davis, Sharon L., Terry M. Curtis, and Rebecca J. Knowles. 2016. Social Organization in the Cat: A Modern Understanding. *Journal of Feline Medical Surgery*, 24, 6(1): 19-28.

Donald, Merlin. 1991. *Origins of The Modern Mind: Three Stages in the Evolution of Culture and Cognition.* Cambridge, MA: Harvard University Press.

Fodor, Jerry A. 1981. *Representations: Philosophical Essays on the Foundations of Cognitive Science.* Cambridge, MA: MIT Press.

Fodor, Jerry. 1983. *The Modularity of Mind.* Cambridge, MA: MIT Press.

Gardner, Howard. 1983. *Frames of Mind: The Theory of Multiple Intelligences.* New York: Basic Books.

Hodder, Ian. 1990. *The Domestication of Europe.* NJ: Wiley-Blackwell.

"Linguistics." *Merriam-Webster.com.* 2024. https://www.merriam-webster.com/. (17 August 2024)

Maslow, A.H. 1943. A Theory of Human Motivation. *Psychological Review*, 50, 370-396.

Mithin, Steven. 1996. *The Prehistory of The Mind: The Cognitive Origins of Art, Religion and Science.* London: Thames and Hudson Ltd.

Sperber, Daniel. 1994. The Modularity of Thought and the Epidemiology of Representation. In *Mapping the Mind: Domain Specificity in Cognition and Culture,* edited by Hirschfeld, L.A. & Gelman, S.A. 39-67. Cambridge: Cambridge University Press.

"Symbolism." *Merriam-Webster.com.* 2024. https://www.merriam-webster.com/. (17 August 2024).

# Act II: REVOLUTIONS

*The further into the future you want to see, the more important it is to look at the past.*

-Sir Winston Churchill

*Keywords: Toolmaking, domestication, the soul, feasting, Solar Cycle, social bonding, ritual, symbolic communication.*

We are them and they are essentially us...

Nam and Muh traveled very well, but they grew tired of it. This is in response to both eco-environmental circumstances and by their choice as motivation to create a better and longer life than the present level of subsistence offered. Their people were the progeny of many generations of elder kin who arose and migrated from their ancestral roots on the African continent to populate the world, as is generally agreed. The Homo sapiens' instinctual mind was expanded to embody a new level of critical thought, raised new awareness of their social, technical and historical cognitive capabilities as products of incremental augmentation by their brain's emergent executive thought centers. This became an evolved developmental plasticity in early humans that was greatly influenced by the various environmental and ecological factors previously discussed. The circumstances allowed adaptations into new realms of life and achievement, the most important of which was maturation into the social creature they became. I will elaborate on the social cultural aspects later in this chapter. For now, I will congratulate them on becoming essentially us.

This chapter discusses the significance of a Revolution of thought, and its growth, that occurred at that time. The backdrop for this mindful evolution leading up to the Revolutions has always contained a necessary awareness to the empirical truth that the life requirements of food and water are our most basic life needs. When considering any period of history or prehistory an obvious reality is that, when these are in readily short supply, or their acquisition becomes problematic, human survival mode attitudes and behaviors will dictate this as the foremost needs requirement to be satisfied.

Support for this biological empiricism comes from inspection of a challenges inventory a species will encounter during its existence. Consider this idea: Long-term survival of a life form requires successful navigation through many existential "great filters." In his 1998 paper, *The Great Filter: Are We Almost Past It?* economist Robin Hanson (1998) wrote that for a species to evolve into a cosmic colonization, it must survive through nine stages where existential barriers can occur. Popular culture and the more learned communities speculate that, simply because "we have no evidence" of an extraterrestrial intelligence that one of his steps, either one of the nine or a tenth that we have not yet encountered as a species, is impossible to survive (Hanson 1998). This is important because Hanson's hypothesis is step wise in nature in that intelligence is required to advance its species to a cosmic existence and to have successfully maneuvered through all the great filters.

Presumptively present in all nine of Hanson's Great Filters is the entanglement that availability of food, water and shelter are continually necessary for any biological species to survive in the moment and through its sustained evolution. This is another influence of Maslow's pyramidal foundation tier of his Hierarchy of Needs Theory, as noted earlier. A new understanding of the Paleolithic-Neolithic Revolutions can be advanced by examining this entanglement. Let me introduce Hanson's seventh filter stage.

This stage lies within the domain of advanced *tool-making* intelligence skills. All nine filters are either constraints themselves or ones that contain filter constraint potential. Nam and Muh's people advanced to encounter this stage and had the following constraint potentials that were as salient for them as they are for us today.

Besides the basic physiological need requirement for and constraints inherent in the acquisition of food, water, and oxygen, humans share a need with other land animals for favorable geological, climatic, ecological, and reproductive developmental conditions to evolve.

Life was a product of Earth's natural geophysical development in the unique way that caused all of us to exist in the forms to which we are known. Flesh-borne creatures on Earth need protein and carbohydrates just as trees and plants need carbon dioxide with which to metabolize for life to continue.

These are some links in the Great Chain of Being. Both need the sun and water with their unique characteristics to allow survival in the fabled astronomical 'Goldilocks Zone' of our solar system. Both sun and water were in sufficient supply to allow the commencement of the metamorphosis of life.

The activities of mother nature caused us and all life to develop <u>in the way it did</u>. Those words are significant because they encourage us to seek and accommodate a scenario where life could exist elsewhere and may not precisely operate with all the nuanced form and functionality as life on Earth.

Lower-level Maslow hierarchy needs such as these were not central to Hanson's Great Filter Hypothesis but treated as an unarguable given. It seems too obvious to speak about this condition, but the fact is that, even today and for our future in the cosmos, the need for food, water and shelter will be omnipresent. Consequently, it will drive human attitude and behavior when a state of insufficient supply exists.

Examples of other more primary influential great filter challenges in which we have evidence to support their reality include the after-effects of cosmic events such as comets, meteor showers, asteroids, and solar phenomena.

These are all catalysts for their effects on the geology, climate and ecology of Earth. Other possibilities for appearance of an evolutionary great filter constraint include the species' potential for self-harm, through violence and altercation, catastrophic biological/anatomical harm from either a microbiological or another animal species.

A worldwide migration of intelligent life began around 2 million years ago when Homo erectus emerged from the Africa landmass to gradually populate all parts of the world. The most advanced Oldowan tool intelligence cult was transported with them. The global theatre was now primed for an evolutionary track that gradually saw the emergence of advanced precursor species to Homo sapiens in social, technical, and historical intelligences. Nature's forces, as I have described, were significant factors in telling the story of how the world grew into what it became at the time of the Neolithic Revolutions. By the time of the Revolutions, it is considered that those natural forces of the cosmos, geology, climate, and ecology combined forces to enable an accelerated pace of advancement in certain geographies. This dynamic infers that the pace of advancement was not uniform around our planet.

We have calculated that the most recent great Ice Age period lasted for over 250,000 years and ended just 12,000 years ago. We know that the biological life requirements include a very rigid architecture of geophysical and ecological variable equilibrium necessary for survival and growth. As these conditions were similarly required for the proliferation of animal and plant life, both food sources for humans, a favorable climate with imposing constraints is vitally important for all of them. Geographies that favored survival and advancement of all requisite species were scarce and built from African influences.

Though they were populated, the climates of the Euro-Asian and the continental Western Hemisphere were less conducive to providing the necessary conditions for an explosion of human development in the contexts of communal living and external material cultures. Therefore, it is not surprising that the earliest records of advanced social and historical cultures have been found thus far on or near the African continent. Recent discoveries from the Jebel Irhoud of Morocco (320,000), the Khoisan of South Africa (300,000), Florisbad of South Africa (250,000), and the Omo-Kibish I of Ethiopia support this argument.

The commingling of forces within our local cosmic infrastructure (the solar and nearby interstellar skyscape) with Earth's geological, climatic, and ecological systems were metamorphic to humankind's evolution in the long-term. However, short-term survival requirements dictated that food availability was a constant consideration. I introduce the food requirement into the formation of a strategic algorithm to illustrate the role these cosmic and planetary forces played in the eventual cessation of the hunter-gatherer migratory subsistence behavior culture. This circumstance, consequently, was an origin factor to the Neolithic Revolutions. Cosmic and geologic phenomena led to regional climatic and ecological changes that had varied and unique effects.

A sequence of events, including a gradual warming of the Earth until around 10,000 BCE, preceded two cooling Younger Dryas Periods, each lasting over one thousand years. They caused a rapid increase in the availability of food, shelter, and favorable climate conditions for life to flourish and advance. The effects of the temperature and glacial meltwater cycles allowed for a volumetric increase in these opportunities. This sequence generated an abundance of animal and plant protein and carbohydrates never experienced by our ancestors. These factors are supported as primary catalysts for the urban Revolutions of humankind, commercial applications to animal and plant domestication, and the eventual worldwide diffusion of these cultures by mainstream archaeology of the later 1900's, including V. Gordon Childe (1950) and Jacques Cauvin (2000), respectively.

The forces of nature, in summary, appear to be a de facto reason as the single most influential and agreed upon catalyst to how life has evolved on Earth today. That said, I can turn to less obvious factors toward formulation of a complete algorithm in an evolution of "us".

## ACT II: REVOLUTIONS

\* \* \*

What caused the Revolutions drama of this time? Insight can be gained from recalling the landscape of discovery already made and wondering about those yet to be made. The Revolutions of human existence contain many dimensions that I will introduce here and some that I treat separately in later chapters.

These Revolutions of thought, attitude, behavior, and existence were a gradual process with each element having its own provenance and compartmentalized within a larger framework. We can confidently infer that humans of the Pre-Holocene Epoch did not possess the intellectual know-how to have a direct immediate and significant influence on super powerful global climate forces that could dictate a particular life style utility. We cannot modify climate today either beyond a miniscule effect of a few hours in a small local geography. Alternatively, we have learned to adapt our living spaces to a peripheral coexistence with nature. This is about as much harmony and balance as we prefer to consider.

Therefore, it is obvious that the forces of nature shaped how food and shelter, as basic life requirements, became more abundant and were used as temperate ecologies became more commonplace post-Ice Age. These developments were characterized by distinct, variable time-to-diffusion trajectories across ancestral geographies. Improved nutrition and shelter opportunities afforded them more time in purpose and lifestyle during their 24-hour day cycle to devote their minds to other pursuits.

Homo sapiens of the Pre-Neolithic period had long been applying their intellectual expansion through step wise advancements in technology and refinements to social, specialized technical, and historical consciousness. By then, our ancestors' brains had physically grown in volume comparably to where ours are measured today. This meant that the brain's core instinct centers, together with the various peripheral cerebral cognitive systems, fully engaged the entire human attitude-behavior perception and multi-tasking cognitive utilization mechanisms that allowed for the functionality of all the intuition/instinctive, observational, perceptual and executive brain decision-making and systematics of memory. These newer adaptations just needed some time cycles of experience to pave the way leading toward today's homeostasis of mind.

Our brain's cognitive Revolutions were shaped through the last grand Ice Age cycle, from about 300,000 BCE to the Early Neolithic. The modern human mind of the proto-urbanization Revolutions was naturally selected and environmentally influenced to transform these specialized brain mechanisms into a more generalized and cognitively fluid one that included the creation of higher-order inference pathways from practice of our perception, analysis, and multitasking skills.

Some in the Revolutions debate argue that Western thought has relied too much on European socio-geography and normative thought to support an explosion of human intelligence that exponentially accelerated the technical, social, historical, and reproductive developmental thought evolution (McBrearty and Brooks 2000, 454). They assert that the foundation for these thought and practice Revolutions was modeled from African history dating back to about 100,000 years ago. Others, like British archaeologist Kevin Greene (1999, 97-109), suggest that "the search for these Revolutions is a search for the *soul*, for the inventive spark that distinguished humans from the rest of the animal kingdom". Still others like archaeologists Steven Mithen (1994, 1996), Paul Mellars (1991), and psychologists William Noble and Iain Davidson (1991, 1996), propose that human Revolutions only arose with the creation of language.

I note here that language is representative of the linguistics tool kit whose development was a significant factor for social interaction behaviors, cultural symbolism, and power and control strategies to come together as future universal cultural norms. The soul is a separate most confounding concept of the mind worthy of exploration, which I will attempt to offer in future works.

Therefore, it is probably too provincial (parochial) and simplistic to argue solely for a single geography as the absolute blueprint source for comprehending the Neolithic Revolutions. The debate contains no overwhelming body of evidence to decide a champion in this regard. Besides the certainty that we won't know "the rest of the story" for some time, characteristic features that add to a definition framework of this theory and the data suggest that dynamics from all continental geographies show universals in the human existence, as well as differences in the pace of Revolutions.

The minds of Early Neolithic man drove a road of steady progress and revealed a Revolution of technical intelligence, in the forms of accelerated tool-making sophistication and mass-production manufacturing, with the latter both in production quantities and resources used. Arrowhead production became more proficient as newer raw materials such as obsidian, combined with metallurgy and fire-treating forgery skills, were utilized. Newer processes meant sharper heads, larger tool construction, and a new industry for domestic tools that facilitated an agricultural Revolution.

An example of this technical Revolution from the prehistory material record portrays a tool advancement in Middle Paleolithic times, to where flake-chipped tips were replaced by a multi-step fire enhanced blade manufacturing and refining. Larger weapon blades slowly replaced more clumsy axe tools that allowed for hunting of larger food game in the same period and through the Upper Paleolithic.

Here is a snapshot of migrations and evidence that correlates to reasonable potential for the various Revolutions of subsistence and the human condition during the last few inter glacial Ice Age cycles of the last 130,000 years. It is demonstrated that they were indeed possible. Recent DNA research has dated the migration of aboriginal AMH (anatomically modern humans) from the African Asian corridor to New Guinea and Australia over 72,000 years ago (Malispinas et al. 2016). Aboriginal edge-ground ax technologies and pigment art (Maloney et al. 2018) and similarly compared art and tool inventories have been dated to over 35,000 years ago (Geneste et al. 2010).

In South America's Serra de Capivera región of Brazil, cave art dated to approximately 30,000 years ago are the earliest finds of a migration to that region about 44,000 years ago from DNA dating of human remains (Guidon et al. 2013). Recent excavations at Tagua Tagua, Chile, have uncovered remains of an Early Neolithic hunting and processing communal settlement with radio-carbon dating to about 14,550 BP (Labarca et al. 2024).

Recent discoveries of human footprints found in the White Sands Basin near Alamogordo, New Mexico, have been carbon-dated to about 23,000 years ago, during the height of the last Ice Age glacial maximum (Pigati 2023). These findings have rewritten the timeline to when this Southwest region was first inhabited, as originally considered to have been part of the Clovis technology culture of approximately 15,000 years ago, as well as the timeline for the great North American migration from the hypothesized Asian-Alaska ice bridge. About 10,000 years ago, near present-day Palm Springs, California, ancestors of the Native American nation of Agua Caliente thrived in one of the scarce temperate environments of the Southwestern United States.

A temporal advancement of the human condition has been recently uncovered at the Neanderthal site near Krapina, Croatia and aligns with a date stamp of 130,000 years ago by ESR and U-series chemistry dating (Monge et al. 2013). It is there where extensive depository remains suggest many advanced hunter-gatherer behavior schemes primarily attributable only to an Early Neolithic time neighborhood about 85,000 to 115,000 years ahead of its time. Among the behavior schemes suggested are advanced tool material cultures (Simek and Smith 1997), social community cultures that included medical care for members (Spikins et al. 2019), personal body ornamentation (Radovčić et al. 2020), possible feasting ritual mechanisms and a potential for cannibalistic and ceremonial burial cults (Ulrich 2005).

A fossil set discovered at the Rising Star Cave in South Africa, preliminarily dated to over 300,000 years ago, belonged to an archaic extinct Homo species, Homo Naledi. Also found were carvings of geometric shapes on cave walls and signs of an intentional ceremonial burial cult and associated meaning-making ritual activities (Berger et al. 2015).

We know that all these lands were inhabited yet nothing in comparison has yet been uncovered to conclude that our entire planet underwent a simultaneous advancement. The influence of natural climatic, geologic, and ecological changes on those locations was sufficient on its own to restrain advancement synchronous with that of the Levant. When specific human cognitive, reproductive development and other cultural characteristics are added to this algorithm it becomes obvious that nature helps select for advantages in certain life regions, from the periglacial to the sub-tropical and desert land masses.

I consider the Levant, now modern-day Middle East, to be a region rich in pertinent data that supports such revolutionary behaviors. This Asia Minor "melting pot" has offered many new insights that, in turn, has led to consideration of a new detailed understanding of the Paleolithic-Neolithic transformation. A region serving as a sample dataset to this explosion of evidence is situated within ancient Anatolia, now modern-day Turkey.

German archaeologist Klaus Schmidt began work at the Göbekli Tepe site (near the city of Sanliurfa) in 1994 in acknowledgment of its significance based on discovery surveys conducted in 1963. Schmidt's work began on the heels of a 1993 resurrection of research at the nearby site of Çatalhöyük by British archaeologist Ian Hodder and others. Dormant since the mid 1960's, additional findings have dated Göbekli Tepe to over 11,000 years ago and the Çatalhöyük site to approximately 9,000 years old.

Göbekli Tepe and Çatalhöyük remain over 95 percent unexcavated to this day. An even older site, Karahan Tepe, aged about 14,000 years, is also about 97% buried. More support to my notion that climate directly influences habitation and colonization behaviors in certain geographical regions at any point in time is present here in Anatolia, where, since the Göbekli Tepe and Çatalhöyük discoveries, many more settlements have been explored, including Çayönü, Hamzan, Harbetsuvan, Nevali Cori, Sefer, Sayburç, and Tasli, among many others.

The single most impressive overarching inference from these discoveries is that they show a widespread distribution of domestic, ritual, spiritual, cosmological, ceremonial burial, food, water, and resource management industry behaviors and activities. Examples of Revolutionary cultural traditions include a tightly packed communal neighborhood network within an extremely populated local geography. These discoveries forced a rethink into the realities of the Early Neolithic dominion. They are all products of an attitude-behavior and lifestyle Revolution that, up to then, were not thought to have been possible.

An inspection of the many artifacts and cult industries from this region, also popularly known as the Fertile Crescent, show examples of early pottery, pestles and bowls (Çelik 2010; Schmidt, 2012), terrazzo style floor surfaces (Güler, Çelik, and Güler 2013), and tool kit resources consisting of hammers, arrowheads, tips, picks and sickles from most sites. A most fantastic research achievement includes finding of the iconic T-pillar monoliths with altars inside circular geometric temple architectures considered to be part of a highly developed spiritual and cosmic ceremonial cultures (Çelik 2011), (Güler, Çelik, and Güler 2012), Karahan (Çelik 2011), (Schmidt 2012) Nevali Cori, Çayönü, Hamzan, (Çelik, 2010), Harbetsuvan (Çelik 2016), (Güler, Çelik, and Güler 2012), and Tasli (Güler, Çelik, and Güler 2013). The finding of sickles and picks, and rectangular spaces used as agricultural tools and storage architecture, respectively, for high output inventory management, lends support to a mindset of agricultural domestication.

From a comparison of the site characteristics in the overview of the Anatolian landscape, it is difficult to infer that the attitude-behavior of the indigenous could be defined within an archaic hunter-gatherer context. The proximity and population densities all settlements could have shown, at the least, reflects a waning of the migratory behavior existence patterns present throughout the last few Ice Age cycles.

The architecture cultures, especially of the many uncovered local ceremonial ritual buildings, show an improbability of completion by small, disparate groups of individuals characteristic of hunter-gatherer phylogenetics without social cohesion and coordination. However, the dating of these sites encompasses a timeline of more than 3,000 years. With the favorable landscape climate and ecological characteristics, it was entirely possible that smaller lineages of advanced hunter-gatherer mindset types migrated just a short distance to another site when the current one outlived its usefulness. Perhaps future DNA dating of remains could provide insight into the phylogenic features in a lineage-matching protocol.

ACT II: REVOLUTIONS

\* \* \*

Consider this attitude-behavior analogy: Nam and Muh had often come to find stone pieces that were more inherently sharp than the hunting and processing tips they were using. The observation behavior strategy was already in place to seek out and either find or manufacture more advanced hunting tips and cutting tools using better stones through trial and error and experimentation. They are also now deploying larger groups, from many examples depicted on cave art, rocks and architectural cultures worldwide, for hunting strategies and newly created food labor employment.

Nam and Muh also observed that available hunting game and edible plants in their immediate location have demonstrated that a life of high food stress and travel was becoming a thing of the past. They do not have to travel great distances to hunt game or gather plant foods as their ancient elders did, as has been the case now for millennia. Their migratory patterns have been altered as opportunities for a more bountiful sustenance became prevalent. This behavior pattern is analogous to and predictive from a similar behavior pattern of an animal herd. Migration and travel for animals are inversely related to availability of sufficient food and water. The less available food, the farther they must travel to satisfy those needs. Referring to my earlier support for regional or global climate change as nature's catalyst for cultural change within an indigenous population, this is just a sample dataset in the larger biological behavior experiment.

This new food economy started to shape their civic cultures in revolutionary ways. Record-based evidence infers that egalitarian-based extended biological family units remained the social norm for a while into the Neolithic. The emergence of better living conditions in the Levant allowed for natural agriculture to flourish. This caused the agrios, the wild environment; including animals, plants, humans, and the weather, to become favorable for a lessening of constant migratory travel behavior requirements. The new food economy freed up more hours in the day for humans to pursue other endeavors, like improvements to both the food and shelter economies, the next most basic hierarchal satisfaction needs.

Because shelter industries are a common life activity, animal behavior analogy is effective in predicting those human behaviors. One big difference is in how animals live and migrate to follow food, water, and weather. In four-season climates, the food cycle waxes and wanes in a recursive annual cycle. Animal behavior is directed from the nature of these agrios, so many are compelled to migrate (or hibernate) on at least a seasonal basis to satisfy the food sustenance requirement.

Humans first learned of this cyclic nature way back in the Awareness period; the great awakening of the mind, as part of their instinctive and cognitive attitude and behavior development, as noted in the *Awareness* chapter. Climate modifications of the Revolutions did not destroy this cyclical nature; it shaped it to humankind's advantage. A gradual exponential increase in food inventories occurred as over time, exploitation of these ecological patterns, in addition to advances in food preservation, agricultural cultivation, and eventually animal cultivation as a form of domestication, laid the groundwork for future cultural advancements.

Shelter cultures are the next most crucial survival requirement. It is problematic for many life forms in the agrios to practice a shelter culture due to biological limitations that make constructing shelters physically impossible. This is why some evolved to inhabit natural formations such as caves. Some that do not possess sufficient biological traits were naturally selected for the instinct to practice migratory attitude-behavior as a survival strategy. Many birds and mammals are classified in this way.

Some that do not possess the necessary biology still can survive even without migratory motivation as long as there are sufficient food, water, and warmth for survival. The North American bison is a species that cannot anatomically construct shelters but can thrive in a temperate to arctic climate due to its metabolic homeostasis. Food sustenance is, however, the most basic requirement and will trump shelter requirement as a matter of basic biology. So, if sufficient food is available year-round the agrios can adapt to a wide range of weather conditions as part of the local climate cycle. All life favors a "Goldilocks zone" for food and habitation survival.

## ACT II: REVOLUTIONS

Atmospheric warming conditions contributed to a wetter climate in the post-Ice Age. As periglacial environments transformed into temperate geographical ones, the foundation for a burgeoning wild agricultural industry was either born or revived. At Grotta Paglicci Cave in Puglia, Italy, stone food-processing apparatus, burial artifacts and illustrative paintings - dated to a Paleolithic time of 32,000 years ago - were discovered recently (Lippi et al. 2015).

Evidence from another 2015 field study uncovered 140 species of cultivated plant and accompanying weed infestation remains in the Ohalo II sedentary camp region of Galilee, Israel dated to over 23,000 years ago (Snir et al. 2015). This discovery predates the popular record of such location finds by 10,000 years or more. As more similarly dated settlements may be the subject of future discoveries, for now it can be speculated that this may indeed be a possibility.

A Solar Cycle exists today that tells us solar activity also waxes and wanes every eleven years, on average. This cyclic activity, when the dimensions of time and severity are proportionally expanded outward onto a longer pattern sequence, may provide much information as to how the cooling-warming rhythm of the Ice Age patterns behaved when scaled up to become cycles encompassing smaller ones. The artifacts and relics at Ohalo II and close-by sites suggest that the ecological conditions for agricultural innovation became favorable 23,000 years ago. The achievements may have been temporary, as mandated by nature, that were favored then discouraged and were re-acquired around 12,000 years ago. We may find that future discoveries came from different geographies as, in the 11,000-year period, food and shelter survival potentials may have driven communities to migrate short or long distances away from Ohalo II, as defined by human behavior.

Did the Revolutions begin with agricultural or food animal domestication? The evidence from Ohalo II suggests that agriculture cultivation industries emerged before wild animal food domestication. This point excludes a domestication of other animal breeds, such as dogs, who served a purpose as more tamed companion than wild prey. The case for precursor animal husbandry is more problematic when we consider the attitude-behavior mechanism in relation to environmental pressures and the psychology of social power and control.

Representational symbolic art clearly illustrates an unhurried metamorphism of the power perception in the agrios wild no matter the same or disparate geography. The timeline for these art examples begins from Cáceras, Spain, dated to 64,000 years ago. The panel depicts an animal in solo without any human portrayal. More recent cave art found at the Sulawesi site in Indonesia illustrates three extremely small human figures next to a predominately large figure of a wild pig dated to approximately 51,000 years ago (Oktaviana et al. 2024). The animal-as-powerful motif continues in 40,000-year-old art found at Lubang Jeriji Saléh cave in Borneo, Chauvet Cave, France dated to approximately 30,000 years ago, and progresses through to the Pillar art at Gobekli, Karahan, and at most of the Tepes in Anatolia of 11,000-15,000 years ago.

A reframing of the power and control perception in the human mind does not become symbolically evident until several thousand years later, as evidence shows from the Çatalhöyük site of about 9,000 years ago. The iconic wild bull is portrayed as being both deified and a manifestation of the great hunt as surrounded by dozens of armed hunters in dancing celebratory ritual (Mellaart, 1967). Therefore, support for an agriculture-animal cultivation-domestication sequence favors the evolution of plant industries thousands of years earlier, perhaps during the prior Ice Age warm-up cycle episode of 25,000 years ago, before the end of the last Ice Age and prior to the first Younger Dryas cooling period.

This sequence should not be interpreted as a degradation to the importance of animal husbandry. Along the way, the multitasking cognitive mind of Neolithic humans opportunistically observed and analyzed certain animal behaviors. Canines, goats, and sheep for example, are known to be among the currently considered earliest domesticated species, recording back to over 23,000 years ago, the time of the last Ice Age Maximum (MacHugh et al. 2016).

Logically, after investigating the extensive record of animal domestication efforts and experiences, we now know that many species can be domesticated. Many examples exist to prove that if an abandoned infant animal is adopted by a human parent who feeds, shelters and cares for it in an appropriate manner, the animal's attitudes and behaviors will drive it to live in a domesticated environment. The food and shelter requisites as empirical life requirement considerations drive a successful strategy for animal husbandry that the Neolithic multitasking cognitive intellect possessed in those times.

I would like to briefly reflect here on an interesting point. If evidence of canine domestication is dated 23,000 years ago, in this case from Siberia, is it meant to presume that all global indigenous simultaneously learned of and adopted this technology? By means of inference, I argue that this was not the case. Today knowledge of any invention can be diffused into global culture faster than ever in humankind's history; in practical terms, this now happens almost instantaneously. The Upper Paleolithic or Neolithic global population, however, is known to have lacked the capability of instant dissemination of information. Three possibilities of information diffusion to have been possible then would have consisted of either: an ability of the inventing culture to communicate this existence to another one, that the invention was achieved by the same intellectual human minds in disparate geographies, or that a third party disseminated the invention to the global population. Given a presumed technological prowess of ancestral traditions diffusion was known to not have been instantaneous.

Recall that this thought experiment would be undermined if there were not sufficient food, water and shelter available for the human practitioners to administer to the animal population. If food and water supplies were in equilibrium with demand, for both humans and animals, then husbandry would become feasible.

An additional consideration should be given to the possibilities of domestication among species classifications. Herbivorous creatures are more conducive to domestication than carnivores. Additional support to the cultivation/husbandry sequence can be argued that, generally the agricultural Revolutions diffused comprehensively into the civilized world before husbandry to give the human practitioners sufficient time to evolve sufficient planting industry processes which would then allow for domestication via a food-and-herding maturation process. This scenario was the case in MacHugh's Siberia canine case (MacHugh et al. 2016); if there was sufficient food, water, and shelter available, the dogs would have developed an attitude-behavior propensity to become domesticated.

\* \* \*

Social communities, reasoned to have appeared 700,000 years after our hominid ancestors disappeared around 1 million years ago, consisted of extended family congregations that are supported by conclusions drawn from fossil remains. Records of these findings are widespread across the globe.

When any group situation is created, the potential life cycle of a new power regime is catalyzed. This attitude-behavior ideology, though, was foreign to the hunter-gatherer group cultures because their sociology was manifested under an umbrella of egalitarianism. A pure form of equality among its constituents was preferred due to many factors. One of these was defined by the overarching requirements of the food sustenance activity. transformative climate change existed as patterns themselves due to the repetitiveness of Ice Age-to-warming cycles that the indigenous survived as early as the Middle Paleolithic of 300,000 years ago. The primal quest for food and water under these circumstances dictated that the indigenous be nomadic with the adoption of simple labor industries that called upon everyone in the group to participate when required. Time allocation to construction of permanent structures was not required then because a village did not remain in one place for an extended length of time.

These groups were much smaller and consisted primarily of extended kin. The ideology of family devotion was an instinctual one carried over from our ancestral species and was also present in the primates dated to 2.5 million years ago during the Pleistocene Era. Because the Paleolithic village consisted of kinship with these behavioral attitudes, the labor industries adopted the egalitarian characteristics of boundlessness and a focused family personality.

Demonstrative support for this sociological characteristic originates from an inspection of modern-day societies that maintain this egalitarian open and open-to-view society concept. Studies of the Inuit Eskimos, Mbuti pygmies, Hadza, !Kung, and Siriono cultures prove that, despite the constant encroachment pressures of neighboring societies with modern sociopolitical influences, these nations have achieved long-lasting success in their efforts.

While their philosophies are of open, no boundaries type, ethnocentric focus is individualized and involves every member, including the aged. The community acknowledges and celebrates the involvement of seniors by enabling them to continue working in whatever labor capacity to which they are capable, such as food procurement, household duties, accommodation, textiles, and those general merchandise manufacturing that are conducive to the capabilities of that demographic. These labor efficiencies have existed since Paleolithic times when elderly members made new points and spear blades for the younger, more physically capable members who participated in the game food hunts. Social power and control regimes, therefore, could not exist in these social environments until another concept of power, that is the imbalance of environmental power and control that naturally existed between humankind and the animal kingdom and living environments, became contested and controllable.

Ancestral clans, analogous to the reality of our contemporary examples, practiced a life purpose whose attitude and behavior mechanism was devoted, driven and resolved by clan status, kinship, age and gender, the latter of whom rigidly practiced many overlapping activities in their day-to-day lives (Gale 1970, 5). A labor equity model like this one required cooperation among hunter-gatherers. Consequently, an egalitarian structure emerged as the prevailing human nature. Examples of this limited social stratification ideology thrived in the Western Hemisphere until just a few hundred years ago, when the sociopolitical power and control orientation of the Mayan, Aztec, Native American, Inca, and Australian aboriginal civilizations flourished.

The marginal cost-of-food acquisition intuitively compelled early humankind communities to behave in this manner. Extensions of this learned behavior pattern compelled ancient societies to create a division-of-labor among the daily tasks required for continued living. Using an earlier version of our cognitive reasoning, intuition, observation analysis, and trial-and-error, these Upper Paleolithic and early Neolithic people segmented labor activities according to talent, productivity, design, and an early form of social engineering. In this way, they also discovered that a type of gender specialization existed to where males were more talented and productive at certain activities and females likewise.

A labor culture was formed this way to produce the most efficient and productive outcomes and not because of any gender bias. It is with this foundation that the genders of all ancient habitation groups "had a great deal of autonomy and influence" (Draper 1975, 78). Survival was the most important factor and motivation. Because of this labor structure, the social culture was decidedly equal among all tribe members.

Features of this labor structure served our ancestors well in adopting a holistic approach to life. A holistic awareness helped them to perpetuate a culture where a solid family structure, sharing, harmony, perpetuating the family tree, appreciation of their environment, and structuring a life compass and worldview according to nature's cyclical processes were the important matters of existence.

The Tree of Life concept was eventually conceived autonomously but universally by all cultures. Recalling my earlier introduction, this was cognitively derived from long-studied manifestations of the tree in nature. The tree grew for many years beyond the lifetime of a single or many generations. This means that elderly children would notice the same tree years later but that it was much larger than when their elders were alive. Trees characteristically grew many branch networks, and they also lose their leaves in the autumn every year in a natural cyclical process. Nam and Muh's people, for example, saw and learned this as a transformational process in their lives in adoption of moral life codes and such. The multi-dimensional transformation of this new version of Homo sapien sapiens is still considered as the single most salient collection of life changing attributes.

This new version of human versus animal duality was one of those revolutionary examples. By this time the perception of the human "self" in relation to the animal (agrios) and to more complex social roles with other people also emerged into the global consciousness. Permanent human communities started to grow; consequently, new labor industries proliferated to satisfy the growing food and shelter requirements of the proto-urban landscape. Permanent building cultures arose in those adopting geographies because of the new social relationships of the neighboring semi-sedentary groups. The relationships, as analyzed from inspections of many Middle East sites, especially the Southeast Anatolia (Turkey) region which includes Gobekli, Karahan, Tasli, Sefer, Hamzan and Asiab Tepes.

These sites are comparatively over 90 percent unexcavated, but we do know that all sites contain ritual building architecture as well as residential accommodations. Some of these housing plots could have been the living quarters of the construction labor that were building the ceremonial temples, as we do know it took many months and years to construct a site with a new practice of cooperative labor among disparate community groups being undertaken. This concept has correlation to other world sites, including Serra de Capivera, Brazil, of 30,000 years and Tagua Tagua, Chile, of about 14,550 years ago.

New depository finds continue to prove and infer that these sites were stages for spectacular ritual (*social bonding*) food and drink ceremonies, in conjunction with spiritual, proto religious functions, and as demonstrations of power and control regimes. What is important here is to recognize and reflect upon the overarching mindset of community, group roles and social bonding and cooperation mentalities that were manifested.

It is possible that the development of cooperative ventures among disparate groups was a first step toward eventual cohabitation and urbanization. Establishment of cooperative hunting and food processing centers was an outgrowth of an existing strategy of food risk reduction in hunter-gatherer societies that created characteristic traits of risk-pooling, resource manipulation, proliferation of regional reciprocal alliances (co-ops) and food exchanges, storage technologies, and expropriation behaviors (Wiessner 1982). In his Feasting Model of Domestication Theory, Brian Hayden (2009) suggests that the size and extravagance of the feast was central to social bonding and engineering strategies perpetrated by the various power elite of trans egalitarian societies. These displays were designed to be ritualistic in their attitude-behavior purposes to achieve and reinforce power and control authorities.

Upon reflecting on the 30,000-year-old relics and fossils from disparate geographies of Tagua Tagua and Serra de Capivera, in conjunction with those of the Middle East of 15,000 years, it seems evident that the Neolithic human mind independently created and practiced the same concepts and inventions as a function of his innate cognitive abilities. This point may also serve as support for the redefining of the Neolithic Period.

\* \* \*

Early humans acquired technical intelligence (such as tool making) first, then historical intelligence; for example, the ritualistic funerary cultures of remembering deceased family members, then social intelligence outside the family tribe. Interactions with and interbreeding of various species over the last 100,000 years encouraged even larger family villages, and the ideology and behavior of proximity habitation, inherent to all species, was adopted. A new culture of building architecture was invented to facilitate an urban lifestyle. This created new opportunities and new challenges for Neolithic man. Ian Hodder suggests that "The evolution of culture appears patterned when the principles of domus (home), foris (door), and agrios (wild) are articulated in social action" (Hodder 1990, 176). In summary, changes to the process of social reproductive development were shaped from changes in the thought Revolutions basic to new attitudes and behavior mechanisms pertaining to food, shelter, labor, architecture and sedentary domestication cultures - essentially the urbanization of the human condition.

As humans found they could better control their environment and exhibit power over both their environment and life (hunt larger animals, cultivate plants), their confidence and power increased. The principle of economic thought was created from the new abundance of acquired and cultivated resources, and of the growth of labor and trade industries. Critical thinking strategies then created concepts of value, inventory, and property ownership. Those who obtained these larger amounts of resource inventory (and those with a propensity toward type-A ego psychological traits; the Alpha male or female) began to use this power and control over other people, thus creating a societal class system.

Other Revolutions that forever changed the tapestry of human consciousness included profound cosmic awareness's and mythology of the skyscape's patterns and cycles; the sources of light, dark, rainwater, birds, the night sky (heaven), life/afterlife, and supernatural spirituality. The ground and water underworld below were additional motifs that performed their own drama. This is where the mythical 'hell' was perceived to reside, populated by serpents, earthquakes, and other "bad" things. All societies, however, recognized the beneficial dual aspects of the world below. For, according to many cultures, this is where plants, food, animals, and people were created and the entry point onto the "path of souls" that dearly departed traveled on their journey to the heavens above. These are all fantastic achievements of the human mind that, in themselves, helped provide the framework for an exponential growth of knowledge, symbolic communication, invention, and life-enhancing manifestations but also came with increased challenges to dealing with a new stress, tension, and fear ethnocentricity.

Due to the sheer complexity of the argument, from the sizable list of variable factors and temporal reasons that could influence a Revolutions history such as this, it seems dubious that a single motivating factor is the "right" one with which to advocate. I argue that the emergence of the early Homo sapien sapiens into the current version of 'us' was gradual due to a sequence of many environmental, ecological, biological, and cultural factors. This can be best illustrated by a diagram of a tree with interconnected nodes where each of these four major catalysts are at the core of the process. This argument aligns with our ancestor's abstract visualization of "The Tree of Life," which represents the four cycles of life, growth, direction, and order in the terrestrial world and the universe.

The first scene of Act II next will introduce the "who, where, and when into my Algorithm of Humankind," the $T_2$ variable of "who we are" into $T_1 + T_2 + T_3$; 'who we were' + 'who we are' + 'who we could be'. Together, these Revolutions are given meaning by the various Revolutions I've just considered. I will be giving identity, location, and a time stamp to some of Nam and Muh's many contemporaries who built a world that both harmonized and conflicted with what the Universe offered; and created a means of sharing their joy of accomplishment and stress of challenge through effective communication that endures to this day.

*References*

Aubert, Maxime, Pindi Setiawan, Adhi Agus Oktaviana, Muhammad Ramli, Budianto Hakim, Andi Muhammad Wahyu Mudakir, Basran Burhan, Yahdi Zaim, and Adam Brumm. 2018. "Palaeolithic Cave Art in Borneo." *Nature* 564 (7735): 254–257. https://doi.org/10.1038/s41586-018-0679-9.

Berger, Lee R., John Hawks, Darryl J. de Ruiter, Steven E. Churchill, Peter Schmid, Lucas K. Delezene, Tracy L. Kivell, Heather M. Garvin, Scott A. Williams, Jeremy M. DeSilva, Matthew M. Skinner, Charles M. Musiba, Noel Cameron, Trenton W. Holliday, William Harcourt-Smith, Rebecca R. Ackermann, Manuel Bastir, Barry Bogin, Deborah Bolter, Julia Brophy, Zachary D. Cofran, Kaitlin A. Congdon, April S. Deane, Marianne Dembo, Michelle Drapeau, Marina C. Elliott, Elen M. Feuerriegel, Daniel Garcia-Martinez, David J. Green, Alia Gurtov, Joel D. Irish, Asher Kruger, Mary F. Laird, Damiano Marchi, Matthew R. Meyer, Shara Nalla, Elen W. Negash, Caley M. Orr, Davorka Radovčić, Lauren Schroeder, Jenna E. Scott, Zachary Throckmorton, Matthew W. Tocheri, Chloe VanSickle, Caroline S. Walker, Pengfei Wei, and Bernhard Zipfel. 2015. *"Homo naledi, a New Species of the*

*Genus Homo* from the Dinaledi Chamber, South Africa." *eLife* 4 (September 10): e09560. https://doi.org/10.7554/eLife.09560.

Cauvin, Jacques. 2000. *The Birth of the Gods and the Origins of Agriculture*. Translated by Trevor Watkins. Cambridge: Cambridge University Press.

Çelik, Bahattin. 2010. "Hamzan Tepe in the Light of New Finds." *Documenta Praehistorica* 37: 257–268. https://doi.org/10.4312/dp.37.22.

Çelik, Bahattin. 2011. "Karahan Tepe: A New Cultural Centre in the Urfa Area in Turkey." *Documenta Praehistorica* 38: 241–254. https://doi.org/10.4312/dp.38.19.

Çelik, B. 2016. "A Small-scale Cult Centre in Southeast Turkey: Harbetsuvan Tepesi." *Documenta Praehistorica*, 43: 421-428. https://doi.org/10.4312/dp.43.21

Childe, V. Gordon, 1950. "The Urban Revolutions." *Town Planning Review* 80 (1): 3-29.

Draper, Patricia. 1975. "!Kung Women: Contrasts in Sexual Egalitarianism in Foraging and Sedentary Contexts." *Anthropology faculty Publications* 45. https://digitalcommons.unl.edu/anthropology/facpub/45

Gale, Fay, ed. 1970. *Women's Role in Aboriginal Society*. University of Adelaide, Australian Aboriginal Studies 36. Canberra: Australian Institute of Aboriginal Studies.

Geneste, J. M., David, B., Plisson, H., Clarkson, C., Delannoy, J. J., Petchey, F., and Whear, R. 2010. Earliest Evidence for Ground-Edge Axes: 35,400±410 cal BP from Jawoyn Country, Arnhem Land. *Australian Archaeology*, 71 (1): 66–69. https://doi.org/10.1080/03122417.2010.11689385

Greene, Kevin. 1999. V. Gordon Childe and the Vocabulary of Revolutionary Change. *Antiquity*, 73: 97-109.

Guidon, Nièdе, Gabriela Martin, and Anne-Marie Pessis. 2013. "Chronology of the Rock Painting in the Serra da Capivara National Park (Brazil)." In *Pleistocene Art of the World: Short Articles*, edited by Jean Clottes, 711–17. Proceedings of the IFRAO Congress, Tarascon-sur-Ariège and Foix: Société Préhistorique Ariége-Pyrénées.

Güler, Mustafa, Bahattin Çelik, and Gül Güler. 2012. "New Pre-Pottery

Neolithic Settlements from Vıranşehir District." *Anadolu* 38 (May): 164–80. https://doi.org/10.1501/andl_0000000398.

Güler, G., Çelik, B., and Güler, M. 2013. "New Pre-Pottery Neolithic Sites and Cult Centres in the Urfa Region." *Documenta Praehistorica* 40: 291-304. https://doi.org/10.4312/dp.40.23

Hanson, Robin D. "The Great Filter—Are We Almost Past It?" Weblog post. Last modified 1998. "Accessed January 4, 2025." http://hanson.gmu.edu/greatfilter.htm.

Hayden, Brian. 2009. The Proof Is in the Pudding: Feasting and the Origins of Domestication. *Current Anthropology* 50 (5): 597-601.

Hodder, Ian. 1990. *The Domestication of Europe.* John Wiley & Sons.

Labarca, R., M. Frugone-Álvarez, L. Vilches, J. Francisco Blanco, A. Peñaloza, C. Godoy-Aguirre, et al. 2024. "Correction: Tagua Tagua 3: A New Late Pleistocene Settlement in a Highly Suitable Lacustrine Habitat in Central Chile (34°S)." *PLOS ONE* 19 (7): e0306861. https://doi.org/10.1371/journal.pone.0306861.

Lippi, Marta Mariotti, Bruno Foggia, Biancamaria Aranguren, Annamaria Ronchitelli, and Anna Revedin. 2015. "Multistep Food Plant Processing at Grotta Paglicci (Southern Italy) around 32,600 cal B.P." *Proceedings of the National Academy of Sciences* 112 (39). https://doi.org/10.1073/pnas.1505213112.

MacHugh, David E. Larson, Greger, and Orlando, Ludovic 2016. "Taming the Past: Ancient DNA and the Study of Animal Domestication." *Annual Review of Animal Biosciences* 5: 329–351. doi:10.1146/annurev-animal-022516-022747. PMID 27813680.

Malaspinas, AS., Westaway, M., Muller, C., et al. 2016. "A Genomic History of Aboriginal Australia." *Nature* 538: 207–214. https://doi.org/10.1038/nature18299.

Maloney, Tim, Sue O'Connor, Rachel Wood, Ken Aplin, and Jane Balme. 2018. "Carpenters Gap 1: A 47,000-Year-Old Record of Indigenous Adaptation and Innovation." *Quaternary Science Reviews* 191 (July): 204–228.

McBrearty, Sally and Brooks, Alison S. 2000. The Revolution that Wasn't: A New Interpretation of the Origin of Modern Human Behavior. *Journal of*

*Human Evolution.* (39): 453-563.

Mellaart, James. 1967. *Catal Huyuk: A Neolithic Town in Anatolia.* McGraw-Hill.

Mellars, Paul A. 1991. Cognitive Changes and the Emergence of Modern Humans in Europe. *Cambridge Archaeological Journal.* (1): 763-776.

Mithin, Steven. 1994. *The Ancient Mind: Elements of Cognitive Archaeology.* Cambridge University Press.

Mithin, Steven. 1996. *The Prehistory of The Mind: The Cognitive Origins of Art, Religion and Science.* Thames and Hudson Ltd, London.

Monge, Janet, Morrie Kricun, Jakov Radovčić, Davorka Radovčić, Alan Mann, and David W. Frayer. 2013. "Fibrous Dysplasia in a 120,000+ Year Old Neandertal from Krapina, Croatia." Edited by Janet Kelso. *PLOS ONE* 8 (6): e64539. https://doi.org/10.1371/journal.pone.0064539.

Noble, William and Davidson, Iain. 1991. "The eEvolutionary Emergence of Modern Human Behaviour: Language and its Archaeology." *Man* (26): 223-253.

Noble, William and Davidson, Iain. 1996. *Human Evolution, Language and Mind: A Psychological and Archaeological Inquiry.* Cambridge: Cambridge University Press.

Oktaviana, A.A., Joannes-Boyau, R., Hakim, B., et al. 2024. "Narrative Cave Art in Indonesia by 51,200 Years Ago." *Nature* 631: 814–818. https://doi.org/10.1038/s41586-024-07541-7.

Peters J. and Schmidt K. 2004. "Animals in the Symbolic World of Pre-Pottery Neolithic Göbekli Tepe, Southeastern Turkey: A Preliminary Assessment." *Anthropozoologica* 39 (1): 179-218.

Pigati, Jeffrey S., et al. 2023. "Independent Age Estimates Resolve the Controversy of Ancient Human Footprints at White Sands. *Science* 382: 73-75. DOI:10.1126/science.adh5007.

Radovčić, Davorka, Giovanni Birarda, Ankica Oros Sršen, Lisa Vaccari, Jakov Radovčić, and David W. Frayer. 2020. "Surface Analysis of an Eagle Talon from Krapina." *Scientific Reports* 10 (1): 1, 5. https://doi.org/10.1038/s41598-020-63294-w.

Schmandt-Besserat, Denise. 1997. Animal Symbols at 'Ain Ghazal.

*Expedition Magazine* 39 (1).

Schmandt-Besserat, Denise. 2013. Neolithic Symbolism at 'Ain Ghazal. *Berlin, Ex Oriente.*

Simek, Jan F. and Smith, Fred H. 1997. "Chronological changes in stone tool assemblages from Krapina (Croatia)". *Journal of Human Evolution.* 32 (6): 561–562. doi:10.1006/jhev.1996.0129.

Snir, A., D. Nadel, I. Groman-Yaroslavski, Y. Melamed, M. Sternberg, O. Bar-Yosef, et al. 2015. "The Origin of Cultivation and Proto-Weeds, Long Before Neolithic Farming." *PLOS ONE* 10 (7): e0131422. https://doi.org/10.1371/journal.pone.0131422.

Spikins, Penny, Andy Needham, Barry Wright, Calvin Dytham, Maurizio Gatta, and Gail Hitchens. 2019. "Living to Fight Another Day: The Ecological and Evolutionary Significance of Neanderthal Healthcare." *Quaternary Science Reviews* 217: 3–4. https://doi.org/10.1016/j.quascirev.2019.06.012.

Ullrich, Herbert 2005. "Cannibalistic Rites within Mortuary Practices from the Paleolithic to Middle Ages in Europe." *Anthropologie.* 43 (2/3): 249–261.

Wiessner, Polly. 1982. "Beyond Willow Smoke and Dogs' Tails." *American Antiquity* 47: 171-178.

# SYMBOLISM

*Symbolism is the Entry Point into the mind of our Ancestors.*

-Keith A. Seland, 2025

*Keywords: Semiotics, symbolic representation, symbolism, multitasking cognitive utilization, dualities, feasting, domus, entoptics, agrios, ideographic linguistics, soul eschatology, power and control.*

Nam and Muh are us, but not quite ready to appear as the latest showroom model...

All the cognitive traits of the mind, except those that arose from new situational occurrences since the urban Revolutions, have been integrated into the consciousness of Nam and Muh's people. Nam and Muh have willfully adjusted to new individual and group behavior roles made requisite by the new sociology and psychology spreading around the world. This is another in the series of gradual adjustments of the human condition into a universal social cultural package, but not yet the last. These new situational awarenesses are embodied in the realm of the most complex socialization modifiers, such as the ritual and sociopolitical sciences that, within their practice, created an ideology of a power and control mechanism experience for humankind.

Artifacts of the solitary human lifestyle were permanently buried into their psyche of core instinctive attitude-behavior. Adding to, but not replacing, their cognitive utilization was an intelligence of socialization. These newly adopted social roles originated in the feasting cults of 30,000 years ago. The record shows many depository remains of not only feasting but also architectural building industries and ritual centers schemed to stage the 'celebration of the feast.' Through many successive generations, these technological and social advancements were refined, introduced, accelerated, and continued to influence successful adaptations to people's new rapidly changing life environments.

This is not, though, the last or solitary monumental behavioral adjustment of the human condition. Here I will introduce the major players in the sequence of this Neolithic Urbanization Revolution drama. The revolution of thought is a governor for these various Revolutions. Our minds shaped the creation, practice of and improvements to our human condition. The process was dictated by the behaviors of our Biosphere's (the Earth's) various geophysical processes. This theme continues as a recurring ritual thought exercise throughout our present and future.

These Revolutions are the growth of food sustenance production, animal husbandry and cultivation sciences, labor and economic industries, social urbanization, domestication practices, feasting cultures, and expansion of semiotic expression and communication as the major players. *Semiotics* defines a practical application of all the tools used to create and communicate information, knowledge and expressions of attitudes, behaviors, and ideologies to others. *Symbolic representation,* as an interchangeable term with semiotics, is one I prefer to use as it expresses both the themes of symbolism (noun) and representation (verb "action" of behavior) in this process.

Semiotic expressions are the product of our thought Revolution. The tools of semiotic expression include linguistics; both verbal and a variety of written, in scripted, or imprinted symbolic representations such as cave, rock, body adornments, tools, utensils, clothing, landscape "art," and building and monument architectures. Interpretive meaning within a semiotic tool use enables people to transfer meaning, information, or knowledge within literal, implied, and/or metaphorical context.

If you recall the popular cultural definition of the term 'symbolism' that I introduced in *The Mind* chapter, and adding what insight has been explored since then, I update the definition as follows: "An activity process of *multitasking cognitive utilization* to communicate information, meaning or knowledge to others via a variety of display platforms". Contexts to which this concept applies in my discussions include cultural/geographic, reproductive developmental, educational, ideological, and influential social domains.

I mention here that because popular culture has favored reflecting upon the concept of symbolism into an association with a concept of art, I will occasionally use or combine the terms "symbolism" with "art." The platforms of semiotic art include linguistic, external material cultures, object/artifacts, building, biological/body art, and monument architecture and can utilize all the biological senses in their transmission and/or meaning. Many universals of usage exist within the domain of symbolism, and symbolic representation such as cross-cultural similarities in meaning, purpose, illustration, metaphorical design, and other cognitive utilization as a product of the human thought process.

Symbolism is a concept made necessary by the motivation to store information and communicate ideas, concepts, data, subjective views, and ideologies, as an activity to promote social behaviors of bonding, cohesion, instruction, ritual, and as a means of engineering social power and control through purposeful attitude and behavior protocols by group leaders or other authoritative figures. A further feature of symbols and their human styles of representation is taken from this quote by Ian Hodder, "Symbols are secondary connotations evoked by the primary associations and uses of an object or word…and refer to abstract and general concepts and they tend to be organized into oppositional structures" (Hodder 1990, 13). These symbols are then given purpose which sometimes depends on the social community involved. The symbolism is manipulated and driven down an 'observation-perception-cognition' pathway, often with the use of the duality ideology (organization of oppositional structures) in the context of "one vs. another".

But it is the social structure that chooses its context and usage options. Once adopted, the context is practiced through rituals, mimicry, or similarly efficacious activities. This is why some cultures gave different attributes to the same animal-as-deity figure in their folklore. But this can be also part of a feedback loop where the process circles back to the earlier cognitive manipulation for modification of the next iteration of this feedback process. This means the social practice can be modified either by discovery of new data, popular change, or by mandate, coercion, or force by those in power or control of the community.

The road to symbolic intelligence was borne out of the observational awareness our ancient brethren possessed of all the objects in the world around them; the earth, water and sky, all the life that acted on their environments and the ways they interacted. Then, using the observation-perception-cognition pathway, transfer relationships were created in their minds via repeated and frequent observations of these objects' characteristics, perceptually and cognitively and associating shapes of similar objects in later observations.

Examples of this could include associating a snake seen in the wild with the Serpens constellation or the Milky Way/Great Rift astronomy, or the Orion constellation cognitively connecting a hunter with a bow & arrow weapon. Patterns were then observed, and the critical thinking compelled them to create the attributions after a time. From there, the stories of folklore-as-instruction, symbols used to impart information, navigation, or mathematical situations were engraved or painted on walls, caves, rocks, buildings, and even the ground.

The buildings themselves served as symbolic representations, architectural objects such as pillars, monoliths, and totems. For example, a significant reason for the adoption of the geometric circle in Early Neolithic building architecture designs was the profound age-old relationship that aligned the circular geometry of such natural objects as the Sun, sky (from horizon to horizon), the stars, moon, bird nests, etc. These were all divine, spiritual abstractions of humans and correlated with a larger ideology that all physical matter in the Universe held and resonated with its own energy frequencies in a continuous transfer relationship with people.

This idea was among the most sacred of human life in those times, and it is where we have coined the phrase 'sacred geometry.' Pottery, textiles, ornaments, and trinkets were also used as objects of symbolic meaning, as were people from their body art. The multitasking cognitive utilization notion stems from the brain's ability to drive this observation-perception-cognition pathway from sensory stimulation through the limbic and various brain cortex systems and finishing as expressive output to what is termed today as art. All symbolism is ideographic in nature and is at the core of the semiotics definition.

Protocol use in the semiotics concept is in a framework of what I call a two-step *ideographic linguistic* system, whereby the author creates meaning from utilizing metaphorical interpretation or direct symbol translation of objects from nature into the story platform and thus establishes usage and context of symbols used in the message. A similar protocol still in use today is a more complex three-step ideographic system, whereby a language is functionally used as the transmitter of the communication's meaning. If the messages are either verbal or in a written language not of symbolic nature, the brain must identify, interpret and translate the original syntax usage as an added step; and, if the transmission requires or elicits either an immediate verbal or written response, a compatible language must be recruited to effectively communicate this reply. Today our civilization makes important use of both mindful protocols as vocabulary and ideogrammatic icons.

Symbolic representations are the objects or iconography that are to be interpreted and to whom its social meaning is derived or given. They possess the context, help us to uncover and demonstrate the motivations and unique customs of the culture under inspection and help us to define universal characteristics of the human elements that created them. Study of these also uncovers the *attitude cues* used that drove the respondent perceptions, cognition and behaviors of ancestral cultures. Implements are the material instruments utilized in the representations' creation.

We have knowledge of representation styles and meaning creation that early humans used going back to over 100,000 years. Key to this discussion is an interpretation that includes examples that the creators utilized to convey their abstract meaning, purpose, ideology, or context representations. We can study many examples of artifacts, such as weaponry, trade tools, clothing textiles and housing materials to which modern researchers can infer about the physical non-abstract aspects of ancient survival and day-to-day living. My thesis concerning how we can learn about ourselves by studying our ancestors is concerned more with ontology and teleology of why and how symbolism was used by them in mindful, cerebral, and abstract ways. It also examines how they conducted their lives, why they were motivated to create, and how they illustrated their symbolism to us.

Inherent in the ideology of symbolic presentations is the premise that, without the human mind interpreting them, their meaning and even more basically, their purpose comes into question. The symbol, then, is just a tool; the mind provides the context and purpose. The practice of symbolic representation requires both a creator and an audience to function. It is logical, therefore, to conclude that symbolism is a social construct for social benefit and loses its meaning if no one is there with which to interpret.

Iconography in the social realm is known to have existed over 70,000 years ago in the later Pleistocene epoch. In my earlier reference to the Blombos Cave symbolism, the discovery of geometric figures, ornamental beads and advanced heat-treated spear tips depict the Blombos cultural achievements and potential transmission of cultural meaning in a form of social status or military power, respectively. The complex hunter-gatherer version of 'culture' here only defines an earlier version of the social community that will inexhaustibly manifest itself by the onset of the Neolithic. Meaning is conferred in all these objects and contains social intelligence, and for some objects, like the spear tips, an additional technical intelligence, as part of Steven Mithen's cognitive mind development (Mithen 1996, 195-198).

The advent of self-awareness beyond core instinctiveness is associated with what I supported earlier to be an initial deployment of multitasking cognitive utilization. We became self-aware long before we developed the cultural awareness that resulted in socialization and the semiotics used to express these social cultures. Our brains possessed, at the outset, the necessary functional elements with which to grow our various intellectual skills; those that enable our utilization of instinct, technical, logical, social, artistic, historical, emotional minds, including a linguistic capability.

However, it was in combination with other naturally occurring environmental, geographical, ecological, social, and anatomical developmental templates that caused the specific development of our mind beyond the instinctive basal brain system. Technical intelligence appears to us here in this example as an evolution of more sophisticated weaponry. The manufacturing process at Blombos Cave that now includes heat treatments was itself a mindful advancement. But modifications to weapon size and raw materials utilization show a newly discovered social symbolism in that the manufacture and design can be associated with new group hunting techniques and social alliances not yet found before that point in time. This made it probable that hunting expeditions of a social nature were undertaken that involved larger prey. This also opened a portal to which a social culture of food sharing became possible.

Additional social intellect can be derived from an inspection of ornamental beads and geometric figure artifacts. The beads at Blombos Cave are part of the record and their depository characteristics show no other utilitarian purpose except as part of social cultural symbolism. The geometric figures also depict a social intelligence as portrayed by their creator(s). Their existence is representative of a purposeful means of communicating information, knowledge, ideas, and relationships to others. These manifestations had evolved from the instinctive ancient development of awareness to the patterns and cycles in nature that programmed the human intellect.

One of these basic relationships that the mind developed as an extension from recognition of patterns and cycles was the ideology of *dualities*. Archaeologist Ian Hodder is among many in the post-structuralist ideology movement of the late 20th century who argued that the principle of universal duality patterns and cycles drove ancient human thought and culture, the "oppositional structures" earlier noted. The dualities of the Early Neolithic shaped human thought and involved the themes of, for example, the male vs. female, life vs. death, and wild vs. domesticated. These are only themes, however, in the broader purpose of cognitive meaning-making and the representational semiotics found in any archaism.

The mind became wired to perceive and relate tangible dualities long before the Neolithic Revolutions. Nature provided us with templates containing inherent opposing duality life codes which became part of our hard-wired instinctive basal brain skills. These dualities, some favorably aligned and some diametrically opposed in form, substance and style, were then perceived, through time, to be repetitive, cyclic, enduring, and with patterned design features. Early man took these witnessed patterns and adopted their use initially as tools for basic physiological survival strategies and then applied them to successful learning of higher-order human needs and evolution, including an existence within complex urbanized social cultures.

For example, early on, they learned how to survive each day by limiting foraging and extensive travel to the daytime and by securing their lives from the dangerous environment at night. By extension, nature's seasonal climate cycles became templates for strategy-building to address constraints of the summer-winter duality cycle. Adoption and adaptation of this mindset contributed to the proliferation of successful food cultivation, preservation, and storage industries. This cognitive utilization was influential to the Revolutions of animal husbandry and agricultural domestication.

When nature's favorable factors aligned - allowing for our Revolutions of thought, behavior, technology, sustenance, and culture - it became opportune for us to form new social allegiances. Our minds steadily proceeded on these dimensions in successive stages of advancement and retreat, like nature's operative forces did during the last few Ice Age cycles. The need for new paths to sustenance drove our mindful pursuit of new technology, behavior and culture. What has been shown to us thus far is a growing catalogue of illustrative insights into the emergent social Homo sapien-sapiens.

# SYMBOLISM

\* \* \*

*Feasting to Social cults of labor, building temples*

The inter group *feasting* ritual activity is an early Homo sapien-sapiens social mechanism that developed from this new path to life sustenance. The last generations of hunter-gatherer societies advanced the basic feasting behavior routine over a few thousand years to a status of a complex ritual social event. I introduce "inter group" activities to emphasize the emergence of a new level of cooperation among otherwise unrelated family communities in those times. This also contributed to formation of a new social concept, that of a trans-egalitarian political culture; the basis of which caused, according to Brian Hayden, "powerful pressures to develop political economies, food production, and ultimately, domesticated plants and animals" (Hayden 2009, 597).

An early known Western hemisphere example came from discoveries at Taguatagua 3 in central Chile, South America, a permanent large-scale hunting, butchering, grains, and red ocher processing center of 14,000 years ago (Labarca et al. 2024). Discovery of associated permanent residence architecture has not yet occurred due to its very recent discovery. However, because of favorable climactic and ecological data of the local geography during those times, it is reasonable to conjecture that a future realization of such finds remains possible.

From the record we also know that a trans-egalitarian feasting ritual cult within a surplus framework was attained at an advanced state of practice in the Levant of modern-day Middle East. The entire Turkey/Syria regional ecosystem, for example, contains hundreds of excavated settlements. The iconic T-shaped pillar-adorned architecture found throughout Pre-Pottery times at Gobekli, Hamzan, Harbetsuvan, Karahan, Sefer, and Taşli Tepes, for example, coexists with extensive animal skeletal depository pits found at Gobekli and elsewhere. Later in the Pre-Pottery period, similar animal remains have been uncovered at sites such as, Çatalhöyük of 8,000 BCE and further south at Jericho.

This suggests that there was continuous social contact in an organized cultural environment within continental geography. Social cooperation roles manifested as shown from feasting remains and in abundant ceremonial architecture left throughout the region. Remains of residential structures are already known to exist from Anatolia at Karahan and are widely predicted to exist from Gobekli, Hamzan, Nevali and Taşli Tepes, among others. While there are sites estimated to be older (Karahan Tepe) than its sister site, Gobekli Tepe, within the modern Şanliurfa metropolitan area, evidence suggests that Gobekli may have been a regional or continental ceremonial center, in addition to a residential community.

The totality of this evidence proves that the urbanization revolution had already transpired in these places by about 10,000 BCE. The fluid nature of discovery and interpretation here gives pause to more permanent far-reaching inferences about how much the effects of the various human Revolutions had penetrated life during the early Neolithic.

New roles of social cooperation and communication were necessary for these new cultures to come into existence. Cooperation meant new labor industry practices among neighboring tribes and a means of communication among them for successful project completion. It is generally agreed that, on a worldwide stage, many tribal communities were responsible for shared construction of ceremonial structures and other monuments that they populated.

Each project consisted of an estimated hundreds or thousands (millions for some of them) of individuals sourced together to erect their architecturally imposing structures that inspire awe and amazement among our reflection today. Consequently, they created ritual traditions as social activities, such as feasting. This required a means of sharing information and cooperation among people to facilitate their interactions and their communal project endeavors. While I will speak more on the ritual concept in the *Ritual* chapter, its behavioral prerequisite was establishment of a system of communication and sociology for humankind.

It will be difficult to achieve enduring solutions to the question of which exact symbolic cultures occurred earliest in time due to the fluid nature of discovery and that new finds of uncovered representations will predate the others. For example, ongoing activity at the Rising Star Cave region in South Africa has uncovered carvings of a variety of geometric symbols as part of an initial dating of 335,000 years ago (Berger et al. 2015). Recently discovered Neanderthal and Denisovan funerary deposits, dated over 100,000 years ago, have uncovered such artifacts as animal skeletons, the arrow tips possibly used to slay them, and body arrangements showing symbolic meaning of spiritual compassion and a mnemonic of remembrance, celebration, and belief in an afterlife of their deceased elders. Remains of tools and ceremonial burial cults were found and dated to over 92,000 years ago at Qafzeh Cave, in Israel near Nazareth. Stoves, human and animal skeletons, and a ceremonial burial site suggest that Qafzeh was a residential village for both the living and departed (Lieberman 1991).

Displays of intelligent meaning and communication inherent within the artifacts left by these groups of people are evidence that a cerebral symbolic perception of the human mind existed at least hundreds of thousands of years in the past. Therefore, these mindful features of human symbolism existed far before a written, language-based historical record, or of a spoken one. Also, of note, is that these ritual cult elements suggest a mimetic correspondence to those practiced in our modern world.

Tomb cults such as this overcame the finality of death in their minds by creating an enduring life of the departed. Therefore, the final architecture of the Neolithic residence, the *domus,* was built in this way to accommodate the living and honor the dead, temporarily transcending the cognition of permanence that reinforced the entire lifestyle of sedentary life. If the Qafzeh research permanently confirms both residence and tomb cults of ceremonial burial ritual attitude-behavior mechanisms, then the symbolic representation characterized by building architecture has a far longer provenance than the explosion of findings in the later Neolithic in the Anatolia region.

As was the case with the Neolithic Revolutions, the attitude of thought and the behavior of action, as part of our human nature, was shaped slowly and gradually by a sequence of seminal evolution, rather than a single eureka event. The intelligent transfer of meaning, information, and knowledge through communicative interactions between people was just another of these Revolutions. As noted, the attitude-behavior mechanism has its roots in Early Paleolithic times and is known to be central to our instinctive brain core biology. Hominid brains evolved to support increasingly more complex attitude-behaviors beyond satisfying the basic physiological drives of food, water, shelter, and reproduction. As reproductive development is one of those basic life drives, the existence of our social drives aligns with this biology and whose growth is its natural by-product. The need for communication among "us" was, in many ways, anthropic.

Our minds were programmed to be pattern-and-cycle driven. This awareness, a continual work-in-progress, allowed beings to interact with and exploit nature, other life and us to survive and evolve past some of the "great filters" of our existence. "Us" was the de facto social dimension of interaction and infers an anthropic existence. This social dimension of interaction has always existed and for us to continue to exist in the universe we had to grow this feature. A unique system of communication was developed by all life forms on Earth; ours has become the most complex.

One challenge of situational bias in trying to obtain insight into ancient symbolism is in remembering that our ancestors were communicating in real time through the eyes of a vastly different worldview. Our mind's worldview today is predominately secular, material, empirical (at least sometimes), and myopic. Our ancient brethren saw the universe as acute observers of nature: highly descriptive and holistic, ecological, immersive, spiritual, and philosophic. Our cultural dissimilarities, our contemporary 'baggage' of critical thinking and other situational biases inherent in many practitioners' historical analyses, often clouds a true interpretation of their symbolic meanings.

Hopefully, you have learned by now that the minds of our Neolithic and Paleolithic kin were essentially the equivalent of ours but with a smaller knowledge base and, consequently, different perceptions of the universe and its operation. They were using the time to build a human version of a basic akashic record, a foundational archive of knowledge, for us to inherit.

The earliest human styles of representation we see were, in a large way, descriptive of mathematical shapes and patterns in nature. Known painted and carved examples of over 77,000 years ago at Blombos Cave (Henshilwood et al. 2001) and 54,000 years ago in the Levant at Southwest Syria (Marshack 1996) illustrate a variety of geometric symbols, including zig zags, triangles and circles, that suggest a mindful recognition of a significant relationship between nature, shapes, and a need to socially share this semiotic information with others. Material objects such as trinkets, beads, body adornments, and the use of paint for pictograph ideological representations also occur frequently throughout the Afro-Asian land mass.

Some have suggested that these early geometric drawings were the result of *entoptic* phenomena, "visually perceived patterns that have a biological basis in the human body and are independent of light from external source(s)…and are motifs of basic grids, hexagonal patterns, parallel lines, dots, short flecks and zigzag lines" (Lewis-Williams and Dowson 1988, 202; Clottes and Lewis-Williams 1998). Many others have inferred a result as manifestation of a variety of mind-altering chemical shamanistic episodes.

I suggest that many underlying interpretations contain a story or informational significance that, from their eyes, had meaning and purpose, and cannot be explained away with just a clinical explanation using tools and views from the menu available to today's observer. All the illustrations are analogous to frequently observed replicas of designs in nature. The landscape was full of geometric forms, and if this was not a large enough palette for utilizing the available inventory, it grew much larger when the artist looked up into the sky. Both the day and night skies provided obvious and abundant inspiration and sensory perception opportunities for their motivated minds to establish lines of social communication using these objects as meaning-makers.

Consider, for example, the serpent/snake form. Why did the serpent acquire its place in universal ancient mythology, ritual and status? First, it became a universal deity; indeed, one of the Great Spirits of ancient prehistory whose lofty status was also awarded to the tree and the Sun at different times. Intuitive reasons for this adornment embody uniqueness of form, substance or style, and could have included:

- The snake being a unique "two-edged" sword of nature. Its bite was often lethal though its venom was also a known cure for many medical ailments, including the poisonous venom itself. Very few, if any, other animals exhibited these dual characteristics.
- It is the only land-based animal without any appendages and, as such, evolved a unique locomotion physiology.
- Humans have held an instinctive mindset through evolution of the snake as a scariest species.
- Not only is a snake associated with the star constellation Serpens, it also most visually resembles the Milky Way and Great Rift. These cosmic phenomena have been observed worldwide since the human time of Awareness. Both are also visually symbolic of the female reproduction apparatus, specifically shaped like the umbilical cord, and often both are interfaced in ritual ceremonies and social celebrations conducted by these cultures. An obvious intuitive pattern of social association through bonding, cohesion, power and control attitude and behavior protocols are inferred when these correlations of ancient cultures between the serpent and these astronomical objects of symbolism are considered.

The serpent was held universally as a spiritual duality of life and death. The finality of an earthly demise was intuitive of their observed reality of bodily death in association with the belief that the spiritual path the departed soul must take to reach, heaven was first underground then to heaven - the Milky

Way. These are intuitive shapes of likeness in nature, between the serpent and objects that made all of them metaphorically special and sacred, and their associations became a cultural essence of ancient humankind's abstract minds if not hard-wired into their instinctive basal brain. All the shapes looked alike and contained many synergistic characteristics that manifested the underlying theory. Our ancestors ascribed symbolic meaning to the shapes they observed in nature and that they deemed vital to their existence. I will explore more of the significance of cosmology and related spirituality in the *Archaeoastronomy* chapter. Notably, our brains still operate in these ways today.

Representations such as these symbolizing the attitude and behavior of both Paleolithic and Neolithic man began when humans still viewed the agrios as a dangerous, wild, dominating place. Depictions of violent animals commanded creation of cave and rock art well into the Neolithic; for over 70,000 years, they were the sole figures to appear in them. Later in the Pre-Pottery Neolithic, humans first appeared but remained pictorially subordinate in power and control. Even as recent as examples from 7,000 BCE at Çatalhöyük, the Great Hunt in the agrios was shown as a small army of smaller armed hunters in a life and death struggle against the mighty bull.

*How our Neolithic ancestors initially viewed balance of power in the agrios*

This was a symbolic representation of the artist. He was literal in describing the event and provided additional metaphoric meaning as to his dualistic interpretation of the prevailing power and control psyche. Power and control are major motivational behavior structures of the human condition. Being that semiotics is an expression form to the dynamic of the human condition; the sacred mathematics is just one segment of the "meta communications" flowchart.

The mathematical shapes of the early Homo sapien sapien mind became salient and transformational in ceremonial and building economies, as well as socially and spiritually. The building and the monument, as another segment of the semiotics flowchart, became tools of semiotics and of human styles of representation. The matured human mind of the Later Paleolithic already possessed the skill to think in patterned, symbolic, metaphorical, and dualistic ways that were motivational factors in the design of early generational architectures utilizing relationships with sacred geometry noted earlier, such as the alignment of the circle with nature's spiritual shapes of the Sun, Moon, etc.

The earliest known discoveries of building architecture came in the form of a central meeting place concept. Ceremonial building design was a first stage in urbanization deployment. The newly permanent social cooperation culture built these gathering sites for celebratory, ritual, spiritual, economic, and industrial purposes. A known large group feasting attitude-behavior cult concept was being conducted regularly on the African, Euro-Asian, South American, and Australian Continental land masses from as early as 25,000 years ago. It is speculated that smaller group feasting activities occurred even thousands of years earlier at various sites where cave art symbolism has been found depicting both animal and human figures. Those sites, such as Chauvet, France, Blombos, South Africa, and Salèh Cave, Borneo, however, do not show definitive proof of building cooperation architecture.

As one of a few examples of building symbolism, consider the funerary architecture cult. Funerary buildings were very costly to design and maintain because they represent, in the eyes of the indigenous, in-the-moment celebrations and ritualistic social bonding, history, and enabled power and control strategies themed as a remembrance of the departed by congregations of descendants long after the departing of the honored soul. Also, these building projects, as findings from across the entire regional ecosystem of the Middle East and South America, among others suggest, appeared not to have been designed for permanent use.

This attitude-behavior mechanism of the builders at such places as Gobekli and Karahan Tepes, Nevali Cori, and Qafzeh each suggest a planned temporary utilization of only a few hundred years, where a building project is completed and used, then buried, as scientific dating techniques have informed us. A major dilemma occurs specifically at Gobekli Tepe where, of the buildings at least partially excavated, all are argued to show a deliberate back-filling manifestation that purposely hid their existence. This sequence is repeated at Karahan Tepe and the other sites. Up to now widespread agreement about the purposes of both the existence of these buildings and their eventual concealment remains elusive. This will be a topic of insight later in the *Archaeoastronomy* chapter.

The permanent residence, a novel form of basic shelter sustenance for the urbanization Revolution, was another building symbolism. Reasons for the adoption of Neolithic circular building geometry may have been driven by practicality, as well as spirituality, as a carryover from the design knowledge and reasoning of less advanced hunter-gatherers. They reasoned that a circular design was easier to construct, roof, and utilize higher percentages of allowed for larger interior space than a structure that was square.

Other practical factors included the knowledge that their ancestors lived in caves or teepees with this circular geometric form that were better equipped to protect them from the forces of nature, such as inclement weather, due to rain water drainage, high winds and storms without destroying the integrity of the structure. For building architecture, the circle geometry was naturally preferred for a time for practical reasons, as well as becoming foundational to the human life ideologies of ethos, spirituality, and religiosity. The sacrality of the circle was born from observation of this geometry in nature as contributing to the harmony, balance, equilibrium, and interconnections of all matter in the Universe as parts of The Great Chain of Being.

The "life vs. afterlife" was another duality pattern of human nature that penetrated the residential building architecture cult. The home building, known as the domus of the living, also became the home of the deceased. Their remains were buried within the domus. The domus took on a symbolic personality that was defined from conscious devotion to the deceased by the living. The building became a generational clock for the living and the dead and was mindfully honored and displayed as the house and the grave. At that time, this was considered a most efficient design among the indigenous.

Then there came a time when, after a few hundred years, many generations of remains had accumulated within the domus. They reasoned, by their attitude-behavior protocol, that an ideological adjustment must be made to better accommodate the practical aspects of funerary cults. Therefore, the design for domestic, as well as ceremonial, social center design was transformative as the now urbanized culture drove from a circular to a

4-sided geometry.

We see many examples of this evolutionary process where the design behaviors demonstrated an original favoritism to the circular geometry for both central ceremonial and the domus structure. I have studied examples of this first hand at Karahan and Gobekli, where others exist at Körtik Tepe (Flannery and Marcus 2012). Later, by the time of the earlier Göbekli Tepe buildings (Schmidt 2012) and of neighboring Çatalhöyük, the popular circular geometry architecture had been largely replaced with rectangular structures (Dietrich, Köskal-Schmidt, Notroff and Schmidt 2013; Kinzel and Clare 2020; Schmidt 2012, 133).

The symbolism cultures of the Levant are shown to exhibit widespread multifaceted design philosophies. The building geometry finds among vast geographies show significant support to a notion of imitative attitude-behavior among many, even unacquainted village inhabitants, a societal norm in the moment of that period where people learned from others, a direct result of more frequent social contact.

\* \* \*

Another symbolic expression transformation occurred simultaneously within these structures along the same timeline. An explosion of illustrative linguistic symbolic representation, what I call *ideographic linguistics*, proliferated depicting subject matter of another duality pattern; the animal vs. the human. From my earlier introduction to the cave illustrations from Middle Paleolithic times, such as at Blombos, Border Caves 71,000 years ago, humankind's illustrated alphabet of the outside world was myopic and inclusive of only animals. The people themselves were not purposefully part of the dictionary, except for the hand print signatories found on many panels. Other early cave art at Cáceras, Spain, dated 64,000 years ago, illustrates an early phase of SR (symbolic representation) evolution with the depiction of a bovine creature, in portrait only, has been generally interpreted as what

I call a "snapshot of an object in reality" as if the creator used a camera to take the image. No metaphorical or allegorical meaning representation is discernible from an inspection of these illustrations. Their author depicted only what he saw as this "snapshot effect," as we often do today when we describe the details of a witnessed event.

But animals were wild, behaved in ways that were gravely dangerous to humans, and required egalitarian group hunting attitude and behavior strategies to procure food sustenance. They were depicted as such through humans' eyes until Neolithic domestication was firmly established. Power duality favored wild agrios animals until Pre-Pottery time. What we have seen in sites such as Gobekli Tepe (Peters and Schmidt 2004, 184), Karahan Tepe, Nevali Cori, Ain Ghazal in modern-day Jordan (Schmandt-Besserat 1997), and Çatalhöyük, Anatolia (Turkey) (Mellaart 1967). Other depictions of food, such as consumable grains, have not been observed in this context because it is reasoned they did not represent an existential power threat to them. Therefore, a predominance of wild animal symbolism exists, but now in a different motif, one with diminished power ratio in comparison to earlier periods.

The artful symbolic expressions of humans acquiring more of that ratio of power and control appear through time. Throughout the pillar icon architecture of the Anatolia Tepe region in the Pre-Pottery period, the animals are still shown as violent creatures but are now posed with humans in a variety of adversarial postures. Transformational attributions now also show humans and animals interacting metaphorically with revolutionary cognitive meanings, in the spiritual, cosmological, and proto-religious motifs. By 9,000 years ago in Çatalhöyük, while the animal (usually a bull which held much additional metaphorical meaning yet remained prey) was still depicted as large and violent, human hunting parties came to dominate the pictographic illustrations.

Verbal linguistic symbolism, which was feasible and available to Neolithic humans, was probably utilized though evidence for this is lacking. Verbal linguistics can include a syntax to convey identification of and meaning to symbols, as well as utilization of a language to achieve the same endpoints.

## SYMBOLISM

We possess no depository records of such verbal linguistics for now. Your name is an example of symbolic identification through language.

External material cultures, including adornments, implements, and amulets represent another segment of semiotic interpretation. This cultural technology gained prevalence when religiosity became part of the supernatural human condition over 100,000 years ago. Body art forms from bone records and folklore, another teaching form of symbolic representation, were known to have existed in aboriginal Australia over 40,000 years ago. Pottery and textile forms were assigned an entire dated cultural classification, popularized in the Levant from around 10,000 years ago. Considered in their entirety, all these technologies infer another Neolithic Revolution, this to a conscious transformation of mindful communication and an unquenched motivation for knowledge acquisition.

It is reasonable to infer that, because no written syntactic text has been found dating to these times, all these material cultures, including building and monument architecture, were the languages themselves that conveyed information, knowledge, meaning, and ideologies. The central ceremonial temple center was known as a main symbolic urbanized survival tool for social activities of all kinds, including bonding, trade and commerce, group feasting, ritual, social engineering, and power and control devices utilized by the power elite. These group sites were full of symbolic representations whose construction, resource contributions, purpose, meaning, and utilization were shared by neighboring village communities.

The domus, like the house, was metaphorical in nature and design, built and decorated as such, by a geometrical symbolism. The domus was also illustrative of a behavioral perception and cognition of status and identity of its inhabitants. Remains uncovered at global locations show that early adopters of the domus were this power elite; the influential leaders of the urbanized community. Examples of the symbolism are attributed to a proliferation of funerary cults in the form of grave goods, typically uncovered next to the remains of the departed. The inventory also includes weapon technologies - used if the honored was a hunter - adornments, skeletal remains specifically associated with a remembrance of the deceased, and other properties of ownership during the life of the deceased.

Remembering the deceased through honorary worship rituals such as this is a manifestation of a *soul eschatology*, a most deliberate and curious behavior pattern for many reasons. These include an exceptional intuition to a universal existence of an afterlife domain, an abstract material cognition to worship and historical meaning for remembering loved ones through time, and their use as learning tools for future generations - reflecting an acutely profound long-term intellectual perspective.

As the concept of soul eschatology and eternal life beyond life on Earth was passed down from its genesis of about 100,000 years ago, the ritual of eternal sustenance evolved. These consisted of regular food offerings and, in later cultures, the mummification of the body that the soul could recognize and re-acquire at its time of ascension, all were created to assist in those endpoints. The symbolism of the domus was suggested by Ian Hodder to, "not only to be the metaphor for change but also the mechanism (of change)" (Hodder 1990, 17). "This 'dual role of duality' was timed correlatively to domestication. It was the domus (a term he created) where the psychology (changing fears, tensions, joys) of everyday life became catalysts for change" (p. 41).

The association of symbolic representation with communication, meaning, and shaping behavior and human nature was contained within its purpose for creation. A variety of platforms were used, and the passage of time shaped their evolution. The purpose could include instruction, identity, navigation, information to be combined with other symbols, or metaphorical "meaning-within-meaning". It is this last purpose that eventually became the most frequently used in ancient civilizations; Egypt was an acute example of this semiotic. The ancient Egyptians of both the Old and New Kingdoms were especially advanced in this technique.

The Neolithic Revolutions of humankind, to summarize, were not just one manifestation of life change, like the agricultural revolution as proposed by popular culture, but of many. If one tried to consider a single domain as a primary catalyst for these Revolutions, I would suggest that development of the human mind is that one. Our maturing observational awareness, perception, cognition, attitudinal primers and cues, behaviors, and capability for memory and relearning produced all these life changes. Our intelligence, as shaped by nature, nurture, adaptability, and the driving curiosity to continue to learn, exemplifies our universe's propensity to embody an anthropic principle. The final achievement of all the Neolithic Revolutions, therefore, can be summarized from this discussion as the information, communication and behavior Revolutions. This is how the Homo sapien-sapien mind hard-wired its social nature into its biology and metamorphosized its existence into a truly cosmological potential.

\*\*\*

*Introduction to Social Power and Control*

To borrow a contemporary phrase from popular culture, "knowledge is power." This concept certainly occupied the minds and strategies of the cultures that grew from the human Revolutions. What this phrase meant in ancient times was that the more knowledge leaders possessed or could scheme to possess, the easier it became to manage the sociology of an urban society. Because the general populace of a Neolithic community possessed a smaller body of knowledge with less empirical understanding about nature and their environments with which to access than we do today, there was far greater opportunity for the power elite, as they became known, to grow this resource capacity with the motivation to unite the congregations under their power authority.

The ritual and ceremony concepts were tools created from another tool, the semiotics of information content, that allowed authorities to gain stature within the community and therefore enable this type of social engineering to exploit the intellectual ignorance of the community at-large and gain their endpoint, which was to control the social community: "The control of the wild is a metaphor and mechanism for the control of society" (Hodder 1990, 12). Hodder continues stating that "Power may be based on the control of social or esoteric knowledge rather than on the control of economic resources," and "Second, goods, labour, and land have to be evaluated within a symbolic system before they can be used as the basis for social domination" (Hodder 1990, 15). Recognition must be awarded to other motives of this control mechanism whose evidence appears overwhelmingly in history and whose attitude-behavior mechanism continues unwavering today in that power and control strategies were formed to control other things about a community, such as resources, geography, etc. but continues to be the symbolic system that is indispensable to this process.

A new concept of power slowly took its creation from the persistent growth of the village family group now genetically diffused by many generations of reproductive development. Application of power and control sociology grew influential within the psychology of societal and individual behavior. A *Power and control* mechanism is an attitude-behavior process that appears repeatedly in the ancient record. The 9,000-year-old illustrations at Çatalhöyük, strikingly show a snapshot in the power and control evolution. This is illustrated as humankind's perceptive wrestling of power and control away from nature, his environment and the animal kingdom.

Power dualities had always existed between animals and humans, and between nature and humans because they were inherent within the food sustenance satisfaction pyramid model. By the nature of his continued survival, man was able, in pre-Neolithic, to exert control over animal prey - at least enough to provide food sustenance and medicinal resources. On some levels this could constitute a successful possession. Again, the wealth of illustrative information left for us from Early Neolithic in the Middle East, Euro-Asia, and the Americas shows the slow, mindful transfer of weighted power and control dominance from the animal agrios wild environment to the human domain.

SYMBOLISM

*How our ancestors' power perception of the agrios evolved*

It was through development of the semiotic form of information and knowledge sharing that helped to allow power and control sociology to eventually dominate human existence. This intelligence grew independently throughout the local geographies. Then, because of continued contact with these people, a diffusion effect successfully spread the ideology to others, as well as new symbol cultures with which to communicate and share those ideas. The receiving culture, for one, must have been perceptive and receptive to the advantages of adopting the new symbolism in the first place for them to have left evidence of its use or practice. Sufficient contacts would initially have been made for this situation to occur.

We see global evidence of these external material cultures and resources appearing in the records of many disparate cultures, resources and artifacts that were not native to the local geography. Therefore, travel among distant cultures was regular and persistent for the commercial trade of resources and appearance of those materials and artifacts to have appeared in those civilizations. For another, the receiving culture may have been vulnerable to a less-than-amenable exchange of semiotics, or that it was an imposition of power and control and not even an exchange that occurred.

As the urbanization revolution progressed, animal domestication and agricultural cultivation industries grew to give rise to a revolutionary new value of property ownership and its adjacent resource and commodity trade industries. The trade and sharing of natural resources and raw materials between individuals or small family groups, pre-urbanization, has been practiced since the Upper Paleolithic period. Urbanization gave rise to a whole new industry of commodity trading which included food, manufactured goods and resources, and material goods with symbolic meaning and attributions.

*Their minds' more evolved view toward balance of power in the agrios*

The Revolutions of urbanized life, beyond the social psychologies among people and their groups, was a transformation that the Universe required to occur in form and substance, and whose style was dictated by the unique homeostatic conditions of the natural environments at that time. A new understanding of the agrios and the domus shows us that our ancestors were developing a thoughtful strategy to sway the balance of power and control in their favor for the first time. Domestic domus structures and ceremonial ritual centers, as community architectures, were a mindful expression of their strategy to combat the wild agrios as a line of battle humans drew between themselves and the animal and environmental stress, tension and fearing daily life situations. They were combatting, or competing against, the cognitive duality titled 'the wild vs. the ordered.' In fact, Hodder thought extensively about this duality, "The wild, nature and death are created (in the mind) to form the domesticated and the cultural, and vice versa. In the opposition and juxtaposition of the cultural (and domesticated) and the wild society is dialectically created out of its own negative image" (Hodder 1990, 11). It is from this model of critical thinking that their plans were formed and that laid the foundation for their strategies at competing against these adversaries.

In summary, symbolism was developed as a tool that allowed one to express meaning from their thoughts, ideas, desires, as well as a representation of what was observed. All the media of symbolism; inscription, artifacts, body ornamentation, structures, temples, monuments, and more recently writing and verbal forms were props and tools that are, at their core essences, extensions of their minds, hands and mouths.

There was pragmatic utilization from many of these objects. Inscriptions, such as petroglyphs, served as navigation instruments, calendars for keeping time, and even disclosing food and water locations. Artifacts such as pottery, were food utility utensils but which bore meaningful metaphorical inscription art. Body ornamentation served a dual purpose as tools for food processing or warfare. Structures, temples and monuments provided habitation architectures, ceremonial, social bonding, engineering, and more diverse manifestations of power and control cultures. But our ancestors, like us today, used semiotics to create and express meaning and make relationships between two existing entities. According to Hodder, "The giving of meaning to the world is no more than a particular reading of it...When we state, 'this means that' we are simply saying that we have just made a relationship" (1990, 274).

The social and material cultures of Neolithic humankind, those of Nam and Muh, were being revolutionized by new weapons of competition, the use of their minds to create expressions of thought. These semiotic-infused weapons would serve them well in the battle against the stressful and fearful duality of man vs. nature. These changes were affected from further development of the $T_2$ variable in my Algorithm of Humankind and that adds much substance and style to the question of "who we are". The appearance of building and monument architectures, as symbolic representations, were aligned with habitation, ceremonial and emerging ritual cultures in mind. Hodder suggests that "Structures have a potential for certain directions of change. They have tendencies which may or may not be acted upon" (1990, 277). These Revolutions, aided in a very large fashion by the invention of semiotic forms of mindful expression, opened many new avenues of sophistication and the development of human beings, as well as many new complexities to the human condition.

It is with this in mind that we now take the leap into a most important revolution of our species, one which has become - the adoption of a "new set of clothes" we still wear today: the ability to socially communicate knowledge, meaning, and persuasion effectively and instantaneously to one another through various forms of symbolic representation, such as the Ritual.

All that is needed for Nam and Muh to become the showroom-ready human model is a proverbial coat of polish and aftercare.

*References*

Berger, Lee R., John Hawks, Darryl J. de Ruiter, Steven E. Churchill, Peter Schmid, Lucas K. Delezene, Tracy L. Kivell, Heather M. Garvin, Scott A. Williams, Jeremy M. DeSilva, Matthew M. Skinner, Charles M. Musiba, Noel Cameron, Trenton W. Holliday, William Harcourt-Smith, Rebecca R. Ackermann, Manuel Bastir, Barry Bogin, Deborah Bolter, Julia Brophy, Zachary D. Cofran, Kaitlin A. Congdon, April S. Deane, Marianne Dembo,

Michelle Drapeau, Marina C. Elliott, Elen M. Feuerriegel, Daniel Garcia-Martinez, David J. Green, Alia Gurtov, Joel D. Irish, Asher Kruger, Mary F. Laird, Damiano Marchi, Matthew R. Meyer, Shara Nalla, Elen W. Negash, Caley M. Orr, Davorka Radovčić, Lauren Schroeder, Jenna E. Scott, Zachary Throckmorton, Matthew W. Tocheri, Chloe VanSickle, Caroline S. Walker, Pengfei Wei, and Bernhard Zipfel. 2015. "*Homo naledi*, a New Species of the Genus *Homo* from the Dinaledi Chamber, South Africa." *eLife* 4 (September 10): e09560. https://doi.org/10.7554/eLife.09560.

Clottes, J. and Lewis-Williams, D. 1998. *The Shamans of Prehistory*. New York: Harry N. Abrams Inc.

Dietrich, Oliver, Çiğdem Köksal-Schmidt, Jens Notroff, and Klaus Schmidt. 2013. *Establishing a Radiocarbon Sequence for Göbekli Tepe: State of Research and New Data. Neo-Lithics* 1: 35–37.

Flannery, Kent and Marcus, Joyce. 2012. *The Creation of Inequality*. Cambridge, MA: Harvard University Press.

Hayden, Brian. 2009. The Proof Is in the Pudding: Feasting and the Origins of Domestication. *Current Anthropology* 50 (5): 597-601.

Henshilwood, C. S., Francesco d'Errico, Curtis W. Marean, Richard G. Roberts, Judson W. Sealy, Hilary A. Yates, Chris S. O. Reynard, Peter J. Henshilwood, and Ian R. Godfrey. 2001. "An Early Bone Tool Industry from the Middle Stone Age at Blombos Cave, South Africa: Implications for the Origins of Modern Human Behavior, Symbolism and Language." *Journal of Human Evolution* 41: 631–678.

Hodder, Ian. 1990. *The Domestication of Europe*. Oxford: Basil Blackwell.

Kinzel, Moritz, and Lee Clare. 2020. "Monumental - Compared to What? A Perspective from Göbekli Tepe." In *Monumentalising Life in the Neolithic: Narratives of Change and Continuity*, edited by Anne Birgitte Gebauer, Lasse Sørensen, Anne Teather, and António Carlos Valera, 29–48. Oxford: Oxbow Books.

Labarca, R., M. Frugone-Álvarez, L. Vilches, J. Francisco Blanco, A. Peñaloza, C. Godoy-Aguirre, et al. 2024. "Correction: Tagua Tagua 3: A New Late Pleistocene Settlement in a Highly Suitable Lacustrine Habitat in Central Chile (34°S)." *PLOS ONE* 19 (7): e0306861. https://doi.org/10.13

71/journal.pone.0306861.

Lewis-Williams, J.D. and Dowson, T.A. 1988. The Signs of All Times: Entoptic Phenomena in Upper Paleolithic Art. *Current Anthropology.* 29 (2): 201-245.

Lieberman, Philip. 1991. *Uniquely Human: The Evolution of Speech, Thought, and Selfless Behavior.* Cambridge, MA: Harvard University Press.

Marshack, A. 1996. A Middle Paleolithic Symbolic Composition from the Golan Heights: The Earliest Known Depictive Image. *Current Anthropology.* 37: 357-365.

Mithen, Steven. 1996. *The Prehistory of The Mind: The Cognitive Origins of Art, Religion and Science.* Thames and Hudson Ltd, London.

Schmidt, Klaus. 2010. "Göbekli Tepe—The Stone Age Sanctuaries: New Results of Ongoing Excavations with a Special Focus on Sculptures and High Reliefs." *Documenta Praehistorica* 37: 239–256.

Schmidt, Klaus. 2012. *Göbekli Tepe: A Stone Age Sanctuary in South-Eastern Anatolia.* Berlin: ex-oriente e.V. & ArchaeNova e.V.

# RITUAL

*Ceremony is a primordial part of human nature; one that helps us connect, find meaning and discover who we are: we are the ritual species.*

-Xygalatas, Dimitris, from *Ritual:*
*How Seemingly Senseless Acts Make Life Worth Living, 2022.*

*Keywords: Generalists, specialists, ritual, building semiotics, power and control, social bonding, Anthropic Principle, competition, mimicry, superpower, shamanism, entoptics, animism, eschatology of the soul, sacred mathematics.*

Nam and Muh are us, and preparing for their showroom rollout...

What a long, strange trip it continues to be for Nam and Muh! Revolutions of sustenance, thought, behavior, technology, social interaction, culture, history, spirituality, and a new profound appreciation of the cosmos have seized their collective consciousness. The pace of metamorphosis in these areas of the human condition for their people was accelerated beyond what could be comparatively shown of past species and civilizations to which we possess evidence.

The rise of these life changes happened because elder Homo sapiens, and related younger hunter-gatherer genetic lineages were able to adapt to nature's ever-changing living homeostasis better than their competitor species. Their perception and cognitive capacities highlighted abilities to be both specialists and *generalists* in matters of intellect, sustenance, technology, history, memory, and adaptability.

While the Homo evolutionary pathway of the last 300 thousand years (kyr), was selected by nature's climactic, geological, ecological, and reproductive developmental forces, many of H. sapiens' adversarial contemporaries - such as H. floresiensis, H. Denisovans, H. Idalou, H. naledi, and H. neanderthalensis - were primarily *specialists* of intelligence. This became existential in the last 100 kyr. when H. sapiens comingled within respective geographies of the others. The instincts of H. sapiens were less sensitive to disruptions in nature and more adaptable to changes in the food and ecological chain mechanisms than they were. The intellectual abilities of Homo sapien sapiens won the competition to essentially become us, bolstered by new tools of inference, long-term mindfulness, and mature historical, technological and social intelligences.

I have enlightened you to the salience of nature's climate dynamics in shaping the onset of these Revolutions. Many speed bumps were encountered in their journey along this road. Among the most severe were the ongoing episodic cosmic and global geophysical phenomena like space collisions, solar particle emissions, cataclysmic earthquakes and volcanoes, and other, more esoteric influences. These recurring cataclysms obviously infected the climatic and ecological environment's reactions to this web of nature's entanglement. When the conditions became favorable for change, humankind's adaptability and adoptability allowed the Revolutions to be undertaken with success at a rate far more than linear velocity as a function of time.

The calculus for the adoption of various technological advances was different among geographical landmasses primarily due to climatic and cultural factors. This also affected ideologies, political matters and economics. The proliferation of the Western Hemisphere's post-Younger Dryas eco-environment took thousands of years longer to allow its natives to adopt an ethnocentricity comparable with the Euro-Asian and African contemporaries. An extreme example would be to compare the Sahara region of 8,000 years ago, which precisely fit the 'temperate' geo-climate classification with that of North America, that was still within the climatic grasp of the cooler Younger Dryas period. Three thousand years later, records left from the Egyptian Grand Unification show a desert eco-environment already overtaking the populace. The situation was similar in the Levant of the Middle East/Asia Minor.

In contrast, Native America, South America, and aboriginal Australia were still immersed in cooler and far wetter climates. Because these people did not possess a favorable technological intelligence, we possess today that could climatically influence any kind of territory, their dependence upon climate drove their sociopolitical and cultural ideologies, ancient traditions, sustenance practices, and overall human condition.

For example, consider the Native American city of Cahokia. It enjoys the distinction of being the largest inhabited urban land space on the ancient North American continent, with a measured area of approximately 7 square miles, and an estimated snapshot population of over 25,000. Its builders started construction around 900 CE, only 1,100 years ago. Cahokia's "shooting star" urban model lasted only about 400 years and was abandoned by 1350 CE. Conversation and debate today rage unabated about the sociopolitical structure, but one factor is present in all of them.

Cahokia illustrated an autocratic, stratified, vibrant economic, and complex government management ideology of a size not seen anywhere else in North America north of Mexico. These factors meet all the criteria in V. Gordon Childe's early 20$^{th}$ century definition of an urbanized community. But this city, now known as East St. Louis, Illinois, only existed after 900 CE; thousands of years after the rise of other analogous locations on the Euro-Asian and African continents. Cahokia's emergence and decline coincided with temporal shifts of flood frequencies on the Mississippi River Basin in the periods from 600-1350 CE (Munoz et al. 2015) and other geophysical phenomena.

Nam and Muh's people now enjoyed the best version of life they have ever known. The best domesticated food and shelter industries have encouraged the most prolific reproduction population development. The tools of semiotics were tasked, by the preoccupation with transfiguring the sharing of information, knowledge and meaning with others, into causing these life changes. These tools of the communicative mind, meaning-making, mindfulness, linguistics, inscription art, building and monument architecture, material cultures and most significantly, a social dynamic existentially dependent upon all these manifestations, were all Revolutions that are attributed to the successes of Neolithic man. Merlin Donald suggests that, as an evolution of culture and cognition, humankind underwent three transitions of memory representations: an episodic-to-mimetic, mimetic-to-mythic, and mythic-to-external symbolic and theoretic cultures (Donald 1991).

My analysis will now closely inspect the social aspects of these cognitive evolutions. The ideas I present next all fall under the social apparatus of *ritual* and *power and control.* I was originally considering using *Power and Control* as this chapter title, but upon reflection, I decided on *Ritual* as a final choice. Here is why: power and control grew to become so behaviorally dominant a practice in all human cultures post-Paleolithic that if one were to debate a determinative hierarchy it could be reasonably argued that power and control is most precisely associated with a totalitarian-influenced cause-and-effect relationship that defines the reality of the situation.

However, egalitarian societies of our hunter-gatherers were unanimously open social philosophies embodying small group dynamics and an indigenous mindset subsisting correspondingly in an unenclosed, unbounded physical landscape, a more inwardly driven ethos and a specialized multi-tasking cognition that did not utilize power and control structures much at all, certainly not in the scope, perspective, and nuance we use today. Power and authority, derived from their ethical and sociopolitical constitutions, were equally distributed, relatively speaking among all hunter-gatherer members, and to which each member held and impressed upon others a responsibility-driven way of life. This was their human condition that was different from the autocratic or representative totalitarian governing principles popular today.

This proto-historic existence was functional and enduring because it integrated well with basic needs for survival and procreation success for that time, given the real geophysical and other survival factors nature presented to them. As I noted earlier, the hunter-gatherer lifestyle was characterized by small community habitation, an egalitarian lifestyle constrained by the inability to establish permanent domestication cultures due to environmental and other constraints.

These constraints favored a mobile existence and no propensity toward the possession and use of personal property beyond those occupational tools each member fabricated and used as compelled to by their culture. Labor industries, an inherently social function, were practiced according to talent, skill, and specialization; all focused on the "one-for-all" as the best need-and-application strategy. The chance for a different social community structure, containing a personal property ethos, industrial channels of mass labor, commodity production, and resource manufacturing to bloom and flourish was not attainable simply because they weren't favored until an accommodating natural homeostasis emerged. Because nature was a power humans could not control, this manifestation often only became established regionally when the periglacial Ice Age cycles trended warmer in a particular locale.

As environmental living conditions encouraged both a shift in migratory behaviors in the contexts of food sustenance for animal prey, as well as human hunters, and favored plant growth, urbanization created the need for new sustainability strategies in all aspects of life. Entire cultural existences adapted to these changes. Certainly, the basic physiological food and shelter requirements took on new dimensions as living space per capita decreased and physical boundaries caused by the creation of *building semiotics* came into existence.

Significant to the move toward urbanization was the onset of living conditions conducive to this change. When the time came for a group of communities, for example, to create a feasting ritual center for food processing, storage, trade, and celebration, it became immediately apparent that living spaces were needed to accommodate the workers during construction activities and, later, permanent habitation behaviors. Discoveries and inspections of a growing number of ancient, sophisticated buildings and monument architecture continue to support the argument that they took a very long time to complete - often years.

Feasting centers, then later henges, pyramids, temples, coliseums, monoliths, and other megalithic designs were central to the creation of the life-in-close-quarters identity as the workers and residents needed nightly accommodations to see a construction project through to completion and for later enjoyment and occupation. The underlying attitude and behavior, perception and cognition pathways were ritualistic features of this mindful human historic time. This mindful system is continually witnessed in contemporary times as part of the tapestry of our lives. We are them and they are us.

I have shown you that the feasting center was a first permanent building concept created over 30,000 years ago and that it functioned as a social behavior conduit whose architecture expressed multifaceted symbolic meaning, learning, communication, and ideology. The first urbanized ritual cultures were born from this creation. Communities of people who cooperated to assemble these cultures used these meeting grounds to share *social bonding*, ceremonial, and commercial pursuits. They fashioned a purposeful ritualistic behavior to bond, celebrate, ask for, give thanks to, remember, trade, and plan future activities.

Ritual cultures predated even basic urbanized boundary-driven power and controlled cultures by dozens of millennia. But they did not much resemble those of the Holocene Epoch (our Neolithic kinship classification) due to the aforementioned egalitarian ethnocentric characteristics of unbounded space and personal responsibility, predominant at that time in small group communities. These are just some of the existing rebuttals to a hierarchy rank-order system of power and control along some dimension. Both are social constructs with no other relevant meaning except for the existing mindfully abstract meaning people assign to them. If people did not exist there would be no meaning to power and control or ritual mechanisms, a thought experiment in the context of the *anthropic principle*.

The ritual protocol possesses a highly complex interwoven psychological fabric necessary to the catalytic features of power and control. Some may think the underlying meaning suggests that ritual <u>causes</u> power and control to happen, but is this really the case?

Power and control, in my view within the context of this thesis, are meant to be conjoined as two terms sharing one <u>meaning</u>. I have earlier introduced some salient characteristics of these concepts, so let me add them to this discussion. Many definitional features of power and control exist, including that suggested by the 20th century philosopher Bertrand Russell who asks, "is power a fact or a potential" (Lukes 1986,19). Hannah Arendt introduces a social dimension by suggesting that "power corresponds not just to the act but to act in-concert…it is a state of being" (Williams 2011, 27).

Anthropologist Peter J. Wilson introduces a belief structure characteristic, "the surrealities of power produce, or reinforce, beliefs in the realities of power without those realities ever having ever to materialize" (Wilson 1988, 118). Power, in this context, is made "real" when the recipients' minds are made to believe or abstractly perceive that power is present. Examples of this potential occur when the recipient's mind is stimulated by pertinent body language, a weapon, speech, or contrived entoptic episodes.

A common thread of meaning is agreed upon that the <u>process</u> of power and control, as provided by my definition here, "is a social construct, with inherent differing perspectives and contexts, of an impression held by a person or group about the ability or capability of an authority, whether an individual or an association acting in concert, to enact a measure of control over another's mindset, or their actions of attitude and behavior". My idea of the concept "impression" is explained in the last sentence of the last paragraph.

In addition, I suggest that power and control is more of a process than a state of being, though its lifespan can consist of a single iteration whereby the power motive disappears for some reason. I use the term <u>motive</u> here to describe a single behavior. This circles back to the attitude-behavior mechanism in that this is an all-pervasive ideology that interfaces within the larger framework of my thesis.

Is power a cause or effect of a control mechanism activity? This may be a case of the "chicken-or-the-egg" paradox, whereby, one examination from the perspective of the party who administers it will arrive at a different result as compared to an examination coming from that party who receives it. The administering party initiates the power, and the receiving party accepts it; or the receiving party projects the impression of power initially onto the administering party followed by the demonstration of the activity in question.

To close this thought and introduce it into a new discussion, it appears evident that power must always be enabled by two or more involved parties to have any meaning or that the mechanism of power does not exist in that example.

Power and control are pervasive, at least in today's world; one might even say they are omnipresent. This is one of many universal existential ties that bind us to our ancestral brethren of the Neolithic Revolution. The requisites of power and control are made necessary by the surrounding circumstances situation. They weren't so in the times of hunter-gatherers as I will suggest below with a monologue of this progression to what "could have happened".

The attitude-behavior mechanism, in association with power and control cultures, was not as power-seeking in the hunter-gatherer Paleolithic. Requisites surrounding a potential power situation were not efficacious, at least in the contemporary sense, because the circumstances were not conducive to its manifestation.

Many studies of modern societies have been conducted that serve as proxies to what may have existed in our hunter-gatherer cultural traditions. Studies of the Mbuti Pygmies of Zaire (Turnbull 1965, 1966), the Negritos of Malaysia (Endicott 1979), the Pandaram and Paliyan of India (Gardner 1980), and the !Kung Bushmen of Botswana and Namibia (Lee 1979; Wiessner 1977), characterize many commonalities toward the forementioned equitable distribution of power, control and a highly individualized, but not selfish ethos prior to the Neolithic Revolutions.

!Kung women were determined to possess an exceptional degree of autonomy and sexual egalitarianism (Draper 1975, 77). The Hadza of

Tanzania, like all these contemporary analogous examples, are nomadic and follow economic ideologies that "prevent saving and accumulation (of property) and impose sharing through mechanisms which allow goods to circulate without making people dependent upon one another" (Woodburn 1982, 433). An additional ancient characteristic still practiced by the Hadza is that their society is an open one whose value systems are non-competitive but limit the development of agriculture because of this economic ideology and rules of sharing. But this mindset spills over onto such areas as limiting care for incapacitation in certain circumstances (Woodburn 1982, 433, 448). All these behavioral characteristics became subject to radical change upon the urbanization of our species.

Upon commencement of those changes, the Neolithic cultures maintained the memory of nature's power and control over them, as was known by their ancestors. However, new power structures had now entered the highway of their existence. These structures were created by other human beings. The powers of nature; the environment and animal agrios, were always reflected upon as being overwhelming to people, but now a new, formidable and overwhelming human administrator of power and control eventually began to assert itself through the semiotics of symbolic representation. For both adversaries of the power *competition*, those of nature and the human ones, the natural ones were still the most formidable. A new, more totalitarian social culture slowly developed from these changes in the dynamics of growing tribal size, acclimation into structured communities that offered more opportunities to acquire and demonstrate power and control authority over others and their environments.

When the urbanization vehicle accelerated, the egalitarian ideology of hunter-gatherers slowly began to fade into a periphery of curiosity (where a random version resides today in some cultures). The appearance of the group concept in life meant that new roles and new behavioral role-playing were created to deal with the consequences. As habitation group sizes increased, assignments of power, property rights and, later, competition potentials also increased. These manifestations were presumptive of the instinctive hard-wired mindset which held that hunter-gatherers perceived nature as possessing power and that an entity existed which was responsible for that power authority. So, a concept of power existed then, but its ideological focus was diametrically opposed to that of the urbanized human.

The new Neolithic cultures expanded their thinking into more generalized realms; a pedagogy of life now with boundaries and a 'larger picture' mentality. There were more things to think about now in a larger and longer-term lifestyle dominion. Whereas the hunter-gatherers devoted more of their time-day to a narrowed perspective of survival sustenance, the urbanized humans now had to work construction, establish a division of labor, and introduce congregational and other social cultures into their daily routines. This sociology and the social cultures were the most taxing on their ontological dynamics.

Their minds reasoned an efficient lifestyle arrangement featuring geometric building designs fashioned from more instinctual mnemonic knowledge and observations of favorable mathematical shapes, patterns and geometry in nature. Early on, the circle was the shape of choice for such structures. Such objects as the sun and moon, the behavior of some animal movements, many species of trees, as well as the stars, were perceived to be circular in shape. These shapes were all transfigured into deified and sacred worship status by the collective Neolithic mind as subservient observers, and not powerful masters of the wild agrios. Consequently, ceremonies of many ancient peoples used a circular worship dance for a variety of purposes, further binding a sacred attribution to the circle geometry.

The overwhelming majority of the early feasting and central meeting architecture has been found to be circular in shape for these reasons and practical ones. For example, excavated ritual centers and residential dwellings at many sites used circular shapes as the most efficient use of the indoor space and because a congregation assembly is most naturally, ergonomically, and securely arranged in circular patterns, for ease of construction or adaptability to various roof components. All these characteristics support adoption of the circle ideology as an ethnocentric shape of choice due to its harmonious equilibrium with both nature and the spiritual realm.

# RITUAL

\* \* \*

The invention of the ritual and ceremony concept gained favor among authorities and their wannabes as a type of social engineering to exploit the intellectual capacity of the community at large and gain their endpoint; that was to control the social community. The ritual was a strategic tool of power and control ideology. The ritual protocol contained its own characteristics; a toolkit of strategies associated with its administration. This toolkit, associated with the practice of the Neolithic contemporary attitude-behavior mechanism included fear and stress, social bonding, mimicry, competition, and exploitation of knowledge, including the suppression of knowledge from the general community. It is interesting to note that all these characteristics are present and practiced in our social behavior today, both individually and in groups.

A ritual attitude-behavior anatomy, whose purpose is to assist in showing the associative elements of power and control structures with what both the Neolithic person and a person today may reasonably experience, is as follows. A ritual event is initiated by an individual or group whose purpose is to address an emotional need. These needs could be for gratification or for reduction of fear and stress in a situation. Because the power and control dynamic are topical, a reduction of fear and stress is the objective of the attitude-behavior mechanism. Often the ritual is learned on the group level, with a generous amount of social bonding attached to its dynamics. The individual ritual activity is often a maintenance regimen prescribed by an authoritative body to uphold the individual's commitment to the group as the social bonding mechanism and to the authority as the sought-after control mechanism. Humans, to whom our ancestors are us and we are them, behave identically in this realm.

Whether the ritual activity is performed by an individual or as a group function, relief of any underlying stress, tension, and fear is essential for a power and control process to work. The authorities want this to happen to maintain control over the group. Social bonding attitude-behavior is a tool used by a leader or authority to directly reduce their emotional stress and fear in a frightful situation and is an interim objective toward achieving a power and control regime.

A "power in numbers" and mindful collective agreement to participating in the group ritual ceremony psychology is impressed upon them and often reinforced by the threat of negative consequences by the authority if the directions are not followed. This strategy works because, among our most basal instinctive brain pathways is the one that addresses the hard-wired socialness of our human nature.

Ancient humans needed social psychology to survive and evolve in the wild agrios of the outside environment. The same foundational stress-induced situations that we face today were encountered by our older kinship. They were all concerned with relieving the stress of death, ill health, survival, economic sustenance, the demands of cooperative group labor, the psychology of habituating in a confined space, security from a dangerous agrios environment, and maintaining harmony with both nature and the spiritual realm. Many of these situations occurred simultaneously in daily life. The human brain was naturally selected to accommodate this social psychology by means of a group construct and residual basal brain drives toward socialness.

Many mammals today exhibit these behavioral characteristics. Primates and humans are of special note when discussing this subject. Because the primate and human brain is larger; specifically, the Neo-cortex region, according to the latest research by biologist Susanne Shultz and biological anthropologist Robin Dunbar, "there exists a statistical relationship between the typical size of a species' social group and the size of its neocortex, ostensibly derivative of selection for specialized cognition required for group living..." (Shultz and Dunbar 2022; Dunbar 2024). This reaffirms Dunbar's research study that spans over thirty years and concluded that "there is a quantitative relationship between brain size and social group size (group size is a monotonic function of brain size) presumably because the cognitive demands of sociality place a constraint on the number of individuals that can be maintained in a coherent group" (Dunbar 1998,

2009).

Stress relief, in the context of crisis resolution via the ritual culture protocol, is made possible by the larger Neo-cortex brain regions of primates and humans that allows for the formation of a group social psychology to deal with these survival pressures. (A note here: A curious speculation could be inferred from findings established in this extensive research to beg the question, what would we observe if the Neo-cortex brain regions were even larger in primates and/or humans?).

Why rituals? The rationale for a person to participate in these ceremonial episodes may include personal fulfillment, empowerment or transformation, social bonding, maintenance of a community order, or even coercive social engineering by a despotic leadership figure. Another reason for our contemporary participation is, "well, I can't really say why, I guess it's something I've seen since my childhood" according to research anthropologist Dimitris Xygalatas (2022, 15). His findings feature an important attitude-behavior association that has existed among all descendants since the second generation of humans who engaged in the ritual activity.

*Mimicry* is another characteristic behavioral property trait in many life species on Earth. Today we witness many examples of mimicry in the mammal biology, as we do in the human world - as our ancestors had observed for millions of years in primates and other indigenous species. Mimicry is an attitude-behavior mechanism practiced by all of us that, according to conclusions by social neuroscientists Eliska Prochazkova and Mariska Kret, helps, "enhance their (receiver's mimicry) understanding of the other's (mimic sender) feelings, emotions, intentions, and actions" (Prochazkova and Kret 2017, 110). Mimicry can be autonomic (Prochazkova and Kret 2017, 99) or unconscious (van Baaren et al. 2009). Both embody the brain's behavioral systems to help the receiver empathize with the sender's mimicking. The mimicry activity begins in an infant's early years as a learning mechanism that continues through one's life.

This process works in conjunction with the ritual function to create strong social bonds and cues the receiver's attitude and behavior mechanism, enabling both recognition of and empathy for another's emotions (Buck

1980). Recent experimental data have shown that, according to Duffy and Chartrand, "Although mimicry is generally facilitated by prosocial motives, a more nuanced view is emerging that shows that antisocial motives, such as power, status and competition can drive mimicry as well" (2015, 112-116). These processes were well understood and strategized by ancient leaders in their desire to contrive - for prosocial and fabricate - for less than prosocial and even antisocial - motives, power, competitive and control-seeking status in a stratified environment.

The exercise of ritualization, according to Xygalatas, is characterized by features of rigidity, repetition and redundancy (2022, 66, 69). The precision of the ritual behavior activity movements (rigidity), its repeatability (repetition), and ensuring a successful endpoint - at least in one's mind - by exceeding the "required" minimum number of repetitions (redundancy) are the functional elements that define this attitude-behavior.

Whether the exercise is performed in private or in a group setting, the profound social bonding 'homework' exercise details find their way back to the group 'classroom' knowledge update setting; the ritual center, temple, cooperative meeting venue, etc., through conversation (a contemporary behavior) or through use of a 'checking in' surveillance mechanism that ensures proper participation by the individual. Xygalatas supports a notion of 'shared arousal' of bond-strengthening through this ritual exercise, "Anthropological insights, psychological surveys, biological measurements and neuroscience data all agree that these rituals create shared arousal that results in feelings of togetherness" (2022, 153).

Does ritualization allow us to establish and practice routines that eventually become force-of-habit? This question circles back to Xygalatas' "wild card" factor for the rationale of the ritual; the "I don't know why I do it, I just do it as I have learned from childhood and/or am told to do it" (2022). If ritualization via repeated exposure and practice does "teach" the student to cognitively assimilate this behavior as force-of-habit, then this supports a theory that humans instinctively rely on conforming to cultural conventions such as rituals as a vital form of social bonding. Xygalatas thinks so. He concludes that "Ceremony is a primordial part of human nature one that helps us connect, find meaning and discover who we are: we are the ritual species" (2022, 268).

Before I proceed on the theme of the ritual phenomenon, I want to establish a perspective on how the environment of stresses, fears and tensions were created and developed in the Neolithic urbanized world. The unique dynamics of Earth's changing ecology post-Ice Age and the Younger Dryas periods, aided by the then current state of technological advancement, allowed for new food & water sustenance and sedentary lifestyle practices. The modification of both animal movement behaviors (dominated by their own basic survival pursuit of food and water) and wild agriculture harvesting potentials precipitated from eco-environmental change, favored a millennium-long transformation from nomadic food collection to husbandry and agrarianism, respectively.

Now, instead of just taking from the land and herd, the new regime had to provide for sustainability of both plant and animal populations. The practice of sedentism, complete with their egalitarian way of life and all its societal embodiment, was adopted as the indigenous found their way toward achieving vastly increased carrying capacities for food, water, shelter, and domestication of both animals and plants (already in practice by the Neolithic but with new motivation and impetus for accelerated advancement).

Breakthroughs such as these were not without the creation of new constraints to 'life in the city'. Resource acquisition and management due to technological requirements of a new urbanized food economy, the pursuit of which also forced society to create new labor specialization and production infrastructures, were just some of the new complexities the people faced. These same characteristics and constraints were present in the building construction economies, all of which were successfully developed through synthesization of socialization concepts with assistance from the various behavioral strategies I am now discussing.

While the carrying capacities for basic life commodities in an increased population density were expanded, marginal costs for managing the resource, labor, trade, and accompanying health infrastructures also increased in complexity in both economic and social dimensions. It is recognized that, in a sense, the concept of economics was created and given cognitive meaning in this period as a definition to the new framework of efficient resource procurement and management.

Egalitarian sociology was transformed by a new critical thinking into adoption of a stratified social group mindset. Food and building management infrastructures were layered into specialized labor groups whose efficiency was best managed or controlled by a group leadership function. Additionally, the principle of property ownership, another concept anathema to the egalitarian 'one for all and all for one's' way of life, was a natural ideological strategy adoption that helped perpetuate the longevity of urbanized resource management infrastructures. These newly created and necessary social connections were indispensable for the survival of the Neolithic city but were inherently complex, without precedent to the indigenous, and brought with them new living stresses, fears and tensions.

The stratification of social groups, as an attitude-behavior ideology, created a new cognitive perception of status to those deemed or elected as leaders of any congregation. The existence of the status concept can be found as depicted in symbolic representations of all ancient civilizations dating back 100,000 years, as noted. Examples include building architecture styles, personal symbols such as carvings, scepters, jewelry, coins, family identity shields, and a variety of body adornments. A most pronounced visible symbolism of the ancient status concept must include the readily identifiable ownership of mansion, palace, and temple real estate by wealthy and royal leaders of a despotic or totalitarian sociopolitic.

As the new civilized ethnography skewed popularly toward a despotic sociology, the new phenomena of increased habitation density, stratification, property ownership, and competition were social constructs that brought new problems. A 'tie that bound' these phenomena together was the transformative new socialization psychology. The attitude-behavior and perception-cognition mechanisms absorbed many new layers of complexity. The creation of property ownership, a new labor philosophy, and the resultant urban lifestyle accommodation require an influential result to deal with the new platform of stress, tension, fear, and the maintenance of harmony among themselves and their environments - social and geophysical. The development of tools and strategies generated by leaders to use for social engineering purposes would come to deal with the ultimate endpoint, the maintenance of power and control.

\* \* \*

What faced our ancestors in the Neolithic model was the desire for status that was borne from competition in many phases of life. The social group dynamic was a new factor of human nature that compelled competitive attitudes and behaviors. Urbanization redistributed the infrastructure of many cultural institutions, customs, and practices. Populations became more concentrated, external material industries such as food, natural resources, commodities, and building trades were congregated and compartmentalized. The notion that centralization and concentration can lead to greater efficiency and increased power potential is inherent in nature's processes.

As far back as the early Paleolithic, inhabitants learned and understood this concept through observation of these natural processes. Examples include intensifying a fire by feeding the core instead of dispersing the fuel around a periphery, group instead of individual hunting to secure larger game, and sharing ideas in a group setting rather than everyone individually tasking all activities in isolation. Our minds resonate with these strategies and behaviors used by our ancestors. The mindset for them to transfer this application of knowledge and thought to a social construct with similar premises and characteristics was a holistic one of generalized intelligence. They created, from witness and application of similar natural phenomena with the associated attributes of power outcomes, new understanding that led to new uses of the power concept.

Power and control through centralization was a direct reflection of ancient knowledge transfer from natural phenomena by the generalized intelligence and that is still evolving today. With so many new social group concepts to develop and learn, from the importance and economics of a centralized power institution was a natural Neolithic thought Revolution away from the incumbent egalitarian, decentralized format. The power institution took on added weight and significance as a successful social engineering strategy when applications were made efficient and effective in all large social, labor, and military associations. Many tools of power and control strategies were synthesized and that are still in use today.

As noted earlier, "knowledge is power." This axiom was abundantly illustrated by all agrarian and post-Revolution civilizations in the symbolic representation record. What this meant in ancient times is that the more knowledge the power elite possessed, the easier it became to navigate the social engineering function of a society. Because our ancient brethren had a far less empirical understanding of how nature and their living environment functions than we do today, they were compelled to utilize a less empirical method to bond their social community under the power authority.

Knowledge became a resource that allowed the power elite to ritualize social activities into cohesion and bonding of the city-state. This bonding strategy was used to ultimately keep the leadership in power, turning knowledge into a tool of coercion to achieve that end. No matter if the activity was designed to elect or keep incumbents in power or to relieve social stress, fear, and tension, the main objectives were the same: the restoration of peace and harmony, and possession of power and control.

As the human semiotic system transformed from simplistic Upper Paleolithic singularly descriptive visual picture symbolism to the Neolithic informational, historical, navigational, mathematical, technological, and spiritual/cosmic metaphorical meaning-making and storytelling semiotic intelligence, knowledge became a tool for the informed elite to exploit.

A phenomenon that existed then and continues even today is that of illiteracy and ignorance. While a statistical calculation may provide that the raw number of people who cannot read or write today is in the billions, its proportion is comparatively far less than that of our ancestors, most of whom could not read, or did not have access to the existing symbolism, or were unable to obtain this knowledge that was in guarded possession by the power elite. It is well documented that the power elite of many civilizations, a popular example of which was Egypt, ensured by force and/or coercion that the public was not allowed access to any of the royal venues where symbolic communication and knowledge resided. This methodology of suppressing knowledge from the public makes it easier for the leader type to establish and maintain control over his or her congregation.

Power and control could also be maintained by the royal elite by demonstrating that they could relieve social stress, tension and fear, and restore a harmonic community equilibrium through additional available social engineering strategies - some of which could be viewed as less-than-prosocial or even antisocial. By withholding knowledge, as taken from above, the leader could establish a cognitive foundation of superiority; hence, power over his subjects - the unwitting public. This concept served both as a stand-alone strategy and as a conduit for other competitive power and control strategies that were more complex in nature.

A more complex concept, known as the *superpower,* was both a large opportunity that came with constraints to the development of the ritual cultural environment by those seeking or maintaining authority. The cast of actors included gods, deities; both human and animal, and other intelligent beings to whom indigenous representatives provoked visitations. Development of this power and control culture by "Type A" personalities of talented genius, motivated leaders diverged away from the previous egalitarian cooperation of the prior social community concept as one constraint challenge. These were selected/elected by the social congregation as possessing unique talents, skills and other demonstrated qualities that led to some type of initial success in the effect of lessening communal stress, fear, and tension. Another constraining challenge was faced when the culture suffered stress and tension that, if severe enough, led to the leader facing existential threats to his power dominion, or even his supplantation with another leader.

Potential leaders, frequently selected because they possessed some exceptional physical or mental traits within their community, were faced with the task of subducting the group's stressful and often fear-inducing perceptions of the otherwise uncontrollable forces of nature to gain authority favor. Perceiving the attitude cues of the motivation and obsession psychology with wanting to be the authoritative figure, these leaders addressed nature's uncontrollable dominion by developing a strategy whereby they could reasonably claim to possess the ability to communicate with these superpowers through a conduit. The conduct of shamanism could successfully drive their endpoint of sustaining power structures as a control mechanism.

The process of adorning royalty, both living and departed, with any attribution was often completed by a process of observing the king or queen's special enduring behavioral and personality characteristic traits that set him or her apart from the populace and assigning to him or her that adornment which is matched best by an animal genus or particular species observed in nature.

For example, in Native America, a fierce, powerful warrior may have a name containing 'bear' or 'lion'. In ancient Egypt, the falcon is another animal indicator of power. This adornment was assigned to the god Horus where additionally his right eye represented the morning sun and his left eye the moon or evening. This adornment contains more metaphorical dualities that include the day-night cycle, the visual sacred geometry inherent within the metaphor, and a tripartite epithet of regeneration and reincarnation of life itself. When an animal was chosen to represent the god/deity, a specimen was selected, and corresponding ritual ceremony was performed to consummate the relationship. In Egypt this activity involved a mummification ritual at the time of its death. The Egyptians (and universally all other ancient cultures) believed most profoundly in the theory of eschatology. Mummification also contained a required biological instruction activity set necessary to be accomplished to successfully complete this adornment ritual.

The adornment ideology was prominently extended to include other environmental attributes. For example, Hathor is worshiped as the ancient

Egyptian goddess of the sky, women, fertility and love. It is interesting to note that by utilizing this mind process whereby constant manifestation and reinforcement of seeing and remembering the departed, royalty and his or her special attributes is maintained whenever a descendant sees the real animal in his or her daily life. This is as much a cognitive and ritualistic mnemonic for humans today as it was back then. Our mind's learning and cognitive reinforcement are pathed in these same ways as those of our ancestors.

*Shamanism*, a ritual practice involving a more knowledgeable/intelligent and/or talented tribe member who utilized his or her seemingly magical "powers" to interface with other-dimensional spirit entities for purposes of reducing fear, stress, and tension via a mechanism of healing, energizing, divination, or consciousness-awareness, depending upon, and as directed from, the unique circumstances inherent in the activity. The physical provenance for this phenomenon currently dates to over 30,000 years ago (Tedlock 2005); with many more examples of depository shamanistic remains potentially dated to over 15,000 years ago (Clottes and Lewis-Williams 1998).

The shaman was the earliest identified version of a high priest, a very important tribe member who enjoyed a high-status identity. This stratification practice was endowed typically to a family lineage. Descendants were blood beneficiaries who learned the practices from their elders as the knowledge pedagogy. Prehistoric civilizations were familiar with power and control regimes and were frequented with the knowledge deprivation exploited by the tribal leaders. This suggests that the attitude-behavior mechanisms driving this ritual psychology were hard-wired into the core brain system or at least the behavioral perception-cognition of early Homo sapiens.

One ingredient conducive to enabling some ritual schemes involved mind altering chemical stimulants that enabled the power elite to show proof of their contact with these superpowers and, using knowledge not necessarily originating from the supernatural realm, did enable successful treatments to cure the symptoms of afflicted, at least occasionally. The use of a mind-altering chemical strategy made it easy for authorities to manufacture regimes that could primarily strengthen their authority over the state but also facilitate the communal social bonds among the congregation members in a way that reinforced adherence to the leader's wishes. Addressing the inability to control all of nature's processes in this way enabled prehistoric leaders to establish their dominion over and proliferation of the later Neolithic urban structure and assisted in the formation of a religiosity social bonding strategy. Utilizing this design enabled early leaders to evolve the success of shamanism.

In their 2005 book titled, *Inside the Neolithic Mind: Consciousness, Cosmos and the Realm of the Gods,* authors James David Lewis-Williams and David Pearce followed original research conclusions conducted by Lewis-Williams and Thomas Dowson in 1988 (Webster 2007, 319), by evolving their still controversial model of *Three stages of Altered States of Consciousness.* Their claim is that it was a tool of social ritual design which employed shamans to fabricate an imposing measure of power and control over his congregation (Webster 2007). A tripartite tiered level belief of the living, the tribe's ancestors, and the gods, deities and animals allowed the shaman to navigate, via biochemical and neurological stress, an altered state of consciousness to compel the tribal members to direct behaviors toward their desired endpoint.

Their main argument suggests that, in the first of these stages, via the biological phenomenon known as *entoptics,* the optic and brain cortex systems perceive shapes atypical of normal sensory stimuli. Taken from the Greek meaning "within vision," the subject envisions geometric shapes that could consist of a hexagonal grid, parallel lines, dots and short flecks, zigzag lines, or nested catenary curves (like flickered zigzags, and filigrees or thin meandering lines (Lewis-Williams and Dowson 1988, 203). Stage 2 involves the subject interpreting the Stage 1 stimulations as a "sixth sense" or "third eye." In Stage 3, the imagery display radically changes, and the witness experiences the iconic rotating circular tunnel or vortex, popular in popular culture today, and which introduces images of supernatural objects (Lewis-Williams and Dowson 1988, 203, 204).

The shamans were considered to have used this three-step geometric vision-interpretation-supernatural contact model to communicate and receive curing knowledge that they then delivered to the patient(s) or congregation in an attitude-behavior engineering modification. This was an important bonding strategy that, if successful in "driving the evil or bad spirits away," could endow tribal leaders with a meaningful reinforcement of their authority to the group.

In summary, the shamans, via sensory deprivation or chemical stimulus, induce these visions. They then interpret them as culturally salient. In the last step of this tripartite interpretative methodology, access is obtained to a tiered cosmology of communication; the realms of their ancestral chiefs, the living and the gods and great spirit, which then allows the shaman to obtain the curative powers/answers to the problem. Access to the trans dimensional sky realm for problem-solving was the achievement of the shaman and he encouraged his audience to adorn him with great powers as a result.

Another significant aspect of the superpower ritual ethnography was the association between animals and humans. The attitude and behavior of power and control psychology competition between animals and humans in the agrios shaped the prehistory of us. Many various motifs of symbolic representation depict a universal adornment bestowed upon the animal kingdom here on Earth. They were admired as originally possessing spiritual power over us. They were dangerous but also memorized instinctively as a life-sustaining force of nature as THE food source for humans.

Among observed animal attributes that were observed, studied, and metaphorically adopted included fertility and reproduction. They knew the human reproduction process was like theirs. Their geometrical body shapes sometimes corresponded to similar shapes in nature; the land, others, etc. An example of this is the serpent, to whom representations were built such as at Serpent Mound in Ohio. The land and earth grew other foodstuffs necessary for their survival. Conjoining perception and cognition of these environments compelled the Homo sapien sapiens superpower ethnography into the ritualization of both animal life and natural landscapes, mountains, earth as both a tool and a belief system.

*Animism* is a belief system whereby all life forms and all majestic natural environment features and phenomena like mountains, waterfalls, land, and earth possess a <u>soul</u> that inhabits both a three-dimensional reality and supernatural world. Further understood by our ancestors was that nature's power dictated an existence of harmony and balance between the interactions of all these elemental features of nature. This equilibrium was the desired status of existence for humans; a kind of homeostasis of the Universe. The various superpowers of nature were those that humankind could not control and, subsequently, looked for guidance and the noted stress, tension and fear reduction mechanism of the social engineering power strategy. Any change, whether sudden or subtle, to this homeostasis by nature were causes of some fear, stress, and tension in prehistory lives. Other changes that disrupted any part of the homeostasis and that were caused by human activities created similar fear, stress and tensions.

The attitude-behavior perception and cognition adaptations to these perspectives motivated them to create attributes for and a supernatural classification to all nature's elements and features that guided their lives and livelihoods and that could be taught to their descendants. The ritual culture was precisely a tool that was utilized to compete against and overcome the great existential filters, the underlying fears, stresses, and tensions inherent in them, and was a source of competition for authorities.

Use of "supernatural" is attributable and related to the Power and Control dimension of the human mind. All these superpower beings, especially animals, possessed features and characteristics that humans subconsciously aspired to for relief of stress or harm and for leadership potential within their community. Therefore, they were awarded supernatural status. 'Status' is a keyword here. This is why many cultures (Native America, Aboriginal, Inca, etc.) named their tribal members according to observed traits taken from these supernatural features of either the animal or geophysical environments. The architectural symbolism inherent in the designs of totems, mounds, body adornments, and other symbolic representations were created to make meaningful identifications (symbolic words for names before the development of language). This is a human psychological response (behavioral) to the Power and Control mechanism.

The *eschatology of the soul* and deification was the design that our ancestral kin awarded to these superpowers. For these ancestral cultures, all terrestrial and cosmic features, as well as all life forms, vibrated with their unique conscious energy. Their intuition, proto-empirical analysis, and reasoning intellect concluded that all life possessed a soul.

Various animals possessed unique superpowers. The serpent, as noted earlier, was sought out by ritualistic activities as a source of stress relief from and harmony restoration to fertility situations. Many large migratory land animals were deified and prayed (ritualized) to as an appeal to their power and control in restoration of the equilibrium. Birds were capable of flight and the largest of them, including the predatory class (eagles, etc.) were similarly invoked for specialized ritualized healing purposes. The vulture is another animal whose physical characteristics of preying over dead bodies was observed, studied and concluded by man to exist as navigators of the soul newly departed from the deceased.

All these examples were intuitively, if not empirically, reasoned to be parts of a ritualized universal creation and birth-life-death-afterlife cycle and pattern of all ancient human civilizations as another universal characteristic of our species.

* * *

More support for the process which led to the universal adornment of the animal kingdom here on Earth comes from our brain's perception-cognition mechanism and the indispensable role this intelligence played in humankind's evolution. The gradual, geologically timed growth of pattern and cycle recognition in natural phenomena was most explicit in the motif of the astronomical heavens above. The concepts of 'superpower' and 'supernatural' mean the same thing to us today as it did for Muh and Nam. These cosmological features of our natural universe are still primarily inaccessible to us, at least physically. We cannot touch them or immerse ourselves in the incalculable wonders of knowledge they physically possess. We do, though have a recognition and appreciation of equally unimaginable beauty, wonder and magnificence and can touch these experiences in our minds through observation and advanced technology instruments. While trying not to overuse the grammar of adjectives, it is safe to say that we react to these space wonders as emotionally as our ancestral kin did.

Their perception-cognition allowed for intelligent and metaphorical recognition of animals, people and well-known objects illustrated in the night skies. Because all these shapes contained the characteristic of movement, except for one recurring exception that had relevance to learning about their symbolic knowledge and communication, and possessed a mathematical embodiment, this made it easy for us to classify these phenomena with a new concept - *sacred mathematics*. Because these wonders of nature were inaccessible to our ancestors in any physical manner, and we always had to look up to see them, the cognitive associations of the terms 'power' and 'super' were molded into our intelligence to become the mental manifestations of power and control when we look "up" at something. So, when we look at an object that is much larger than we are and/or that we must look up to, our mental pathway takes us to the power and control protocol.

All space objects move both spatially and in a repeatable, cyclic and harmonious manner; even these during the daytime. Groups of these star objects contain patterns of recognition that appear as replicas of the shapes we observe around our terrestrial environments. The one exception, relatively speaking, that appears not to move is the North Star - Polaris in the Northern Hemisphere. Unfortunately, residents in the Southern Hemisphere do not enjoy a similar exactness to this, lack of movement characteristic as they cannot see Polaris from their vantage point). Additionally, there is no star celestially positioned to achieve the same effect it produces.

We know the North Star does move, but it takes such a long time (over seventy years) to move significantly enough to make it observable that the perception of the real-time witness infers it does not move. This uniqueness created enough interest for ancient humans to integrate symbolic representational meaning into some of their architecture and help develop their eschatological dogma, as this will be a point of discussion in the *Archaeoastronomy* Chapter.

I propose that the sky was a most, if not THE most important requisite for ancient life and their survival. Our awareness of mind and thought were encouraged by the continual bombardment of celestial observation through geologic time. The infiltration of this cosmology into an anthropic development of the minds' capacities allowed the attitude-behavior and perception-cognition processes to mold the human brain into its instinctive, general, specialized, technological, historical, and emotional intelligences our ancestors passed to us.

The Revolutions of thought, mind, lifestyle, ethos, habitation, and culture were motivated significantly by the presence of outer space - the skyscape. The subjects of symbolism and ritual were those expressions of our intelligence that shaped our unique form of communication, and which signify our special identity as Earth's most intelligent species set apart from the rest of its life forms. To my Algorithm of Humankind has been added a more complete meaning to the $T_2$ variable of "who we are" by adding a more foundational enrichment to the "who," "what," "when," "where," "why," and "how" dimensions that make us 'us'.

Let us now move into another realm of collaborative knowledge and insight into how our lives were shaped by inspecting Nam and Muh's archaeoastronomy of Neolithic history.

*References*

Arendt, Hannah. 1958. *The Human Condition.* Chicago: University of Chicago Press.

Buck, R. 1980. "Nonverbal Behavior and the Theory of Emotion: The Facial Feedback hypothesis." *Journal of Personal Social Psychology* 38 (5): 811.

Clottes, Jean and David Lewis-Williams. 1998. *The Shamans of Prehistory.* Harry N. Abrams Publishers.

Cosmides, L. and John Tooby. 1992. Cognitive Adaptations For Social Exchange. In *The Adapted Mind,* edited by J.H. Barkow, L. Cosmides and J. Tooby, 163-228. New York: Oxford University Press.

Donald, Merlin. 1991. *Origins of the Modern Mind: Three Stages in the Evolution of Culture and Cognition.* Cambridge, MA: Harvard University Press.

Draper, Patricia. 1975. "!Kung Women: Contrasts in Sexual Egalitarianism in Foraging and Sedentary Contexts." *Anthropology Faculty Publications* 45. https://digitalcommons.unl.edu/anthropologyfacpub/45

Dunbar, R. I. M. 1998. "The Social Brain Hypothesis." *Evolutionary Anthropology* 6 (5): 178-190.

Dunbar, R. I. M. 2009. The Social Brain Hypothesis and Its Implications for Social Evolution. *Annals of Human Biology* 36 (5): 562–572.

Dunbar, R. I. M. 2024. "Structural and Cognitive Mechanisms of Group Cohesion in Primates." *Behavioral Brain Science* (in press). Doi: *10.1017/S014 0525X2400030X.*

Endicott, K. M. 1979. *Batek Negrito Religion: The World-view and Rituals of a Hunting and Gathering People of Peninsular Malaysia.* Oxford: Clarendon Press.

Gardner, P. M. 1972. The Paliyans. In *Hunters and Gatherers Today.* edited by M. G. Bacchieri. New York: Holt, Rinehart & Winston.

Lee, R. B. 1979. *The !Kung San: Men, Women, and Work in a Foraging Society.* Cambridge University Press.

Lewis-Williams, James David and T.A. Dowson. 1988. The Signs of All Times: Entoptic Phenomena in Upper Paleolithic Art. *Current Anthropology* 29 (2): 201-245.

Lewis-Williams, James David and David Pearce. 2005. *Inside the Neolithic Mind: Consciousness, Cosmos and the Realm of the Gods.* London: Thames & Hudson.

Lukes, Steven, ed. 1986. *Power: Readings in Social and Political Theory.* Oxford: Basil Blackwell.

Malinowski, B. 1960. *A Scientific Theory of Culture.* New York: Oxford University Press.

Muñoz, Samuel E., Kristine E. Gruley, Ashtin Massie, David A. Fike, Sissel Schroeder, and John W. Williams. 2015. "Cahokia's Emergence and Decline Coincided with Shifts of Flood Frequency on the Mississippi River." *Proceedings of the National Academy of Sciences* 112 (20): 6319–24. https://doi.org/10.1073/pnas.1501904112.

Pearce, David and David Lewis-Williams. 2005. *Inside the Neolithic Mind: Consciousness, Cosmos and the Realm of the Gods.* London: Thames & Hudson.

Prochazkova, Eliska, and Mariska E. Kret. 2017. "Connecting Minds and Sharing Emotions through Mimicry: A Neurocognitive Model of Emotional Contagion." *Neuroscience and Biobehavioral Reviews* 80: 99–114. https://doi.org/10.1016/j.neubiorev.2017.05.013.

Shultz, S., and R. I. M. Dunbar. 2022. "Socioecological Complexity in Primate Groups and Its Cognitive Correlates." *Philosophical Transactions of the Royal Society B* 377: 20210296. https://doi.org/10.1098/rstb.2021.0296.

Tedlock, Barbara. 2005. *The Woman in the Shaman's Body: Reclaiming the Feminine in Religion and Medicine.* New York: Bantam Books.

Turnbull, C. M. 1965. *The Mbuti Pygmies: An Ethnographic Survey (Anthropology Papers American Museum of Natural History.* 50 (3). New York: American Museum of Natural History.

Webster, David S. 2007. "Review: *James David Lewis-Williams and David Pearce, Inside the Neolithic Mind: Consciousness, Cosmos and the Realm of the Gods* (London: Thames & Hudson, 2005)." *European Journal of Archaeology* 8 (3): 317–319. http://eja.sagepub.com/content/8/3/319.refs.html.

Wiessner, Polly. 1977. *Hxaro: A Regional System of Reciprocity for Reducing Risk among the !Kung San.* PhD diss., University of Michigan.

Williams, Garrath. 2011. Hannah Arendt on Power. In *Encyclopedia of Power.* edited by Keith Dowding, 26-28. Sage Publications.

Wilson, Peter J. 1988. *The Domestication of the Human Species.* New Haven and London: Yale University Press.

Woodburn, James. 1982. "Egalitarian Societies." *Royal Anthropological Institute of Great Britain and Ireland,* 17 (3): 431-451.

Van Baaren, Rick, Loes Janssen, Tanya L. Chartrand, and Ap Dijksterhuis. 2009. "Where Is the Love? The Social Aspects of Mimicry." *Philosophical Transactions of the Royal Society B: Biological Sciences* 364: 2381–89.

Xygalatas, Dimitris. 2022. *Ritual: How Seemingly Senseless Acts Make Life Worth Living.* New York: Little, Brown Spark. Hachette Book Group.

# ARCHAEOASTRONOMY

*For archaic man, reality is a function of the imitation of a celestial archetype.*

-Mircea Eliade, historian from
  *The Myth of the Eternal Return: cosmos and History, 1971:*
  Princeton University Press.

*Keywords: Path of Souls, pareidolia, animism, animal symbolism, Four Cardinal Directions, Father Sky, Middle Earth and Mother Earth, land of the dead, shamanism, heaven and hell.*

Nam and Muh are us, but need an after coat...

I propose that the presence of the skyscape was a most, if not THE most aspiring feature of Nam and Muh's human condition. The Revolutions of thought, mind, lifestyle, ethos, habitation, and culture were motivated by the continual bombardment of the celestial presence and wonder of outer space - the skyscape. Social cultures, symbolic reference, and ritual were expressions of our intelligence that shaped humans' unique form of communication, and which signify our special identity as Earth's most intelligent species set apart from the rest of its life forms.

However, when they looked up into the sky, Nam and Muh always saw a most mysterious, often stressful and unattainable domain. This experience elicited a mind full of curiosity, stress, tension. and a heightened awareness that the 'others' were often directing their actions. They were aware that the light by which the Earth's surface and land below could be seen and felt came from the sun above. In nature's ritualistic display they witnessed the cycles of light each day and the tiny shimmers of patterned lights that each night filled the sky (Earth's rotation).

They quickly developed awareness that these cycles, patterns, and shimmers moved around the sky in longer cycles themselves. All but one of the stars moved in this way, the North Star, and some of them disappeared altogether for a while before reappearing again in the next yearly cycle (Earth's orbit around the sun). An additional aspiring awareness came about when they saw that those same shimmers of starlight not only moved around and sometimes disappeared, but that groups of them would come to occupy a different segment of the night sky grid and a different star would seem to stop motionless for a duration much longer than their lifetime (Precession of the Equinoxes).

Nam and Muh were profoundly aware of the above world and its rhythmical patterns and cycles but were prevented from touching the sky themselves like their interactions with the rest of their eco-environment. This exasperating feature drove the existential need, navigated by the function of their mind's perception and cognition pathway, to create an entire worldview and ethnocentrism according to the directives of the cosmic skyscape and its physical representations.

The changing patterns of the celestial grid were perceived to be the 'writing of the Gods,' a stage populated by laws and knowledge that were dictated to Nam and Muh and their people in profound and meaningful ways. Ancient treasures contain an uncountable number of such examples. In this production, the human mind concocted numerous skyscape symbolisms from the pattern-making perception and cognition pathway of man's brain. Today we identify many of these symbolisms with carryover names from early language like the Pleiades, Orion, Leo, the Zodiac signs, Hercules, Milky Way, etc.

Perhaps a provenance to the creation of language came from the perception of these illustrations, perhaps from elsewhere. Certainly, many other forms of communication resulted from the locking of the mind's eye with the theatre of space; a magnificent interstellar mural that has inspired and enlightened you and I and to which caused the Revolutions of Homo sapien sapiens in the unique ways they did.

Existence of the celestial realm, THE most referenced natural environmental platform by all ancient civilizations, guided the social dynamics of semiotics, bonding, engineering, ritual, language, religiosity, and the eschatology of life and the afterlife. Our engagements today at star parties, eclipses, and planetarium night sky talks, in part, are a direct reflection on this ancient astrology and folklore, that was originally purposed as a first symbolic modern textbook of spiritual life and learning, with the same brain hardware, software and programming, and the same mnemonic patterns our ancestors used for recall and understanding.

Space today contains the same features and characteristics that were so worshipped by our ancestral kin. The most prominent celestial objects, in order of luminescent magnitude, to both modern and historical observers include: 1 – Sun; 2 – Moon; 3 – Milky Way; 4 – Constellations. This order of visual saliency is due to both the brightness and geometric appearance of the sun and moon, being the largest and most visible, easily defined in the minds' eye as immediate due to their awareness of its physical proximity.

Their celestial motions evoke characteristics of repetitiveness, rigidity, and redundancy in Xygalatas' ritual concept (2022, 66-69). Humans are compelled to 'describe what they saw,' and the brightest objects they saw were the daytime sun and nighttime moon. Their minds - like ours in this example - took these attitude cues and developed the cognitive behavior pathway that is the ritual function. Their purpose, for our ancestors, was developed from this celestial agency.

This celestial agency was important in providing Neolithic man with spatial, environmental, and temporal dimensions of intellect as well as sociologic metaphorical transfer of new knowledge and meaning contexts that I call a four-dimensional axis of perception and cognition. The spatial and environmental dimensions represent the three-dimensional environment while the fourth, time, made up the mindset of this celestial agency.

With these thoughts captured, our ancestors could use what they saw in the heavens to create the agency that helped them understand their place in the moment, the environment around them in that moment, and the historical and future aspects of 'what was,' or prospects of 'what could come to be,' respectively. It also allowed for the growth and maturity of humankind's historical memory intelligence; the part that drove their behavior for remembering things and most importantly, people from their past, the latter of which is suggested by the semiotic cultural traditions of life, death, and the afterlife.

This apparatus enabled the creation and practice of the symbolic representations embodied by communication and social relations, the latter of which is supported by archaeologist Stanislaw Iwaniszewski, "Human societies often people their skies with super naturals, ancestors or mythological heroes to whom they become related through family ties, mythological narratives, political alliances or power relationships" (Iwaniszewski 2011, 31).

With witness to the night sky's rigid, repetitive and redundant nature, our ancestors left us many reminders of how their minds manifested this reality. A keen recognition of the celestial patterns and cycles reinforced practice of the social cultures and their subsequent symbolic documentation for educational/historical purposes.

For example, the sun, as the only celestial object whose appearance did not change except during a solar eclipse, was intuitively reasoned as giving life, and as a life form of a superpower. Its light and warmth caused all life to exist on Earth. This was part of their instinctive consciousness.

Observation of the sun's cyclical daily reappearance and disappearance was a part of that critical writing of the gods because when a cloudy day, an earthquake, or an eclipse event occurred, the sun went away. The perceived chaos disrupted nature's homeostasis, so its occurrence was stress and fear-producing. Sometimes the event disrupted food sustenance.

The longer events produced famine situations. Famines in the Neolithic drove a ritual behavior response strategy because they were otherwise physically powerless to control the sun's activities for their purposes. They could not touch the sun, and that motivated their minds to develop a worship cult of the sun as a god. The best and maybe only strategy to interact with the sun was, in their minds, to appeal to this god for survival as a means of stress, fear, and tension relief.

Perspectives such as this were also part of relationships with the moon. Its nightly visitation was erratic in appearance due to its ecliptic light-shielding characteristics but was recognized as possessing its own cyclic patterns; and, because it could not be touched, also became adorned as a god. The periodic full moon drowned out visibility from a lot of other stars in the night sky. God was giving more instructions for them to follow. It motivated and enabled our ancestors to conduct ritual activities on dates of the full moon for a variety of purposes, including appeals and strategies designed for greater food harvests, giving thanks, and to honor, and encourage future repetitive activities. It was also considered a conduit for a safer path to eternity and to heaven for dear departed souls.

The Milky Way was, to prehistoric man, another manuscript of the "divine creators" that also appeared differently because of its spatial orientation in the sky. Its annual cycle of appearance was due to the simultaneous forces of various physics influencing Earth's orbital trajectory. Their perception and cognition of the constellations were conceived as the most prominent objects of the ritualistically organized night sky as their intelligence again utilized the pattern-making mental neurology that we use today.

To summarize, the common characteristics and attributes of these four cosmic phenomena remain there now from millennia ago for your inspection. I encourage you to visualize yourself observing the sun, moon, Milky Way and constellations over time. You will note their constant movements, consistent with what was seen for over a million years; and, only after repeated study, will all of them be observed to resonate with a cyclical nature that harmonizes with your existence and that of all other matter in the Universe. The interface of all these cosmic objects was perceived and became known to our ancestors as the most quintessential tapestry of creation, birth, life, and afterlife to them and to their souls.

\* \* \*

As we inspect the knowledge left to us through our ancestors' interpretations, we find the record more abundant in more recent times. Records from all the recent cultures make a most compelling case that humankind's attitude and behavior in matters of social cultures, ritual, bonding, funerary, spirituality, leadership, competition, and power and control customs remained equivalent to what we experience today of the same. I will now discuss the special characteristics and attributes that archaeoastronomy offered to influence those dimensions selecting from a palette of many examples afforded by our ancestral brethren.

The patterns and observations of the night sky (and the daytime sun) correlated with those of terrestrial shapes and patterns, such as animals, landscape features, and so on. Consequently, the propensity for their minds to make sense of the patterns by creating known shapes and objects from their visual observations has become known today as *pareidolia*. Pareidolia is defined as, "the tendency to perceive a specific, often meaningful image in a random or ambiguous visual pattern" (Merriam-Webster, 2024).

This trait, triggered by the brain's compartmentalization neurology, became their cognitive basis for an assignment of names, functions and special life and spiritual adornments to the celestial objects. This happened in all cultural traditions and involved protocols, such as matching animal shapes by star placements to real animals and humans of the same process. The Milky Way became interpreted as "heaven and hell" to them; and the term *Path of Souls* describes the road to that destination. This led to adoption of an ethos of harmonious universal earthly order in their minds that readily aligned with the order present in celestial agency and whose understanding their minds could grasp.

Two interesting thought experiments come to my mind that may help enlighten you to a reality that modern man has much to learn from this inspection.

Experiment # 1: Visualize yourself in a space ship traveling out of our solar system and into our galaxy. When you get a few light years out, look at the starscape panorama. Would you think you could see the same patterned star shapes in the constellations as you do when you view them from Earth? What can be learned from this?

Experiment # 2 is this: Do humans today know much at all about what lies out in our Milky Way galaxy, or - much less - beyond?

Using the four-dimensional axis of perception and cognition noted, a foundation of archaeoastronomy meaning can be investigated that tie in all matter, organic and inorganic, to an assessment of our ancestor's mindful and critical thinking process that drove to the creation and shaping of the social psychologies of semiotics, bonding, engineering, ritual, language, religiosity, and the eschatology of life and the afterlife.

A universal metaphysical belief of all ancient peoples was that of *animism*, where all matter and places in the ordered universe, organic and inorganic, contained the spiritual essence of an immaterial soul that resonated with its own unique energy frequency (Stringer 1999, 541). This defined energy possessed an agency which guides its actions and the free will to do so. A belief of intrinsic value to all matter was also practiced by its earliest adopters.

The ethnocentric essences of the spiritual realm included the belief that a soul was real, it existed as an ontological force that inhabited every being and could not be felt by the physical senses, but only reachable in the abstract mind. The most significant contributor to the study of animism was Sir Edward Burnett Tylor. His theory established relationships between the dimensions of death, dreams and apparitions. He proposed that the reality for indigenous to dream of their dead kin was proof to the existence of souls.

Tylor extended application of his theory to the animal kingdom and to terrestrial structures. He proposed that, because all indigenous dreamed in this way, as we do today, our abstract reasoning, the perception-cognition pathway, processed the soul to become a reality of substance and not just of abstractness (Tylor 1871). This theory also applied to consideration and outreach for establishing the existence of the soul as an entity to be considered for all entities and matter as well. With growing evidence that an ontology existed central to a sacred worship and memory cult of deceased relatives from over 100,000 years ago, as proven by the record of other symbolism and external material cultures, reasonable progressions can be made to align later practices of animal worship, deification, and the other knowledge transfers that document associations between animals, the celestial skyscape, and influencing the lives of ancient leaders of all civilizations as a universal attitude-behavior mechanism.

These relationships were merged into a religiosity and an ethos of behavior that was practiced within an earlier egalitarian framework many millennia before the Neolithic Revolutions. ~~By~~ In this time, the mechanisms of attitude-behavior and perception-cognition gradually shaped the structural philosophy of animism into a new domain of physical religion. What resulted were new design strategies to cope with and to restore life order and harmony to all matter and address the new fears, stresses, and tensions to daily urban existences to accomplish the same. These strategies became the social ritual cultures, inherent within the archaeoastronomy framework and with whom we bear witness to in the study of their remains and artifacts. With the celestial skyscape as the stage, the indigenous inserted protagonists such as animistic metaphysics and the intellectual assignment of knowledge and meaning to the matter of the physical world, such as animals, landscapes, architecture, external symbolic objects, and social relations to manifest these potentials.

Our ancestral kin were keen observers of all things in their ecological and natural environments, as part of the animism knowledge. There were practical, spiritual, cosmic, and eschatological purposes to this metaphysics that motivated their active participation, in some realms from over 100,000 years, as suggested by philosopher Tiddy Smith (Smith 2023). An eschatological mindset created, as one of these realms, the opportunity for Homo sapien sapiens, Neanderthals, and Denisovans to participate in funerary cults such as mindful underground body burials as a return of the soul to the creation realm, grave goods considerations, and a perception-cognition of historical intelligence that allowed for ceremonial remembrance rituals. The funerary aspect of animism practiced by humans, therefore, was shown to have existed at least that far back in time.

When defined by a power characteristic derived from the concept's supernatural nature, the practice of animism in the Upper Paleolithic regarded the indigenous animal as possessing this attribute as dictated from the spiritual realm. A reason for this power attribute is contained in Upper Paleolithic cave symbolic depictions of the still forming cult of power and control competition between animals and humans in the agrios. Examples include the Sulawesi depictions of pigs and human hand signatures of 45,000 years, (Brumm et al. 2021) and the Altimara, Spain cave art of bison dated to 36,000 years ago (Pike et al. 2012, 1409-1410).

More modern Neolithic examples abound, especially in the Levant at Gobekli Tepe, Çatalhöyük, and around the Mesopotamia Fertile Crescent. A design evolution occurred in this period as the animal motifs became almost universally violent in their portrayal. This design may have existed as a prop for a ritual activity to increase chances to increase the size of the herd or for success on a planned hunt (Tributsch 2018, 91).

A more widespread interpretation of evolutionary *animal symbolism* is derived from this notion. The purpose for this type of prehistory semiotics, in support of my power and control thesis, was as a survival strategy and not because they suddenly had an isolated inspiration to engage in an artful activity (Tributsch 2018,123). This was brought about due to the following factors. First, the animals in the Early Holocene agrios were a main survival source but held competitive power over them and were, consequently, difficult to deal with. Secondly, visual stimulus of the celestial star patterns was abstractly connected with those terrestrial animals; but, as noted earlier, all celestial objects were physically inaccessible to them except through visual contact. These connections were interpreted as necessary premises for pursuit of a survival mechanism to the ancients in some way. They had to find an answer to this dilemma.

Their minds' perception and cognition, as an answer to this dilemma, bestowed life on these constellation forms in a cosmic realm as a method of obtaining a more profound relationship contact. Eventually, these celestial objects were elevated to spiritual and supernatural status by a mindful consideration of them as intrinsic life forms that regularly communicated with them; akin to a feature of animism that all matter in the Universe possessed energy resonance, a spirit, and/or an immaterial soul. The process concluded with introduction of an attitude-behavior strategy for competing against the powerful authority the prey animals had over them.

It took many millennia for cave art utilizing this symbolic communication to catch up to the intellectual advancements ancient humankind made regarding the practice of animism as a proto-religious way of life. Lack of discovery is a reason we have uncovered no archaeoastronomy alignments with the animal kingdom from the earlier Paleolithic that would enrich our interpretation of this practice. The mindful dynamic showing the human intellect competing for power and control from the wild animals only begins to be symbolically illustrated by depository architectures of the Upper Paleolithic and that shows an increased popularity from remains uncovered at the various Tepes in ancient Anatolia (modern-day Turkey and Syria), that depict strikingly violent animal motifs. I will discuss in detail some of these later in this chapter.

Ancient humankind recognized and observed the seasonal and annual cycles in the weather patterns that drove migratory and wildcrafting behaviors in animals and plants, respectively. As the power and control pendulum between humans and animals slowly swung into our favor, supported by the transformative progress made by advances in animal domestication, a mindful adoption of new intrinsic values created opportunity to view the animal kingdom in a different light. As urbanized life moved from innovation to commonplace, advanced food and labor industries created new daily idle time to pursue different directions of thought, study, and reflection upon a new empiricism of living conditions, nature, ecology and spirituality. New resultant animal relationships, partnered with a continued deep-seeded animistic interpretation of the night skyscape allowed for new comprehensions that involved animals, and a four-dimensional nature of the Universe previously noted.

The shapes of the constellations in the night sky and the real animal body contours affected this relationship, whether from the biological effects of pareidolia or from other phenomena. New algorithms of comprehension were discovered and shaped that merged building architecture design, the skyscape, and the landscape as defined here to include cosmic and terrestrial landscapes, with the critical utilization of design structure, space, direction, and timing. These dynamics were combined to produce the first noticeable forms of organized religion and astronomy, known as the first natural science disciplines.

Animals were used as props for all the human thought endeavors of the skyscape, landscape, ecology, spiritualism, creation, life, health, and the afterlife. They had starring roles in ontological and creation stories, strategies for livestock and agricultural food procurement, as calendar makers, identity assignments, timekeepers, life and the afterlife, deities in such theatrical productions as the ritual and ceremony customs, spiritual intermediaries for shamanistic practices, architectural dimensions, and for ritual strategies by authorities as instruments of stress, fear and tension relief. Examples of this ancestral occupation are universal and used temporally into modern-day times of just a couple of hundred years ago. They are all characterized with the requisite acuteness of intelligence and intuition that marks our ancestors as particularly appealing as a resource for learning about ourselves.

Examples of a food procurement strategies, in close alignment with calendrical and timekeeping systems, include the Aboriginal Australia who linked its indigenous redback spider with the star Arcturus, the thorny-devil lizard with the Pleiades, the celestial emu from the darkened spaces within the Milky Way, and the wedge-tailed eagle with the Southern Cross. The Norse named the Pleiades constellation *Sjaustirni,* while in ancestral India, recognized as part of the *nakṣatra;* a cyclical threshold into another repetition or 'New Year.' Similarly, the Temple of Hathor in Egypt is profoundly adorned with Pleiadian symbolism, aligning with the new growing season and a variety of ritual activities. In Japan, they called them *Mutsuraboshi*; now known as *Subaru*. One can readily recall the interpretation of the Pleiades symbol blazoned on every automobile today of the same identification.

The Mayans deified Ku'kulkan, their serpent god, as the messenger of food procurement (and many other indigenous adornments) and ritualized these honored celebrations around the celestial equinox dates in March and September. Many symbolic architectural design examples of Ku'Kulkan exist at sites such as Chitzen Itza, Mayapan, and Uxmal. Ku'kulkan enjoys a similar status as the Aztecs' Quetzalcoatl.

Calendars and timekeepers were universally used in connection with time and the seasons. For example, the Lascaux Caves in France contain hundreds of paintings over 20,000 years old illustrating celestial, animal and calendar symbols with a predominant calendrical nature. Important constellations drawn at that site include Taurus, Orion, and the Pleiades; all visible if not dominant in that prehistoric sky. In more modern times of the last 2,000 years, the Ojibwa nation of the Upper Midwest, for example, revered the turtle in many ways. Their natural shell design matched observations of the moon's annual new (or full) moon cycle that equated to a 364-day year and the lunar cycle of 28 days. The Mayans utilized Venus as its information source to obtain calendar dates for the social engineering of special tribal ritual exercises or celebratory events.

Animals' attributes were often assigned as names to certain people of the community based on their perceived qualities that matched that of the animal. Throughout Native America brave warriors were given names of indigenous animals that, for example, contained 'Wolf' to identify a great, fearless tribe member. 'Bear' for a powerful leader-type; 'Eagle' for the strongest, bravest member and for its connections to the Creator (it flew the highest and closest to the sky and the heavens), and 'Deer' for its agility and grace. These match up with Ursa Major (canine dog or wolf), Canis Major (bear), Aquila (eagle) and Orion (deer, though not a universal attribution). Ancient India also perceived Orion as a deer; the Rigveda ancient scripts refer to the Orion Constellation as *"Mriga".*

Ancient Mesopotamia used bulls, lions, and scorpions as representatives of a metaphorical power that was assembled as the main adversaries in the animal-human power struggle of the agrios environment and the Universe. Constant reminders of the bull, lion, canine, and scorpion were seen by natives in the constellations Taurus, Leo, Canis Major, and Scorpius, respectively. It is interesting to note that throughout ancient Mesopotamia before 3,000 BCE, a popular motif was the depiction of naturalistic wild animals being killed by human warriors, heroes, kings, and gods.

This motif further supports the ideology that the pendulum of power and control, as applied to the competition between animals and humans, was universally influential to the emergence of the human mind from prehistoric to modern perception and cognition intelligences. In Persia, the mythical bull Taurus was known as *Gavaevodata;* a dog-bird, Canis Major as *Simurgh;* the *Jinn* as a supernatural dual-purposed god; the *Azhi-Dahaka*, a three-headed dragon (Draco), and a *Manticore,* a lion's body with a human head (Leo). The latter symbol has no modern generally agreed upon name, but the Egyptian term "shesepankh" is often used as a phenomenon of the pre-Bronze Age Mesopotamian/Egyptian corridor.

The animal-human synergy motif was repeated in all ancient cultures. In ontology matters the ancient Hindu of India writings told of the story of Arundhati and Vashishta, who transcended time and cosmic forces to become eternal lovers depicted as the twin stars of Ursa Major. This celestial alignment holds profound significance in Hindu tradition, where it is believed that the couple's enduring unity symbolizes the virtues of marital bliss, loyalty, and mutual respect. Ways of life were universally memorized to include the landscape and skyscape, noted earlier, as cardinal points of direction of sacred mathematics not only for navigational purposes, but also for definitions to ways of life, living, and the eschatological paths of the soul through eternity.

Ancestral Native America profoundly used the Medicine Wheel and Tree of Life as such multiplicative representations of the four cardinal directional points, in conjunction with the three cosmic platforms known as Mother Earth, The Center, and Father Sky, as mnemonic exercises of north, south, east and west, seasons, and colors of life - the ethos of living the correct life in harmony with all other matter in the Universe. These three vertical directions are also known as the below world, the living world, and the upper world, respectively. The ancient Chinese worshiped the Four Guardians or Four Gods; the Azure Dragon, the Vermillion Bird, the White Tiger, and the Black Tortoise of the East, South, West and North, respectively, like that of Native America and the rest of the prehistorical world.

This tripartite relationship cohorts with the concept of the *Four Cardinal Directions*, with which a different contemporary meaning is associated. The ontology of the Four Cardinal Directions to Neolithic and Bronze-Age humankind was much more sacred and worshiped as a quintessential consciousness; a compass of universal existence to whom all life's natural forces were embodied and whose harmony and resonance with all other life and matter was practiced as natural religiosity. This was the law of nature and the law of man until modern times.

Cygnus, the great bird constellation most immersed spatially within the Milky Way, holds significant worship in many ancient cultures, including Hinduism, Native America and some considered but controversial attributions as far back in time as Gobekli Tepe in Anatolia. Canis Major, the patterned star design that includes the Sirius star family, and whose brightest member is the Dog Star, is another universally adorned cultural symbol of spiritual and celestial influence. Draco the dragon constellation attributes its popularity as an animal deity only in post-Levant history in the Far East and in some later archaic Native American cultures.

Creation stories are another repetitive theme of the human mind, going back to before the Neolithic era. The Hindu *Saptarishi* represent the Seven Sages and seen by them as the Big Dipper constellation. These sages guide the course of time and creation and is foundational to all the Hindu sacred writings. The *Matsya Purana* tale of Brahma and Saraswati, the Hindu Creator god and goddess, is said to revolve around the constellation Cygnus. Brahma, disguised as a swan, surveyed the cosmic seas in quest for a suitable location to insert the cosmos. A lotus flower was Brahma's choice and was joined by Saraswati as the chosen site for creation of the cosmos.

The serpent motif is frequently known as a Creation theme with similar qualities. *Ometecuhtli* and *Omecihuatl* were the Aztecs, *Itzauaná* the Mayan, *Viracocha* the Inca and many other pre-Inca Andean belief systems, *Pangu* in China, *Izanagi* in Japan, *Ptah, Ra and Atum* in Egypt and *Odin, Vili* and *Ve* were regarded as the Norse Creator gods. Greece and later Rome, however, created a new interpretation of this motif by assigning humans to that position - *Zeus* and *Jupiter,* respectively. In the Zoroastrianism religion, *Ahura Mazda* was known as their Creator god as revealed from the texts called the *Avesta.* Additional attributions to the dragon concept are contained in the Babylonian creation story of the *Enuma Elish* where Tiamat, the dragon of creation, is represented by the constellation Cetus. Cetus was also deified by the Sumerians of an earlier Neolithic time.

The Yellow Dragon in China is an animism metaphor for the Yellow Emperor, the central figures in Chinese creation mythology and religion. The Yellow Emperor was the offspring of Fubao and was the manifestation of an immaculate pregnancy by observing a yellow ray of light (sunlight) around the Ursa Major constellation (Big Dipper). The Yellow Emperor was born about 24 months later. A further significance to the color known as yellow was that it is the Chinese color for the earth on the four dimensions of cardinal directions of life (Tan 2015).

The *land of the dead* was a predominant thematic association of both the building and monumental architecture and the life, afterlife and reincarnation motifs. Consequently, building locations with these attributes were typically found in their urban geography south or west of their cultural center structures. Verified examples include the site locations of a variety of funerary mound architectures at Cahokia, and Serpent Mound in Ohio, many sites in Meso-America, the Aztec sites of Chaco Canyon, New Mexico, and most profoundly, in Egypt.

The Egyptian primordial god Nut was central to the ethnography of our history's most prolifically documented civilizations. According to the ancient text *The Book of Nut,* her attributes are numerous. Mentioned here are her connection with the Milky Way as a guide for the newly departed soul to the afterlife in the Milky Way, and as a provider of food for those souls, known as their *Ba;* the spiritual soul force of the departed. Nut was also depicted as a pillar of support for upholding the Universe and ensuring its uninterrupted rhythmic forces of day and night, including the solar and lunar cycles, and assumed many other animal attributes, including a cow, hippopotamus, and a vulture. These attributes have been associated with many constellations, including Cygnus, Taurus, and Ursa Major, where the Big Dipper was the foreleg of a bull in the Egyptian texts (Graur 2024, 32-35).

All these sites existed around the Milky Way as a focal point of ritual cult practices. At Cahokia, Mound 72, a mass grave which was located directly south of the Grand Plaza and Monk's Mound, palace of the chief, and Mound 66, also known as the ritual center of Rattlesnake Causeway, traversed south from Mound 72. Rattlesnake Causeway has come to be known also as a Path of Souls highway that allowed for the social bonding ritual remembrances of past and newly departed souls and their guidance into the eternal afterlife. This path was along an 185-degree compass point coordinated to the Southern horizon and whose visual trajectory connected during the year to a terminus of the Milky Way (Romain 2022).

Egypt created and humanized classes of both animal and human deities and gods. Their library history is as extensive as any throughout the ancient world. The souls of all dynastic pharaohs were risen to this deified, eternal status upon their earthly demise. Among them were Anubis, deity of the underworld and mummification and whose powers were adorned to Osiris, the human god of these ontological features. The celestial reminder was readily available using the mnemonic of the constellation Canis Major. Another example of this ancient Egyptian animal-human-cosmic cohort identified Thoth, god of writing, knowledge, medicine, time, among others with Anubis, Ibis and Babi, the deification of the hamadryas baboon.

The Norse anthropomorphism list, though found not to be as extensive, includes Freyja, goddess of *Kvennavagn*, the woman's chariot (Ursa Minor constellation) and *Freyja's Girdle* (Orion's Belt).

The puma was a terrestrial divine representation symbolizing strength, wisdom, and agility. In Incan iconography, it was believed that the puma influenced the morphology of the ancient city of Cusco, where

Sacsayhuamán represented its head and the Coricancha, its tail.

In general, all ancient rulers utilized leadership power and control strategies throughout their reigns to obtain and maintain authority over their societies. A tool that comingled with archaeoastronomy, animals and power strategy was the practice of *shamanism*. The practitioners of shamanistic episodes sought to heal the sick via spiritual transport into the 'other world' to appeal for assistance from power animals or other deified spirit forces, or often to chauffeur the soul of a recently departed to the 'after world'. This process is believed by many to have been facilitated by psycho-chemical stimulation techniques, and to which similar techniques are used by modern-day practitioners. Such spirits were solicited to influence unconscious psycho social aspects of the practitioner toward the desired endpoint (Winkelman 2004, 203). This usage represents another utilization of animism that links archaeoastronomy and spiritual realms with the importance of animals to our ancestral kin. The earliest undisputed evidence of Paleolithic shamanism was the discovery of a shaman grave in the Czech Republic dated to over 30,000 years ago (Tedlock 2005).

While considerable debate continues around defining shamanism, historian Mircea Eliade provides a short but meaningful definition as "a technique of religious ecstasy" (Eliade 1972, 3) utilized to alleviate trauma by mending the soul (Eliade 1972, 4-7). Tribal leaders were keenly aware of the challenges to abating the traumas, stresses, and fears of everyday life as was commonplace during both Epipaleolithic and Neolithic urbanized periods by seeking techniques to exert a social engineering agenda. Shamanisms' purposeful existence was generally agreed upon to "exert control over the superstitious and feeble-minded community" (Winkelman 2018, 206), and as a biological healing strategy. The process involves "community bonding rituals" (Winkelman 2018, 204) whose driving force "was the need for integrating groups, making community out of strangers, and… brought humans to an awareness of the living planet and all of its creatures" (Winkelman 2018, 225). The shaman in pre-urbanization hunter-gatherer times provided "charismatic leadership," informal political power, and initiated many egalitarian-influenced banded pursuits, including hunts, proto-religious and group movement activities (Winkelman 2002, 1875).

The association of animals and shamanism was widespread in the ancient world. Among Pre-Colombian tribes in South America the shamanistic trance journey included his body changing into animal form, the type of which was dependent upon the purpose of the ritual episode activity, and his transported soul, now separated from his physical body (the effects of psycho-chemical stimuli), appealing to that animal spirit for guidance and answers to the dilemma of the episode. The communication entailed using a "secret language" of the animal only known to the shaman and sought after because "the animals know the secrets of life and of immortality" (Williams 1973). Many Western Hemisphere cultures, as agreed by many scholars, "included among the criteria for shamanism a fundamental emphasis on transformation, especially human-animal transformation" (Klein et al 2002, citing Furst 1976). Birds, for example, were used as a prop (and exploitative tool to the authority elite) that guided the shaman soul up to the other realm(s) because "birds fly and sing, as does the spirit of the shaman on his journey to the spirit world" (King 2002).

Shamanism, in summary, was a universal institution among Paleolithic and Neolithic civilizations enabled as a social bonding, engineering, and power and control tool by tribal leaders designed to protect the community against the evils of the world, to keep the sacred world of the cosmos in order, and consequently restore harmony and balance binding this spiritual realm with the tapestry of all the universal energies and forces in nature, a version of The Great Chain of Being. Shaman practitioners in the Paleolithic were essentially the leaders of their pack, and in Neolithic and later times were members of the ruling family elite class. The ties that bind both eras together in the shaman realm were the extent and certainty of knowledge that were uniquely possessed and that profoundly influenced the socialization of egalitarian and totalitarian societies by the exploitation of that knowledge to achieve lasting authority, group control, and any other societal bounties that existed.

Architecture design of many prehistoric civilizations was deliberately coordinated with a purposeful cosmological orientation, connection, and meaning. According to archaeologist Christopher Hawkes' 'ladder of archaeological inference' as among the most difficult associations with which to derive meaning, "I believe, unaided inference from material remains to spiritual life is the hardest inference of all" (Hawkes 1954, 162). Anthropologist Fabio Silva and colleagues infer a growing relevance between intentional, "connections to celestial objects in the architecture" and that "it (associations between celestial objects and the architecture) opens research into the minds of prehistoric societies or, at the very least, into those parts of their world(s) that we call the sky and the celestial objects" (Silva, Pimenta and Tirapicos 2021, 472).

The practice of cosmologically influenced architectural design in ancient times can be reliably determined to have existed using probabilistic reasoning due to the testable recurring pattern of comparative data samples in the record. The observation of repeated correspondences between structures with provable celestial alignments contains both worldwide and temporal orientations by nature, the reality of which is both obvious and ubiquitous if not yet generally accepted. Buildings, monuments, and geoglyphs all held profound purposeful meaning aligned with cosmic features, and many contained a tripartite metaphorical attribution that included animals as well. Popular celestial targets included the sun, moon, planets and constellations as reasoned and worshiped by many indigenous as 'God's handwriting'. By charting a course of evidence backward in time, the library of possible mentions here is exhaustive as to be obvious in inferring a reliable and credible conclusion as to the validity of the theory that their relationship with the skyscape was the most important to our ancestors' existence.

One of the youngest and complex associations of a tripartite animal-architecture-astronomy motif is found at the Cahokia site, near present-day St. Louis, Missouri. The city of Cahokia existed from 900-1350 CE and was the largest urban landscape in North America comprising a real estate grid of over seven square miles. The indigenous were of generally unknown origin, as the database is not as extensive in this area with which to draw reliable conclusions, but suggests an ancestry of the Mississippian, Hopewell of the Ohio Valley, and a speculation of some Mayan migratory influences.

This tripartite relationship aligned with the serpent, climatic seasons, and people. The snake, in the North American geographic landmass, lives above surface (the living world) in the summer and goes below ground (the below world) in the winter. A correlation occurs with the star constellation Scorpius, which looks like a snake/serpent, is visible in the summer, and whose tail disappears below the southern horizon in the winter months. A special biological feature of the snake, which attributes use of both above-ground and below-ground to their survival, also correlates with the cosmological mindset of adornment ubiquitous in ancestry as the three archetypes of *Father Sky, Middle Earth and Mother Earth*. Additional celestial blueprints at Cahokia come from the Monks Mound, the Grand Plaza, and the Rattlesnake Causeway site and the Path of Souls, aka Mound 66, and Mound 72, as noted earlier.

Contemporary to the Cahokia empire, three civilizations: the Forbidden City of the Ming Dynasty, China, the Chaco Canyon nation of New Mexico, as the home to Puebloans and Hopi starting before 900 CE, and early Archaic-Basketmakers cultures in the prior 1,000 years, followed these astronomical architecture protocols. The entire architectural layout of Chaco Canyon was built from mostly solar and lunar alignments (Sofaer 1997; Fagan 1999). An older example of this sacred architecture is located at Serpent Mound, an Ohio effigy mound site utilizing the tripartite associations of geoglyph-animal-celestial influences.

The Serpent Mound community also contains a terrestrial association ingeniously created by the Native Americans during the Fort Ancient period, anywhere from 1,400 CE back to over 300 BCE (Monaghan and Herrmann 2019). The project consisted of erecting the mound atop a naturally contoured mountain ridge that, in an aerial view, embodies the shape of a serpent. The mound itself, over 1,400 feet long, is also shaped like a serpent. Both body contours correspond with astronomical alignments of the setting solstice sun, the three cardinal points of the solstice and the two equinox sunrises, and the Milky Way at summer solstice. The serpent, as noted, held the status of deification and even as the Great Spirit god in many cultures.

Many birthing and creation folklore traditions that Native American clans taught to their younger generations are contained as an additional ritual motif observed in the Serpent Mound history. Further correlations are speculated to include attributions of the snake's physical shape to that of the Milky Way (also observed at the Dendera Crypt in Hathor Temple, Egypt) and the human female umbilical cord as a cognitive creation symbolism.

Snakes indigenous to this geography included species with an oviparous reproduction biology by presence of an egg, and a viviparous reproduction biology without use of visible eggs. Associating the shapes and contours of the serpent, the celestial Milky Way, and the female umbilical cord through repeated observations as far back as the early Paleolithic, gave the human mind sufficient exposure to develop a general association of meaning among these three phenomena.

Because the creators of Serpent Mound lacked the more empirical understanding to the existence of these phenomena that we possess today, it is reasonable to infer these speculative meanings and purposes as mindful meaning-making of relationships on their part and that was the intent of the messages they presented to their descendants, and by extension, to us through their symbolism. This perception-cognition process often led to creation of other cultural customs that became profoundly influential in how our ancients viewed the universe and all its environments.

Further south in Meso-America, the Mayan civilization trace their extensive archaeoastronomy pursuits back more than 2,300 years, including uses for crop management (Van Stone 2016), use of solar, lunar, and planetary astronomy-based observations to create their renowned calendar and time measurement system (Foster 2002, 251-262; Demarest 2004, 179, 201), and astronomy-influenced social ritual events (Aveni, H. 1986; Aveni, A 2001). Ancient India used the solar, lunar and star alignments, such as the Pleiades, and knowledge of the 4 cardinal directions alignment to design their urban architecture from over 4,000 years ago, as written in the Vāstu Shāstra (Kak 2010).

Much Egyptian architecture, from the iconic Pyramids to the Great Sphinx of Giza, utilized an astronomical blueprint, as is also illustrated at such famous "henges" sites at Stonehenge, England, America's Stonehenge in New Hampshire, and Woodhenge at Cahokia. More obscure examples of archaeoastronomy in ancient architecture include many sites in Portugal and Spain dating back to 3,600 BCE (Silva, Pimenta and Tirapicos 2021), the lowlands region of Uruguay (Gianotti et al. 2023, 3), the Villa de Leiva region of Colombia, Chankillo, Peru (Gianotti et al. 2023, 2-3), and throughout worldwide pre-history.

In conclusion, the ancestral cognitive practice of devotion to the cosmos was universal, profound to all, and temporal through the existence of our species.

\* \* \*

A much older, but similarly enriched landscape example of archaeoastronomy focus is situated in southeastern Turkey at the location of Gobekli Tepe. Investigating the details of Gobekli Tepe from the collective perspectives of anthropology, archaeology, architecture, engineering design, etymology, psychology and archaeoastronomy, assimilates all the evidence and features of its existence, meaning and purpose to conclude the most accurate determination ever presented. I start this investigation utilizing such a strategy.

The book of inquiry and insight advancing the depth and reliability of meaning at Gobekli Tepe remains divergent within the dialogue of updated discovery. Contributory factors include that, to date, over 95 percent of this Early Neolithic "city" remains unexcavated. The hundreds of sites in the Turkish Tepe region share this scenario. Access to archaeology and anthropology, believed to have existed with many other neighboring sites in this region of the ancient Levant, currently influences the path of these inquiries, as do the consequences of modern sociopolitical decisions. For example, the 1991 decision by the Turkish government to create the Atatürk Dam that flooded the Nevali Çori and nearby ancient sites for use as a modern dam aquatic reservoir (Atatürk Dam, *Britannica* 2025). Ramifications of these decisions, as well as the recurring challenges of cultural situational bias that will remain present among human research, serve to retard the progress of inquiry that led to meaning and knowledge.

The Tepes of the Levant maintain their fascination among all research communities because their known dating alignments, from 6,000 to over 13,000 BCE, are currently correlated as the earliest depictions of many Early Neolithic cultural characteristics. These characteristics include Revolutions of sedentary lifestyle, archaeoastronomy, socialization attitude-behaviors, and the perception and cognitive intelligence as practiced by the contemporary human being. It is left to a future enduring consensus that many of the tepe mound locations also served as residential habitations, specialized workshop areas, and open courtyards as communal living spaces (Peters and Schmidt 2004, 180).

The spatial landscape of Gobekli Tepe, as correlated with prevailing universal attitudes and behaviors throughout ancient times and today, and practiced as such, is situated at the highest altitude in the surrounding landscape. The attitude and behavior of the mindset to be "closer to god(s)" confirms the psychology embedded with the meaningful construction of structures in high places that is confirmation of a purposeful functionality of a temple. The indigenous Gobekli Tepe cultures also opted to purposely situate these buildings on high places as ritual places and cosmic projections that served as power platforms and supports my assertion to be closer to the gods and heaven for worship practices (Peters and Schmidt 2004,209).

Each building at the site displays two central T-pillars on a raised altar platform surrounded by a circular geometry with up to twelve or more peripheral pillars and seating benches for ceremony participants. Extensive animal and anthropomorphic motifs are represented among the entire Gobekli Tepe temple complex, identified in the research as Buildings A through H. The most popularly depicted life form symbolism includes hoofed livestock, canines, horned boars, serpents, aviary, and an occasional bear; all reasoned to be representations of existing wildlife in the wild agrios of the time (Peters and Schmidt 2004,184-185). This motif is represented at the hundreds of other Tepe sites in ancient Turkey. They include a striking theme of violence, fear, and stress embodied within and their depictions are illustrated to communicate these themes. I noted earlier that this was an evolutionary step in humankind's reconciliation of the power and control competition between man and the wild agrios of the animal kingdom.

The central T-pillars are stelae that approach 20 feet in height. Many of them depict a single statuesque human anthropomorph, complete with many phenotypical characteristics such as arms and legs and adorned with many animal figures that suggest an animal-human duality of identity attribution or other sacred animism. This aligns with the traditions of tribal leaders depicted in younger cultures, such as Native America, by correlating personality traits of these people with similar animistic characteristics and subsequently adopting their identity attributes. The relief figures are symbolic memorial attributes of these animals as having had a significant part in the life of the honored, and as part of ancestral worship, social bonding and social behavioral ritual cult psychology. Thus, I assert that the Gobekli Tepe enclosures were characteristic embodiment of a proto-totem concept that served to memorialize the status of royalty within that culture, as well as serving other functions.

For these memorialized ceremonial activities, the central T-pillars were the totem's foundation, and the peripheral pillar designs functioned within the ceremonial complex as guardians, protectors and guides for the activities that were undertaken. These activities included, but are not exclusive to, ceremonies for The Path of Souls of their departed royalty, as well as related communal social bonding and engineering events to memorialize whatever deities and other super powerful beings they worshiped. The theme of a power and control competition is also present at the Gobekli Tepe semiotics as the creators chose to depict the power characteristics of the animals as reflections of both the wild agrios nature of the animals and their surrounding ecological environments. These mindful competitive activities had been practiced for tens of millennia, as the ancient records show.

But this direct, urbanized, close quarters rendition was new in its time and suggests a slow change in the competitive balance mindset that by now began to tangibly favor the human over both the animal and many environmental adversaries. This was due to the many technological and social advancements made, as I previously noted. The ritual cults of feasting, bonding, stress relief through deity appeals and social engineering by tribal leaders are also evident within this activity process and appear to have been unique in their design. These activities may have been comprised of common themes; ancestral worship ethnocentricity and of the skyscape phenomenon that specifically synchronizes with a certain part of the night sky. My research data suggests that this region was the Milky Way, and its many cosmic inhabitants.

These central T-pillar stelae sit atop altar platforms and contain tripartite totemic meaning showing their mindful association with a rites-of-passage ritual custom linking the underworld to the "living" world (Peters and Schmidt 2004, 210). Likewise, it has been suggested that the pillars also connected the rights of both the underworld and the terrestrial world to the skyscape, or upper world (Bischoff 2002). Data I have collected in conjunction with extensive field work conducted at the site provide support to the notion that this upper world; the celestial world, was profoundly meaningful in the minds of the inhabitants as a link in the chain of a vertical axis mundus.

Archaeoastronomical relevance at Gobekli Tepe is derived from a nuanced inspection of the architecture at Buildings A-D. Construction of buildings A, B, C, and D were believed to have been undertaken between 9,900-8,000 BCE with D being the oldest and A the youngest (Dietrich 2011; Schmidt 2012; Dietrich et al. 2013). The central T-pillar stelae, as the tallest monoliths in each building, illustrate full-bodied anthropomorphs adorned with various animal bas reliefs and a belt-like device wrapped around its waist. These belts also show many symbols strongly resembling linguistic characters or letters, as depicted in the associated photos.

*Perimeter Pillars at Gobekli Tepe*

*Animal morphs and 'letters' on central T-pillar*

*The agrios animal morph pillar totem*

The pillars surrounding the outer perimeter of each building serve as the guardian/protector symbolism, show similar adornments as the central stelae, but also show human anthropomorphs with heads and features curiously absent from the central T-pillar monoliths (Schmidt 2010, 246).

I suggest that the construction of each temple building complex and the central T-pillars served tripartite purposes, motivated to depict and attribute worship to a collection of tribal leaders, the assortment of deities and super powerful beings in their ceremonial inventory, and for other feasting and social communal bonding attitudes and behavior cults within their ethnologies. While the peripheral pillars may yet be discovered to identify specific tribal royalty, each of the central T-pillars are metaphorically tasked with symbolizing more than one godhead of that culture.

I would like to state at this time that my work in the subject of the Tepe sciences of ancient Turkey is ongoing, and that presentation of more detailed knowledge is beyond the scope of this writing. This discussion is an educational primer of understanding designed to properly orient you to the larger study of human beings as your ancestors and as a guide to help you start to better understand yourself. I will offer many more related detailed discoveries in future work.

I can now synchronize the archaeoastronomy and all the other forensic and scientific evidence left by the peoples of Gobekli Tepe. I remind you from earlier that a significant factor during cognitive development of our ancestors was the reconciliation of dealing with the skyscape as a physical space in the Universe. They could not touch or feel this space like the other two elements of the vertical axis mundi chain; the terrestrial landscape and the below groundscape. Therefore, they developed the skyscape connections in their way by cognitively creating patterns and relationships between the terrestrial and underworld landscapes with this celestial skyscape. This development was both cognitive and neurological in nature. My conclusion has multidisciplinary support, most recently in statistical hypothesis testing by physicists and systems engineers Martin Sweatman and Dimitrios

Gerogiorgis of the University of Edinburgh (Sweatman and Gerogiorgis 2025).

I begin by assigning celestial correspondence and correlating these findings with date stamp data for each enclosure (Köksal-Schmidt and Schmidt 2010; Dietrich 2011; Dietrich et al. 2013). This data replication confirms that the central T-Pillar design, when studied across the collection of buildings A through D effectively served as star trackers to establish their purposeful construction, meaning and attitude-behavior orientation with specific features of the night skyscape.

Below is a table showing my data collection of the relevant data streams of geo-compass coordinates and dates aligned with each of the Building Enclosures.

Table 1: Gobekli Tepe Building Enclosures,

Geo-compass Coordinates & Construction Dates

| BUILDING | GEO-COMPASS COORDINATE | DATE OF CONSTRUCTION |
|---|---|---|
| Building D | 353° | 9,700-9,900 BCE |
| Building C | 347° | 9,500-9,700 BCE |
| Building B | 342° | 9,300-9,500 BCE |
| Building A | 327° | 9,100-9,300 BCE |
| Copyright Keith A. Seland | 2025 | |

This detailed star-tracking analysis confirms the discovery of a valid celestial alignment of these data points with the star constellation Hercules in-situ. They provide a matching correspondence with the time dating parameter data. Also, an association with Hercules' neighboring constellation of Corona Borealis, and both constellations' very close proximity with the Milky Way complex, are supported by the data. Both analyses confirm a relationship between living man, his eschatology, spiritual meaning and the cosmos. These features add an additional dimension to Gobekli Tepe's tripartite metaphorical meaning. Factors that confirm these associations are numerous and transferable to practices of other ancient civilizations.

First, the mindful prevalence of human sacrality beliefs inherent within the data is illustrated by knowing that, at the times of their use, each central pillar altar, as the prominent feature of each building construct, was centered in sight line alignment directed toward the North Celestial Pole. This means the anthropomorphs, as the pillar stelae, were meaningfully fixed in that direction.

In the study of the cosmos, activities where the cognitive mind is called upon to detect patterns in stimulus phenomena can identify anomalous features in a skyscape. Our minds are, and theirs were, wired to witness and memorize these features. By immersing yourself in that situational awareness to the time of 9,500 BCE, the skyscape would show that all the celestial objects would move about the grid of the skyscape (God's Keyboard), except for one. As I discussed earlier, the North Star would appear relatively stationary and appear to move every 72 years. Today's representative, Polaris, for example, will move about one degree to the west during this time, as does with every candidate. This is due to the Precession of The Equinoxes phenomenon that cycles a recurring iteration of the same candidates roster approximately every 25,776 years. Polaris, when it leaves its status as the North Star, will not cycle back to this celestial orientation for about that length of time.

At the time of Building D's construction, the star Iota in the Hercules constellation was positioned as the North Star. To the inhabitants of the Gobekli communities, in a situation where they witnessed movement of all other star objects, Iota Hercules (ι Her) did not; a peculiar attention-grasping event in the minds of the indigenous. It is easy to infer profound psychological meaning and purpose being derived from this cognitive sequence. On a grid where all celestial objects except one constantly move, notice was taken. Modern-day humankind still practices this cognitive intelligence today.

When time progressed, after a few hundred years, Iota Hercules moved to the west in the sky. When this movement was deemed sufficient, the users deliberately buried the entire Building D space. They then built another one next to the now defamed Building D. We have named this structure Building C. The process repeated with successive burials and construction of Buildings B and A, respectively. This sequence of events proves the importance, meaning, and devotion to the Hercules constellation and the surrounding region of the cosmos as eschatologically vital to the existence of all ancient civilizations.

The road to discovery in this analysis continues. The Hercules and Corona Borealis star groups are celestially situated very close to the Milky Way. Another even more prominent eschatological phenomenon that had a far longer history of sacred meaning to ancient humankind were the manifestations of heaven and hell, their locations, and the destination for a Path of Souls journey. Again, these were physical three-dimensional galactic locations that people's living senses could not touch or feel; they made sense and sensory meaning from these data in their ways to perpetuate the religiosity, eschatology, and psychology of dealing with potential conflict, danger and physical harm to their earthly lives. The entire leadership power and control mechanism operates from application of these premises.

In addition to the location, behavior and perception of its North Star Iota, the Hercules grid, was and still is visualized as a large symbol 'H.' The Corona Borealis constellation has a pattern shape that appears like the symbol 'C.' A curious association is considered between this information and the widespread presence of the 'C' and 'H' symbols on both the belt-like waist devices and elsewhere on many of the pillar stelae, including many of the peripheral guardian pillars. These also contain symbol collections in the combinations of 'C', H,' and/or 'I.' The 'I' could have held more visual appeal and thus was adopted because often the Hercules and Corona Borealis constellations appeared in that orientation; the position of the open segment of the 'C' along a sideways position of Hercules, depending on the time of year they were observed. This would be meaningfully expressed in the form of 'C-I-C' on the belt symbolism as contrasted to a 'C-H-C' iconography.

*T-Pillar 'letters' with hand of anthropomorphic figure*

We know that the North Star moves out of its' "stationary" position by approximately one-degree every 72 years. We also know that each new building enclosure has been dated to have existed a few hundred years later than its predecessor. This time elapse would have led to their observations that ι Her would have moved by three or more degrees to the west. The natives tracked the path of ι Her through generations of mnemonic cognition. Each successive building construction project was tasked with an incorporation of the central pillars to be celestially aligned a few degrees further west, reasonably tracking the movements of this North Star, Iota Hercules, as it falls away from this unique position.

A fourth factor of attribution is inferred from our continued modern observations of a star in the Corona Borealis group. T-Coronae Borealis is a binary star system that goes nova every 80 or so years, particularly close to the witnessed motion pattern of the North Star. Another nova event was to have occurred in either 2025 or 2026. Astronomers have documented this event from repeated observations over hundreds of years. One would observe this star, with a natural magnitude of about 10, to be dimly visible to the naked eye, then suddenly increase in magnitude to about two or one at nova for a week or two. The event catapults T-Coronae Borealis into an observational status of being among the very brightest stars in the night skyscape. This event would have led to another divine interpretation and would have served to further capture the eschatological attention of the indigenous and drive their corresponding attitude and behavior regimes.

The Hercules and Corona Borealis constellations were spiritual, ethnographical and practical in profound importance to all ancestral traditions. These star groups, due to their size and celestial orientations, were and are visible to all humans, including the aboriginal Australian terrestrial landscape. While meaning can be nuanced among some cultures, their intrinsic importance was universal. Another feature of cognitive adaptation concerns the geometry of the modern-named Hercules Keystone. This is illustrated by the trapezoidal rectangle that forms the core asterism of the Hercules constellation.

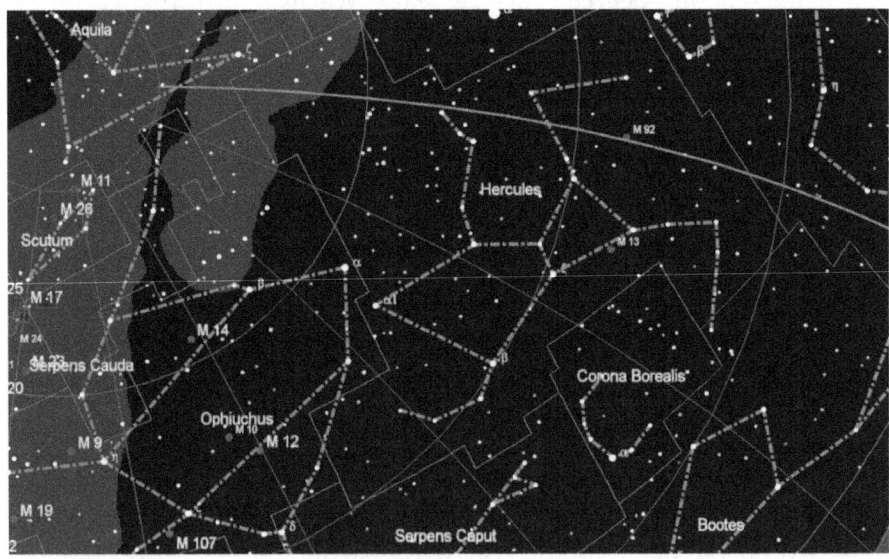

*The Hercules Constellation with Milky Way and Corona Borealis 9,500 BCE*

*Peru ceremonial 'portal' likeness of Hercules Keystone*

*Peru 'portal' representation of Hercules Keystone*

*Ollantaytambo, Peru 'portal' likeness of Hercules Keystone*

*Ollantaytambo, Peru more 'portal' likenesses of Hercules Keystone*

*Machu Picchu, Peru ceremonial 'portals'*

The geometry discussion of Hercules features the "H"-shaped configuration that has attributes to the Gobekli Tepe letter iconography. The contours of the pillars themselves are shaped as isosceles trapezoids, the quadrilateral rectangles that conceptually correspond with the Hercules Keystone asterism. Moreover, a broader application of this concept provides evidence as to the purposeful application of this geometry to many other ancient structures, such as the "windows" depicted in many Andean cultures of South America, Meso-America, Native America, Egypt, and the Euro-Asian landscapes, as shown below.

While the broader square design was an easier architecture to craft, the widespread use of the trapezoidal geometry contained special meaning that aligns with both the celestial design mimicry psychology of Hercules as well as the geophysical placement and alignment of these openings with climate-control and spiritual meanings, respectively. Our modern-day window concept does not use this trapezoidal geometry as we do not mindfully share these ancient beliefs. But the practical design concepts of 90 degree-angles are still in full use.

The special use of this geometry can also explain the cognitive development of the stargate portal concept of ancestral traditions. They purposed use of the Hercules Keystone as a geometric application of the shape as a resonating feature to an eschatological meaning of the Path of Souls journey. The Hercules Keystone was, in their minds, the part of this journey that was ritualized as the "portal" or stargate to heaven. The soul of the departed tribal royalty was guided through this portal. Successful navigation became the premise for ritual, repetitive honor and celebratory behavior as ancestral worship and tradition. The world archaeology and symbolic representation confirm universal adoption of this cognitive development of geometry with spiritual, eschatological and practical applications.

*Puma Punku ceremonial 'H' blocks*

In summary, there exists a rich and multifarious expression of archaeoastronomy symbolism at Gobekli Tepe. Building replacement projects followed a temporal synchronicity with the fluid nature of the skyscape; in this example with the Hercules, Corona Borealis and Milky Way as the apex of the three vertical dimensions that constitute the axis mundi. Each building was a grand plaza of celebration, social bonding, engineering power and control, and conflict resolution. They perpetuated a psychology that combined activities of the living as well as ancestral worship memorialization for spiritual, eschatological, ceremonial, sacrificial, and medical purposes.

The altar and central T-pillars were surrounded by up to over a dozen circularly shaped peripheral pillars. The central T-pillars each memorialized the lives of departed royalty as deities alongside other godheads and served as totems for celebratory, memorial, or more immediate functions such as fear and stress relief, as well as social engineering attitude and behavior processes. These grand plazas of worship also functioned as the starting line for the Path of Souls sequence that both guided the soul of the newly departed and laid the road for filling the future needs of that soul that perpetuated an eternal existence. The central T-pillars, therefore, are not necessarily identified with a single ancestral life, but representative of many lives - some humans, some not.

The symbolic iconography is all supportive of this theory. The archaeoastronomical focal point was the T-pillars. The tripartite metaphorical meaning of earthly life worship (human and animal), divine life worship, and the cosmic meanings were woven into one tapestry by the indigenous of the Gobekli Tepe complex. This was surrounded by all the circular peripheral pillars that served as guardians, protectors and guides for those ceremonies and celebrations, and included participant seating for those involved in the various events. The iconography is expressed as a record of these events and the meaningful props in the production - the animal, headed anthropomorphs and related symbolism encrypted on each pillar.

The anthropomorphs mindfully existed as parts of either a sacral animism or a totem cult, with the stelae as the honored leaders at the time of each building's construction. The animal motifs helped to tell a rite-of-passage life story in remembrance of the deceased tribal royalty. Rituals, including feasting ceremonies and sacrifices, were regularly conducted and served the power elite of the new urban culture as tools of social bonding and governance that included celebrations of the underworld, the living world and the upper world. The Path of Souls guided the newly departed soul, by various animal spirit representatives and guides, as the eschatological transport into the heavenly realm known as the Milky Way, via the road that transported it through the Hercules-Corona Borealis star region.

\* \* \*

Many more revelations await discovery at the Gobekli Tepe site and throughout the many hundreds of Tepes in the Fertile Crescent of the Levant. The correspondence between this early global communal worldview and the deep relationship with the cosmos continues to gain support from all these ancient traditions; only a snapshot has been presented to you. The recurring takeaway, thus, is correlated to that of all the other discussions. That is, your elders possessed under acknowledged intelligence, resourcefulness, curiosity, motivation, holism, peace, and harmony in recognizing and striving to maintain the cosmic equilibrium the Universe demanded of them. This was despite their wide range of responses, ranging from the practical to the spiritual, cosmic and religious, to the chaos, stress, fear, and tension that disrupted this cosmic equilibrium, and by extension their lives, as communicated to us by their external material remains. I encourage you to consult my list of contributors who support this theory for additional data on any of the subtopics raised throughout these discussions.

My Algorithm of Humankind, version 2.0, is now complete. The $T_2$ variable, comprised of the 5-w's and 1-h subroutines of "who we are," is now fully functional and can serve as an addend to the $T_1$ variable of "who we were" of the same constituency. You now possess a total picture of the theater production that is, "This is Your Life". Most of the actors have been welcomed onto the stage. The earliest "us," later "us," and how we perceived, behaved toward, and reacted to the world around us, the underworld, living world and the upper world, and all its constituent organic and inorganic matter forms, compel this stage to be a large one. But some, though not all, of the remaining room is reserved for the latest version of "us," expressed by the dependent variable "who we have become".

I introduce this additional dependent variable because, recalling the numerous references to time in my discussions, a long chunk of time elapsed from then until now. Due to its dependent nature, I am conjoining "who we have become" to "who we are" in the same $T_2$ variable and not as a stand-alone unknown. The people of $T_1$ were too different from us to be compatible; the people of $T_2$ were us and existed as us in every ontological way.

There is one indispensable variable yet to be considered; the $T_3$ variable of "who we could be." We possess the same observation skills and attitude-behavior mechanisms, driven by the same attitude cues that Nam and Muh's people possessed. Our involvement in competitiveness, power and control spheres-of-influence remain their equivalent. These drive similar perception-cognition and mnemonic processes, though our means of communication is now radically different. So is our toolkit of knowledge. Or are they so different?

*References:*

Aveni, Anthony F. 2001 *Skywatchers: A Revised and Updated Version of Skywatchers of Ancient Mexico*. Austin: University of Texas Press.

Aveni, A. and Hartung, H. 1986. *Maya City Planning and the Calendar*. Philadelphia: American Philosophical Society.

Bischoff, D. 2002. "Symbolic Worlds of Central and Southeast Anatolia in the Neolithic." In *The Neolithic of Central Anatolia: International Developments and External Relations during the 9th–6th Millennia cal. BC*, edited by F. Gerard and L. Thissen, 237–51. Istanbul: Ege Yayinlari.

Brumm, Adam, Adhi Agus Oktaviana, Basran Burhan, Budianto Hakim, Rustan Lebe, Jian-xin Zhao, Priyatno Hadi Sulistyarto, Marlon Ririmasse, Shinatria Adhityatama, Iwan Sumantri, and Maxime Aubert. 2021. "Oldest Cave Art Found in Sulawesi." *Science Advances* 7 (3): eabd4648.

Demarest, Arthur. 2004. *Ancient Maya: The Rise and Fall of a Rainforest Civilization*. Cambridge, UK: Cambridge University Press.

Dietrich, O. 2011. Göbekli Tepe. In PPND - The Platform for Neolithic Radiocarbon Dates. http://www.exoriente.org/associated_projects/ppnd_site.php?s=25#.

Dietrich, Oliver, Çiğdem Köskäl-Schmidt, Jens Notroff, and Klaus Schmidt. 2013. "Establishing a Radiocarbon Sequence for Göbekli Tepe: State of Research and New Data." *Neo-Lithics: The Newsletter of Southwest Asian Neolithic Research* 1 (13): 35–38.

Eliade, Mircea. 1971. *The Myth of the Eternal Return: Cosmos and History.* Princeton: Princeton University Press.

Elaide, Mircea. 1972. *Shamanism, Archaic Techniques of Ecstasy,* Bollingen Series LXXVI, 3-7, Princeton University Press.

Encyclopedia Britannica Editors. 2019. *Atatürk Dam.* March 15, 2019. https://www.britannica.com/topic/Ataturk-Dam

Fagan, B.M. 1999. *From Black Land to Fifth Sun: The Science of Sacred Sites.* New York: Basic Books.

Foster, Lynn. 2002. *Handbook to Life in the Ancient Maya World.* New York: Oxford University Press.

Furst, P.T. 1976. "Shamanistic Survivals in Mesoamerican Religion." In *Actas des XLI Congreso Internacional de Americanistas.* vol. 3, 149-157.

Gianotti, Camila, A. César Gonzalez-Garcia, Nicolás Gazzán, Cristina Cancela-Cereijo, and Moira Sotelo. 2023. "Knowledge of the Sky among Indigenous Peoples of the South American Lowlands: First Archaeoastronomical Analyses of Orientations at Mounds in Uruguay." *Land* 12: 805. https://doi.org/10.3390/land12040805.

Graur, Or. 2024. "The Ancient Egyptian Personification of the Milky Way as the Sky Goddess Nut: An Astronomical and Cross-cultural Analysis. *Journal of Astronomical History and Heritage,* 27 (1): 28-45.

Hawkes, Christopher. 1954. "Archaeological Theory and Method: Some Suggestions from the Old World." *American Anthropologist* 56: 155-168.

Iwaniszewski, Stanislaw. 2011. "The Sky as a Social Field." *Proceedings of the International Astronomical Union* 7 (S278): 20–37. https://doi.org/10.1017/S1743921311012440.

Kak, Subhash. 2010. India, In *Heritage Sites of Astronomy and Archaeoastronomy in the context of the UNESCO World Heritage Convention: A Thematic Study,* edited by Clive Ruggles and Michael Cotte. Paris: International Council on Monuments and Sites (ICOMOS) and the International Astronomical Union (IAU).

King, H. 2002. "Gold in Ancient America." *The Metropolitan Museum of Art Bulletin,* 59 (4): 5-55. Doi: 10.2307/3269153.

Klein, Cecelia, E. Guzman, E. Mandell, and M. Stanfield-Mazzi. 2002.

"The Role of Shamanism in Mesoamerican Art: A Reassessment." *Current Anthropology* 43 (3): 383–419.

Köksal-Schmidt, Çiğdem, and Klaus Schmidt. 2010. "The Göbekli Tepe 'Totem Pole': A First Discussion of an Autumn 2010 Discovery (PPN, Southeastern Turkey)." *Neolithics* 10 (1). https://www.researchgate.net/publication/271500663.

Merriam-Webster. n.d. "Pareidolia." *Merriam-Webster.com Dictionary.* Accessed August 15, 2024. https://www.merriam-webster.com/dictionary/pareidolia.

Monaghan, William G., and Edward Herrmann. 2019. "Serpent Mound Still Built by the Adena, and Still Rebuilt During the Fort Ancient Period." *Midcontinental Journal of Archaeology,* 44 (1): 84-93.

Peters, Joris and Klaus Schmidt. 2004. "Animals in the Symbolic World of Pre-Pottery Neolithic Göbekli Tepe, South-Eastern Turkey: A Preliminary Assessment." *Anthropozoologica,* 39 (1): 180-218.

Pike, A. W. G., D. L. Hoffman, P. B. Garcia-Diez, P. B. Pettitt, J. Alcolea, R. De Balbín, C. González-Sainz, C. de las Heras, J. A. Lasheras, R. Montes, and J. Zilhão. 2012. "U-Series Dating of Paleolithic Art in 11 Caves in Spain." *Science* 336 (6087): 1409–1413.

Romain, W. F. 2022. "Following The Milky Way Path of Souls: An Archaeoastronomic Assessment of Cahokia's Main Site Axis and Rattlesnake Causeway." *Journal of Skyscape Archaeology*, 7 (2): 187–212. https://doi.org/10.1558/jsa.18926

Schmidt, Klaus. 2010. "Gobekli Tepe-The Stone Age Sanctuaries. New Results of ongoing excavations with a special focus on sculptures and high reliefs." *Documenta Praehistorica* 37: 239-256.

Schmidt, Klaus. 2012. *Göbekli Tepe a Stone Age Sanctuary in South-Eastern Anatolia.* Berlin, Germany: ex-Oriente e.V.

Silva, Fabio, Fernando Pimenta, and Luis Tirapicos. 2021. "Symbolism and Archaeoastronomy in Prehistory." In *The Oxford Handbook of Human Symbolic Evolution,* edited by Nathalie Gontier. Oxford: Oxford University Press.

Smith, Tiddy. 2023. *Animism and Philosophy of Religion (Palgrave Frontiers in Philosophy of Religion).* Palgrave MacMillan.

Sofaer, A. 1997. *The Primary Architecture of the Chacoan Culture: A Cosmological Expression.* University of New Mexico Press.

Stringer, Martin D. (1999). "Rethinking Animism: Thoughts from the Infancy of our Discipline." *Journal of the Royal Anthropological Institute,* 5 (4): 541-556.

Sweatman, Martin B., and Dimitrios Gerogiorgis. 2025. "New Paper Submitted: Origin of Some of the Ancient Greek Constellations via Analysis of Pillar 43 at Göbekli Tepe." Manuscript submitted for publication, May 20, 2025.

Tan, Shirley. 2015. *Chinese Auspicious Culture.* Singapore: Asiapac Books Pte Ltd.

Tedlock, Barbara. 2005. *The Woman in the Shaman's Body: Reclaiming the Feminine in Religion and Medicine.* New York: Bantam.

Tributsch, Helmut. 2018. "Shamanic Trance Journey with Animal Spirits: Ancient 'Scientific' Strategy Dealing with Inverted Otherworld." *Advance in Anthropology,* 8: 91-126.

Tylor, E. B. 1871. *Primitive Culture.* London: John Murray.

Van Stone, Mark. 2016. "What We Think We Know About Maya Mathematics and Astronomy." In *Inspiration of Astronomical Phenomena VIII: City of Stars.* 501:265.

Williams, P.V.A. 1973. "Myths, Symbols and the Concept of Immortality among Some Amerindian Societies." *Folklore,* 84 (4): 327-338. doi: 10.2307/1259838.

Winkelman, Michael. 2002. "Shamanism as Neurotheology and Evolutionary Psychology." *American Behavioral Scientist* 45 (12): 1873–85.

Winkelman, Michael. 2004. "Shamanism as the Original Neurotheology." *Zygon* 39 (1): 193–217.

Winkelman, Michael. 2009. "Shamanism: Ancient and Future Survival." In *So What? Now What? The Anthropology of Consciousness Responds to a World in Crisis,* 204–29.

Xygalatas, Dimitris. 2022. *Ritual: How Seemingly Senseless Acts Make Life Worth Living.* New York : Little, Brown Spark and Hachette Book Group.

# Act III: UNIVERSALS

*When we understand our purpose here,
we will respect and care for all life.*

-Anthony Douglas Williams,
    Author - *Inside the Divine Pattern*

*Keywords: Eschatology of the soul, anthropic principle, anthropocentrism, agrios, the Overview Effect, Earthrise, Akashic Record.*

We are them and they are us...

Up to now I have been describing you and me as a prodigy of Nam and Muh's people. The showroom after coat has now been applied. The being that is us now becomes a maintenance and tune-up routine. Nam and Muh's people were adopting and enlarging their platform of understanding in the evolutionary track to naturally select for our level of the "knowledge of things". This is just another dimension for higher intelligence.

    I have made great efforts and offered many details to support the theory that in every way, shape and form our ancestors aligned with us in what they experienced, observed, perceived, and interpreted in developing the same attitudes and behaviors as we experience today. There is still a lot of research data available for your inspection and enlightenment that I could not include in this limited space. We are them and they are us in every meaningful way. You can consider these 200+ pages as sufficient evidence to form a credible basis of your own informed interpretation.

To study and learn about them is to know them far better than you may have been led to believe, and, by inference and insight, to get to know us better. My thesis proposes that these dimensions of human heritage should be considered more expansively and critically to assist us in charting our present and future course as a species.

To drive this inference of how our minds work today, insight into their ancient traditions shows in the record a significant analogous resonance of mind that was universally practiced. Their minds worked the same way as our minds do today. We can compare and contrast our thought processes in the details of similar scenarios and conclude, in most every case, that their attitudes, logic and behaviors served as the equivalent of ours in many dimensions.

For example, in a practical context the residential living homes at the Tepe sites in Turkey were deliberately built on the leeward sides of their host mountain as one of many common-sense strategies to shelter the structures from the prevailing climatic western and northern winds. Cultural social centers and residential architectures here and many other global ancient sites vibrate with the same intuition, building resourcefulness, and correlated intellect to how we would think today. Food storage and waste buildings in the earliest urbanized societies were situated away from habitation structures as another example to prevent the otherwise potentially harmful intrusions by hungry wildlife invaders, or by odoriferous smells within their habitat that were unfavorable or unpleasant to ingest, and for other localized security and spiritual reasons. We both would chase attitudes and behaviors as refugees or combatants if a famine or war did or were to occur in our home communities. We are also kindred beings in matters of fear, stress, tension, ritual, competition, power, and control.

We are cohorts in the use of my Multitasking Cognitivity Utilization Model of the mind when tasked to develop new innovations, discoveries, and inventions of new devices, processes, or "things". However, our ancestors did not always drive these achievements at the same accelerated speed as we do today. They used positive feedback loops of critical thinking to feed the discovery and invention of new ones, just as we do today. Their tools of production, architecture, commerce, health, and weaponry sometimes showed a continual, though slow and rhythmic innovation by comparison. Other situations, however, defied this steady progress.

A visually appealing example of this unsteady pace comes from inspecting the first generations after the Great Unification of Upper and Lower Egypt of the late third millennium, BCE. King Djoser, with much assistance from his vizier, Imhotep, created the first pyramidal architecture with their mastaba-influenced levels of construction. Just one generation later, King Sneferu used Djoser's and Imhotep's innovations to invent three new architectural creations utilizing radically improved technologies and design engineering, and accelerated velocities. These "out-of-place" artifacts of innovation included the pyramids at Meidum, and the Bent and Red pyramids of Dahshur. Sneferu's son, Khufu, used this critical thinking mechanism to build, just a few decades later, the iconic Cheops, or Khufu pyramid at Giza that has survived and is universally known today. Monumental structures such as these were created along a highly accelerated innovation timeline using inventions that were conceived at a similarly accelerated velocity, by whatever compelling influences became known to them. It remains fantastic to our minds that this architecture still exists today.

Just a few decades later, we learn of Egypt's demise into their first sociocultural disaster of many known as the Intermediate Periods. A cessation to the accelerated pace of innovation and progress became a cultural "great filter" that they could not overcome for hundreds of years. Their recovery itself was another fantastic accomplishment when contrasting comparable stories from modern day cultures. The Egyptian record illustrates many of the universal characteristics, lifestyles, spiritualism, customs, rituals, ceremonial practices, and existentialism of pre-modern humankind. Reflecting on any example of the Egyptian heritage, reveals their very great and prideful devotion to the *eschatology of the soul* and its eternal life centered around the notion that the Earth, and by extension themselves, were the center of the

## ACT III: UNIVERSALS

Universe. Their tourist industry of ancient heritage remains Egypt's main socioeconomic engine today.

The Neolithic Revolutions of humankind were not just one manifestation of life change, but of many. As others have tried to infer a single phenomenon, such as the development of agriculture as the primary catalyst for these Revolutions, I continue to argue for an inclusion of other catalysts, the total purpose of which was with their meaningful purpose of improving the societal human condition. These included Revolutions of food, building, ecological, spiritual, external material, and social culture trajectories. In substance and form, our ancestor's maturing observational awareness, perception, cognition, attitudinal primers and cues, behaviors, and capability for memory, general and specialized intelligences, and relearning produced all these Revolutions.

The elder minds dealt with the various cosmic and terrestrial forces, as put to them, in their own way. These intelligences, as shaped by nature, nurture, adaptability, and the driving curiosity to continue to learn, fashioned our Universe's propensity to embody such an *anthropic principle*. The final achievement of Neolithic humankind, therefore, may be summarized from this discussion as the information, communications, and social behaviors Revolutions. Information drives innovation as does the increased capacity for unfiltered access to effective communication and agreed upon social protocols that facilitate this effectiveness. The ancients' social nature became hard-wired in their biology and metamorphosized its existence into a truly cosmological consciousness.

Human mind's functional framework can be illustrated metaphorically in the portrayal of an object from nature - the honeycomb. A primary objective in developing the Honeycomb Model of The Mind is to suggest that all six factors needed to be present for the proliferation of the successfully evolved mind in a gradual but continuous process of deployment and development of cognitive intelligence that led to new knowledge. These six factors include neurological, instinctual, environmental, social cultures, life experiences, and emotional. Application of my Honeycomb Model is universal.

It is conclusive, therefore, to state that the similarities of our perceptive and cognitive memory pathway with our older kin are the correlative foundation by which we can both develop a keener synergistic awareness and understanding and use this as a rationale for our future guidance. They endowed to us a foundation of basic knowledge that shaped our mindful expansion of such and shaped our more reasoned human condition and human natures. In another way I state that, if our early Holocene brethren possessed the same tools of technology and knowledge as us, then their situational awareness, attitudes and behaviors might have very much resonated with ours, given the same eco-environmental life conditions.

Of course, there will be divergences in the trajectories of the critical thinking between our ancestors and modern man. This 'apples vs. oranges' debate are knowledge-based to a significant degree and occurs due to the unique set of circumstances inherent in comparison of any two situations. The behavioral trajectories of our eco-environment, the celestial appearances of existential great filter phenomena, of others, including their combinations, were different. If one variable of this experimental protocol were changed, the results would probabilistically be different.

Certainly, this knowledge difference was one divergence. Consequently, it would only be natural that our thinking would lead to different epistemologies. But it is still enlightening to learn that many similarities exist ubiquitously between the two versions of us. The framework and inspiration remained the same and have been repeatedly shown to us. We still eat the same food, breathe the same oxygen, socialize in the same way, still worship on at least a basal social cognitive level, and build our homes with the same core architectural theory as they. A laudatory takeaway here is that we can still study their architectural theory today as it has survived for tens of thousands of years!

* * *

Other similarities that fit under this framework include predictable behaviors when there is a continued scarcity of food, water, or security of mind and body which will drive modern cultural behaviors into a 'fight or flight' mode as influenced by our attitude cues exactly as they were experienced by our ancestors. We still honor and remember our deceased with the same customary historical intelligence in ceremonious ritual fashion as they did. Our civilization still reflects upon the existence of additional dimensions of spirituality, cosmology, and ontological being that transcend the three readily observable dimensions of height, width and depth. We also still practice the conventions of competition, leadership, power, and control on the same mindful levels that they did. In summary, our attitudes, behaviors, perceptions and cognition, critical thinking, and memory storage recall and usage are practiced on the same universal fundamental levels.

Recall from earlier the influence that the fluid dynamics of climate, geology, ecology, cultural reproductive development, and nature played in our Neolithic Revolutions, as well as the 'game' of competition, power and control between us and the agrios that needed to be played to ensure survival and advance our ancient traditions. It is through the endpoint of this grand competition that we could also find a providence to the psychology of *anthropocentrism*; the mindset that our species reigns supreme at the core of life, that humans are both figuratively and literally the top of the food chain among life forms. The biased nature of anthropocentrism continues to manifest itself in many myopic applications, perhaps because of the runaway cognition effect that the proliferation of the 'game' has had on our brains from these ancient sources.

When this lengthy competition was won and the balance of power was shifted from agrios animal to man, the symbolic record tells us that human intellect adopted this perception and cognition to become basal to our human nature and personality. The behavioral "chest thumping" that a human being would do when he or she is declared the winner of a competition on any landscape today resonates with that of the statement, "We won the battle with the agrios." Many examples with this motif exist from as far back as the Levant in Çatalhöyük, many of the Tepes in Anatolia, the Annunaki in Mesopotamia, the Narmer Palette in proto-dynastic Egypt, uncounted examples in later Dynastic Egypt, the Mayan, Aztec and Pre-Colombian cultures of Meso-America, and Native America reaching far back in the archaic classification symbolism.

Further evidence to the contestability of power and control throughout the Holocene is shown in many external material cultures when inspecting the tool kit and weapons industries, technologies and advancements. Specifically, the continued development of increasingly more effective weapons for hunting, violence, and war demonstrates an eventual shift to anthropocentric psychology resulting from the increased accelerated effectiveness of these weapons to obtain food and other material resources for acquisition of new and better material resources not obtainable through invention or friendly interaction.

What does the *agrios* mean in our world today? It seems illogical that the ancient application to "the wild and violent outdoors" or the 'Outback' to Australians would fully describe the situation in a modern society with many technological tools at their disposal. Certainly, physical security within a large wilderness environment can easily be threatened for the unprepared. But these scenarios begin as recreational pursuits gone wrong and not as survival domains faced by ancient man.

So, what is the wild environment that each of us faces today during our waking hours? The classic agrios of animals and environment probably does not apply in today's world except for the scenarios just noted.

The wildcard variable is the one of *us;* a consideration of our advanced knowledge intelligence and human nature. Does today's urban lifestyle reflect the daily challenges we face due to living in close quarters and societal norms, the trials and tribulations of daily living? This includes our intellectual awareness, its desired pathway toward strategic potential, propensity for exploitation, and a myopic lack of the big picture, known as The Great Chain of Being. It is the structure of our social brain framework that defines us as instinctively social creatures (Dunbar 1998; 2009; 2024). The baggage from this framework still exists and resonates today, as I have noted. This is perhaps the most volatile and dangerous variable under discussion.

ACT III: UNIVERSALS

The attitude-behavior and perception-cognition pathway of competitive thought in any social culture today can be analyzed reflecting upon some repetitive activity behaviors and competitive mindsets, like driving to and from work, behaviors within work environments, in an athletic pursuit, the first-in-line scenario or the first-in or earliest-to complete a task, etc. This attitude-behavior pathway, influenced by the stimulus of attitude cues as recalled from the basal brain, the interface of past knowledge, memories, and experience in the process, will determine the behavior structure of all or part of this; the thinking process that guides an individual through a particular event. In the macrocosm, the collection of the situations and environments helps to define what is meant by a competitive mindset. These were present in ancestral urbanized societies because they all participated in large group labor infrastructures.

Just as our daily life experiences and cultural pressures have influenced our competitive nature, so too were they experienced by our elder species. The Revolutions of the Neolithic fertilized the competitive mindset by adaptation to and adoption of property ownership, household specializations, agricultural intensification, and their inheritances. I have often suggested that motivational factors contributing to this mindset included omnipresent features of climate, geography, and socially driven power and control procedures, "even mild and short climatic conditions (i.e., a 2-year drought, leaving no evidential trace), or small intra-group developmental pressures (i.e., charismatic shaman or ambitious ruler coalescing group identity) may have driven such changes" (Shavit and Sharon 2023).

As urbanized individual habitation and food processing requirements rose in complexity to satisfy an ever-growing population base, the homes became owned property and food processing required more specialized machinery that became unequally distributed among those who worked with the machines. Often this specialized labor industry became owned and occupied by a family lineage (Wright 2014). These behavioral ethnocentricities became a universal trait among ancient traditions worldwide (Fibiger et al. 2023). Seemingly inherent problems embedded within the Revolutions of food and communal living economies were unavoidable in germinating the phenomena of inequality, interpersonal conflict, stress, tension, fear, social states, and warfare in those transitional times (Allen 2024).

\* \* \*

We have been existentially influenced by the cosmos' effects on our physical environments throughout time. Our moon controls our oceans' tidal forces. It, like our sun, has a significant influence on Earth's daily rotation and other natural forces. The unique geo-physical entanglement of our earth's movements through space have been naturally selected to determine and enable our unique biological circadian rhythms; the homeostasis of our daily existence (another pattern cycle to which our ancestors long ago were intuitively aware). If we resided on any other planet, our circadian rhythms would have evolved to become synchronized with the host planet's requisite rotational pattern.

Our ancients sensed these phenomena through their mindful powers of observation, intuition, perception and critical thought. The locational and situational information they acquired through time caused their attitude-behavior mechanisms to interact with these phenomena, as well as all the other underworld, living world and upper world matter we have studied, that gradually kept making their lives better.

Our social landscapes, real in form but abstract in their substance and style, function largely in the behavioral realm and dictate the tapestry of life for each of us. Social cues are taken from what the other says or does to shape a situation and our response. How we react to these physical and social landscapes remold our human conditions as ties that bind the different versions of us together into a single relatable species.

Much of any perceived difference between them and us is sourced to knowledge and technological intelligence. Because of these realities we can reflect upon what they have meant for us and what this advanced state of knowledge and technology may mean for us today and going forward.

## ACT III: UNIVERSALS

We know their condition guided them to observe and process a holistic, balanced, harmonious, peaceful, and interconnected universal equilibrium. The guidance of both sets of existences can be visualized by an analogy of piloted airplane flight. If our ancestors relied on the powers of observation to access their critical thinking to help live, they would metaphorically align and identify with the pilot who flies within the concept of "visual flight rules" (VFR), under clear skies. The deleterious effects created upon adoption of advanced technological infrastructures into our society have been mostly exploitative and symbolize a pilot flying within the concept of "instrument flight rules" (IFR). The intimate feel for and resonance with the surrounding visual sky gets lost when you lose sight of its awareness.

We, today, are facing an existential change to our human nature and human condition with the proliferation of a digital space where our social psyche is being newly challenged by lost awareness and understanding of this holistic interconnectedness and by the desocialization effects that this technological intelligence has affected on the mind, whether foreseen, planned, or entirely unexpected.

This state of condition resonates in the cosmic context as well. We can use our instruments to superficially measure miniscule parts of the outer space phenomena, but we cannot 'feel' it like our ancestors could because we have turned our focus away from that awareness. We also cannot touch it with any physical meaning or purpose except vicariously through the reports from our astronauts who have physically touched the surface membrane of Earth's orbital space.

A phenomenon known as the *Overview Effect*, discovered in the 1960s, describes the universal perception-cognition shift to a state of reverence and transcendence all astronauts feel when they touch the membrane of Earth's orbit during their space missions. Many describe an unexpected and unintended interpretation of the Earth as a breathing life form itself, globally interconnected with all the life forms below (Stepanova, Quesnel, and Riecke 2019). All of them have reported a permanent transformation in their view of life that takes on a whole new significance of peace, harmony, balance, and a fragile terrestrial equilibrium (White 2023). Recognition of Earth as a link in The Great Chain of Being is being recalled by the astronauts who experience the Overview Effect.

It has not yet been explored to what form a similar exercise would take if we were to conduct another experiment where we were looking up at the cosmos instead of down at the Earth in these ways. How would our thoughts be driven when asking about the same views of life that our ancient forefathers, i.e., 'they,' had uncovered from Earth below?

A thought experiment may help in uncovering insight into the features of our current existential life dilemmas. The subject of this experiment is how 'they' and 'us' perceive(ed) the features and uses of a variety of objects and symbols. Table 2 below lays out the data in grid form:

Table 2:

Cultural Perceptions of Things

| Thing | Us | They (Nam & Muh) |
|---|---|---|
| A tree | Wood, graffiti, or an umbrella | Interconnectedness, Spirit, life-giving |
| A swastika | Symbol of evil, denial, fear | Good fortune, health, luck, well-being (Sanskrit) |
| Animals, fish, plants | Food, aesthetics, healing | Food, healing, aesthetics, worship, all connected to them and the Universe |
| Cosmos, planets, asteroids | $$$, knowledge | Knowledge, guidance, healing, eternity |
| Fear, stress | Prevalent | Prevalent |
| Gratification, want' behavior | Prevalent, immediate | Doubtful, but not empirically certain, more data needed |
| Grave robbing | As recent as yesterday | Egypt-Old Kingdom/Mesopotamia and earlier |
| Control of agrios | Yes, but anthropocentric | A new phenomenon |
| Are we alone? | No, in most minds, but stigmas in the public persona persist | No - symbolic, documented, testimonial records - do we know all? |
| | Copyright Keith A. Seland - 2025 | |

This comparison can be compartmentalized as, 'short vs. long-term,' 'myopic vs. farsighted,' 'narrow vs. holistic,' 'closed vs. open minded' etc., where 'Us'

216

are the former vs. 'Them' the latter.

Today, we recall no natural empirical physical symbolism, nor much of an intelligent abstract one, for what a tree would represent, except as building material, or for food. The wooden structure built from trees is not much of a permanent one at that, relatively speaking. Another mimetic recall for a tree is that of a canvas with which to etch graffiti of a highly individualistic form and substance, such as a romantic "I love you". Another universal use of a tree is as an escape from a rain shower. This is the extent of meaning our population bestows on a tree.

This exploitation is far different than the purposes ancestral cultures perceived in a tree. Their tree was once a Great Spirit, served as The Tree of Life, a moral compass to purposeful existence, which was worshiped for being part of the Great Chain of Life connecting all matter forms together, and helped celebrate life's meanings. They also possessed the intuition of, but no empirical means by which to prove, the reality that a tree fits the form, substance, and style that epitomizes the essence of life itself because it provides oxygen for all of us to breathe and to exist. We know this but we never recall this most basic purpose and function of a tree.

The swastika symbol contains another divergence of perceptual thought. The modern mind fixates on the meaning we know from 20$^{th}$-century Nazi Germany; Nam and Muh's meaning was quintessentially diametrically opposed. Ancient Hinduism, Jainism, Persia, the Norse, and all other universal ancestral traditions, adopted this circular-shaped motif as generally a good luck or energy symbol (Davis 2000; Mundorf and Chen 2006).

We still use animals, fish and plants in food, healing, aesthetics, and escape cults. Many, if not all, of these utilizations are basally hard-wired into our brain biology. No known alternatives to the food-and-healing demands placed upon them for our species' survival exist. This rigid set of requisites appears to be similarly established, in our mindful search for other life in the Universe, as the untrustworthy perception-cognition mechanism to have become the design basis of virtually all empirical search strategies. Their use of plant-based chemical substances for mind-altering purposes held more profound spiritual and cosmic meaning through shamanistic use that differs from today's preselection for recreational and psychosomatic uses.

While we cannot yet institute an enduring practice of economic power and control to outer space activities, our minds have not wasted time envisioning its financial potential, to the criticism that we have not yet rigidly considered any of the design, operational, and management factors inherent in making reality of such a monumental undertaking. Our ancestors did not think of the cosmos, planets, and asteroids as commodities to be exploited. They did not need these resources, as from their perspective in these areas the living world gave them all that they needed. The skyscape contained the forces of life, healing and eschatological eternity, and it talked with, instructed and appealed to them through a consciousness holistic connection and through their "writing in the stars". They were inspired and stimulated by the celestial skyscape as a compulsion to communicate with the gods and spirits through their rituals, semiotic ideography, and later linguistic semiotics. A new level to Maslow's Needs Hierarchy Model and reallocation of some conceptual information may be needed to accommodate both a cosmic needs dimension and a more synchronous cultural meaning.

Archetypes of fear and stress have not disappeared with our newest Revolutions of knowledge and technology. They have just shifted causes, cessation strategies, and resolutions. Cohorts to these maladies include denial and tension.

Life was and is hard. While stress and tension serve as applied forces to the body, as their triggers, fear and denial are known as defense mechanisms of the mind, biological tools to give instructions in lessening the underlying malady. As part of our baggage as social creatures, all humankind suffered and healed from all these maladies and resolutions, respectively. The causes were more Maslow-based for our ancestors: questionable access to food, shelter, health, and security. When today came, these causes were not entirely extinguished but to which were added the fears and stresses of knowledge and technology. I noted that knowledge is power, and that technology can deliver that knowledge better as innovation is allowed to interface. Does this point to a reason why that, with the proliferation of the digital ether, people are drawn to triggers of stress and tension as attitude cues that magnetize them to digital use behaviors, or by mind-altering chemicals? Both serve as stress-relief mechanisms that also cause them to disconnect, dissocialize, and escape from the difficulties of real life and to escape into the world of the hard drive and virtual reality to avoid this difficulty.

With the ability to obtain more things today at a faster pace than ever before arose the personal dictate cultist behavior of immediate gratification and want. Some argue the immediate gratification syndrome of modern attitude-behavior is pejorative and excessively competitive in its axis of influence. This is evidenced by the reflection upon many examples from everyday life behaviors. For example, the obsessive rush to rise and deboard a landing airplane while it is still moving on the runway, or the compulsive rush into a parking lot traffic jam upon leaving a crowded group meeting venue are identical behavior anchors of this trait. Or the omnipresent attitude-behavior episode of unloading the contents of a grocery cart onto the checkout belt while there are still two or three orders ahead of the shopper on the same belt and many minutes before his or her order can even be tended, are all examples of immediate gratification with deleterious effects on our individual psyches. Life today is full of these situational mimetics.

Grave robbing, as a proxy for thievery behavior, was known to exist from our earliest recorded history. The Code of Hammurabi served as an ethos to discourage and punish the crime of theft for the Sumerian and Akkadian civilizations. The Egyptian larceny economy behavior is another well-documented subject that was a main reason a revolutionary change in the funerary and burial institutions occurred. This resulted in the extinguishment of pyramid-building and the creation of the Valley of the Kings and Queens for reasons of sociocultural security (and security of the power elite). These same behavior regimes exist universally today, the provenance of which could trace back through to the competitive landscape of earlier Neolithic environments. This creation story was born in their minds when society was getting used to life in the sociology and conceptual frameworks of property ownership, and trading of commodities and resources for extrinsic value. It was an attitude-behavior development that created an imbalance between the haves and have-nots of a community (a power and control motif), and between an individual's haves and have-nots (a trigger for force and tension attitude cues causing an activation of fear and denial strategy tools).

I touched upon how the meaning and scope of the agrios are different today. The most acute aspect of these changes is, in recalling an earlier quote stating, "the control of the wild is a metaphor and mechanism for the control of society" (Hodder 1990, 12). I suggest that the agrios have absorbed ecological fear and stress through the recent popular phenomenon known as climate change. The global "sphere of influence" among prehistory societies was small when contrasted with the landscape of today's meta-web of global interactive entanglement. They were as social as we are, in their own smaller worldscapes, without the meta-influences of global interaction involvement magnified by our progressive ease-of-accessibility to communicate and interface with each other. Global climate change is only one example of the many ways global entanglement has both benefited and hurt the many autonomous cultures that now exist. Even as natural climate change existed in all ancient histories as a foundational challenge factor to our ancestors' survival and evolution, we have developed the apparatus to intelligently influence climate, as a proxy for the agrios, with mostly deleterious outcomes at accelerated velocities.

*＊＊*

We can recognize that the homeostasis of our species today is truly a global web of entanglement. Along the dimensions of life today exists the same duality of opportunity and challenge as has existed for tens of thousands of years. You know what ontology was to our ancestors. Their fabric of ontology was a tapestry cross-stitched with a vividly eschatological cosmic and agrios perspective. Both realms possessed profundity of destiny and soul.

## ACT III: UNIVERSALS

The minds knew that the agrios (living world) and the cosmos (skyscape) operated under a code of all-inclusive consciousness that connected them both in-the-moment and across time and space with all other life: life that surrounded them, came from them, came to them, preceded them and were now in eternal life.

I have forwarded, thus far, a theory of how it became a web of entanglement. When we include these perceptions of things as agents toward a worldview of us, a glaring omission becomes transparent. I have sparingly hinted at the nature of this omission. The concept of agrios has been a recurring theme throughout. Today's "2.0" version it is different and more expansive than it was in the before time. If our ancestors possessed the requisite technology, they also could have included the celestial skyscape as part of their agrios. They were mindful of its importance, but they could not physically touch it. So, they improvised a way to touch it and connect with it through their minds. Maybe they had more intuition, empirical understanding, or help about grasping the equivalence of physically touching the skyscape through their minds than we want to give them credit for. The sum of these thoughts is that we were shown their worldviews about the agrios and the skyscape.

Our contemporary global worldview of the framework and the interconnection between the living world and the cosmic agrios is underdeveloped. Does it require a global perspective and motivation for us to begin a cosmic awareness? Will reflection upon these situations create new attitudes and cue a new reflection on the state of our cultural and sociological morale as intelligent living creatures? Could concerted learning, adoption and adaptation of the Overview Effect also cue an emphasis on a desire to absorb the Universe's natural connections of consciousness? Would dissemination of an updated Maslow's Needs Hierarchy model effectually help us discover new insight and understanding of the state of Us?

The cosmos could be part of our new agrios. There is an ontological logic to this state of our human condition - an existential eventuality. As the late Carl Sagan suggested, "The cosmos is within us. We are made of star-stuff. We are a way for the universe to know itself" (Sagan 1980). We know our ancestors knew this. We are obviously more intelligent than they were on the sheer weight of our advanced knowledge and technological intelligence. When we see the Earth from the Overview Effect perspective, and that of the iconic *Earthrise* imagery from the Apollo 8 astronaut lunar mission, our minds begin to form new meaning around this terrestrial agrios. We also know that when the astronauts turned their heads and cameras in the opposite direction, they saw a great extension of the cosmic version. These are the ties that bind all of humankind together - Us, Them, all other life, and all their multi-dimensional, vibrational, conscious interconnectedness.

Are we alone in the Universe? Up to now I have used 'them' in reference to our ancestors. As the last of the data points in the Cultural Perceptions of Things, logical and empirical accommodation irrefutably must be made for a detailed inspection on this question. The short answer is, yes.' 'Life' consists of us and the millions of other biologically diverse examples that have been known to us throughout the fourth dimension of time. Nature's supreme ability to enable so many different forms which are open to our inspection is one of numerous proofs of reality that are contained in an anecdotal *Akashic Record*, that ontological library of all knowledge that is contained in the Universe.

Another construct of nature, the form of mathematical inference used in the *anthropic principle*, delivers more proof to the physically real examples of diverse life forms. Probability mathematics tells us that, yes, these life forms should exist; and because they do, the argument is resolved. A logical extension to the anthropic principle delivers still more support to the notion that, because uncountable numbers of other planets exist that could be called home to other life forms, that mathematical inference determines that other life **does** exist.

The $T_3$ variable of "who we could be" must be added to the $T_1$ and $T_2$ variables of "who we were" and "who we are" in My Algorithm of Humankind as consideration to those eventualities of the human condition with which we may have to come to terms. If 'who we could be' means venturing into the vast knowledge base that exists outside our planet's atmosphere, we have a rather large learning curve before us; a type of existential 'Great Filter'

## ACT III: UNIVERSALS

whose barriers exist in both the physical and cognitive realms. Both offer imposing barriers to transit. We are in the infancy of knowledge acquisition regarding the physical barriers. The cognitive barriers pose, in my view, a greater challenge.

In the context of the vast universal skyscape beyond our atmosphere, our cognitive worldview has become infected by a fear and a stress of acknowledgment, accommodation, and lack of planning for the possibility that the many accounts of observation and interaction with physical and anthropomorphic phenomena – both historical and contemporary – are, in fact, perpetrated by other life beings. How are these fears and stresses made to exist? Many factors are in play.

First, from the inability to correctly explain these situations and conditions to the satisfaction of some intellectual methodologies, our explanatory techniques when using some of these methodologies are like a proverbial "fitting of a round peg into a square hole." Our ancestors would have better appreciated a reversal of the geometry, in that, because they gave sacral adornment to the circle geometry, that "fitting a square peg into a round hole" would ring more intuitive and intelligent to them. Modern humankind is either not aware of or has lost this perception in translation.

Another reason why some of the methodologies are incorrect is because they try to explain observation scenarios that are not as much associated with purely physical events made possible by purely physical phenomena in nature as opposed to those events whose initiations and trajectories are conducted and influenced by intelligent beings within those physical environments. Think here of the classic unidentified aerial phenomena and the intelligent beings who pilot them.

Third, when we consider only the knowledge that is made available to us in academic, informational or practical settings throughout our lives, maybe our species does not know nearly enough about these subjects to eliminate the possibility of having the label of ignorance place on us.

Fourth, when considering the existence of extraterrestrial intelligence (ETI) do we suffer from the same barriers to knowledge, denial, fear, stress, and tension, orchestrated by social engineering strategies of our modern version of the power elite, that our ancestors did? Are some of those non-believers constrained in their acknowledgments by peer pressures, biases, restrained and handcuffed by the methodological and authoritative sources of their personal fiscal pursuits?

The landscape of denying extraterrestrial intelligence contexts is populated by the rhetorical argument that everything has a natural explanation; often fallaciously. So often is the case that the human mind, as a proxy for intelligence, can manipulate, using physical objects or phenomena, some event situations so that they appear to occur naturally. If a person throws a rock, it is not the rock that is throwing itself. If an airplane flies over your head, it is caused by an intelligent intervention; nature did not build the plane and flew it over your head. Similarly, if aerial objects that cannot be identified fly over your head or land on the ground to where physical remains are left for inspection, it cannot be explained away that nature caused the entire sequence of events in every case situation. There is a life form influence of intellect on all these examples. And there have been millions of documented events throughout our history. Too many are prone to dismiss, in an off-handed way, both the credibility of every single witness and the natural mathematical inferences that argue against any such conclusion.

It is with these premises that we move forward into a deeper inspection of 'who we could be'.

*References*

Allen, Robert C. 2024. "The Neolithic Revolution in the Middle East. *The Economic History Review"* 77 (4): 1154-1196.
  Davis, B.L. 2000. *Flags of the Third Reich.* Oxford UK: Osprey Publishing.
  Dunbar, R. I. M. 1998. "The Social Brain Hypothesis." *Evolutionary Anthropology* 6 (5): 178-190.
  Dunbar, R. I. M. 2009. The Social Brain Hypothesis and Its Implications for Social Evolution. *Annals of Human Biology* 36 (5): 562-572.

Dunbar, R. I. M. 2024. "Structural and Cognitive Mechanisms of Group Cohesion in Primates." *Behavioral and Brain Sciences* (in press). https://doi.org/10.1017/S0140525X2400030X.

Fibiger, Linda, Torbjörn Ahlström, Christian Mayer, and Martin Smith. 2023. "Conflict, Violence, and Warfare among Early Farmers in Northwestern Europe." In *Anthropology*, edited by Clark Larsen, vol. 120, no. 4, 1–9.

Hodder, Ian. 1990. *The Domestication of Europe*. 1st ed. Oxford: Wiley-Blackwell.

Mundorf, Joanne, and Guo-Ming Chen. 2006. "Transculturation of Visual Signs: A Case Analysis of the Swastika." *Intercultural Communication Studies* 15 (2): 33–47.

Sagan, Carl. 1980. *Cosmos*. Arlington VA: Public Broadcasting Service.

Shavit, A., and G. Sharon. 2023. "Can Models of Evolutionary Transition Clarify the Debates over the Neolithic Revolution?" *Philosophical Transactions of the Royal Society B* 378: 20210413. https://doi.org/10.1098/rstb.2021.0413.

Stepanova, Ekaterina R., Denise Quesnel, and Bernhard E. Riecke. 2019. "Understanding AWE: Can a Virtual Journey, Inspired by the Overview Effect, Lead to an Increased Sense of Interconnectedness?" *Frontiers in Digital Humanities* 6:9. https://doi.org/10.3389/fdigh.2019.00009.

White, Frank. 2023. 4th ed. CA.: Multiverse Media Inc.

Wright, Katherine I. 2014. "Domestication and Inequality? Households, Corporate Groups and Food Processing Tools at Neolithic Çatalhöyük." *Journal of Anthropological Archaeology* 33: 1-33.

# EXTRATERRESTRIAL

*We are all one. Only egos, beliefs, and fears separate us.*

-Nikola Tesla

*Keywords: Conflict resolution, inference by analogy, magic of life, fear factor, anthropocentrism, acceptance by analog, Akasha.*

Are we them and are they us?

Sharing my work has introduced you to many ways we became the product of our ancestors, from practical to spiritual and mythological. Through shared anatomy, evolutionary track, sociocultural growth, and a few millennial's accumulation of incremental knowledge expansion, we found and grew an empirical intelligence that helped immensely toward becoming conscious of many of nature's processes. Consequently, only very recently did we acquire a level of awareness about applying the discipline of empirical thought to universal laws. We are still in our infancy understanding the implications of anthropic matters that govern life within this set of laws, and a ubiquitous consciousness and understanding of the total set of these laws is very far off in the future. Still, ancestral traditions paved a vital road for us thousands of years ago by imagining blueprints for such monumental proto humanisms as a Great Chain of Being, Tree/Flower of Life, an eschatology of the soul, an afterlife, and other ethnocentric life compasses. Introduction to empirical thought came later and is still in the developmental process.

Who are you? Where did you come from? Did you have help in becoming you? What future will engage and shape your awareness and human condition? As we look at the anthropic nature of our lives in the Universe and the human condition, can our minds accommodate an existence of life forms outside the Earth's eco-structure? Despite our current reflections upon The Great Chain of Being, all other things esoteric and the expressed anecdotal prerequisites for it to exist, our recent activities in seeking other life forms are proof that these features are part of our awareness.

Our brains are hard-wired to detect patterns in the phenomena we observe, then assign conditions of normalcy to them. This process goes far to explain an individual's mental lack of elasticity toward accepting new interpretations and existences. The methodology for the scientist, researcher and forensic investigator is an intricate one in which answers to their questions often take a long time to determine. This is due, in part, to the systemic nature of their methodological investigation set. When looking for other life forms, the only pattern their professional minds are permitted to understand is the one that matches biological life on Earth and its unique cocktail of ingredients. That pattern necessitates precise amounts of oxygen, water, temperature, and pressure to enable reality. But is this form of conscious reality only accepted to serve as a catharsis to our anthropocentrism?

With this body of knowledge, intuition, and self-imposed criteria, however rigid and unadaptable, some state, at least publicly, that we are alone in the Universe. Our minds are inescapably shaped by biology, ecological life experience, sociocultural and intellectual training; the attitudes and behaviors, perceptions and cognitive intelligence that uniquely define each of us and how open we are to considering new ones that we encounter. Our willingness to consider such potential gives existence to a closed-minded or open-minded approach to perception and cognition. It is ubiquitous, however, that none of us consider, or can consider, every possible perspective when inspecting the efficacy of any idea as expansive as existence of other life. A thought experiment may help us here. Maybe the question of "are we alone" in the Universe could be posed to an artificial intelligence platform for examination of any conclusions it may derive. Or we can consider a multidisciplinary approach to the question; a sharing of open-minded inputs whose results would be greater than the sum of its parts.

Ancient man did not possess our intelligence as they were too busy adding to that book of knowledge for us to exploit today. Those older minds, because of their ignorance, were often overpowered by many manifestations of their environments, particularly of the cosmic above world. The cosmos was awe-inspiring, magnificent, overwhelming, unexplainable, and entirely physically unreachable except in their abstract minds.

As I noted earlier, it was the perception of these non-material objects which they could not physically feel, touch, approach, or interact with that motivated their embodiment of a mythological framework for a psychological resolution or cathartic response to the situation. Without the ability to touch and feel, and to only be able to see and reason its features and purpose, they were left with making meaning of the sky world only through their eyes and minds. The result was a workable cosmic relationship in which humans, animals, and all other organic and inorganic matter participated.

This ordered structure worked because the human brain became wired to detect patterns and a cyclic nature to environmental phenomena. Another dimension came from our hard-wired perception to award who or what they physically had to look up, to observe as being more powerful; a superpower or a being that sometimes became deified. Additional support comes from the reality that extraterrestrial intelligence would come from above the observer, down to their location in an interaction. When all these factors and emotions combine to manifest this cosmic perception, it is not surprising that ancient humans reacted the way they did.

Our ancestors witnessed incidents whose circumstances and features broke this observational methodology. In response, their critical thinking assembled a religiosity of gods and deities. Beings appearing from the skyscape, which demonstrated acts of a fantastic or otherwise impossible nature for their reasoned intellects, was potentially such a circumstance. Ancestral knowledge was insufficient to reconcile what was happening within their level of ordered analysis. The power these beings demonstrated was beyond human control, so the concept of superpower deification was mindfully assigned. This mindset applied regardless of whether these super powers were the result of chemical interference, reached from a trans dimensional phenomenon, or real in-the-moment physical visitations. Our ancestors could have seen the attributes of all these metaphors and manifestations as real-time events in the stars, in ET visitations, or both.

\* \* \*

Do we function as individuals and as groups, in a preoccupation of tension, stress, fear, and denial?

A historical compare-and-contrast exercise to these four dimensions of *conflict resolution* inquiry would reveal these factors. Our psychological makeup, key to this analysis, anatomically aligns with that of our forefathers, as taken from their external material and symbolic communication histories. Perception and cognitive intelligence data would suggest obvious differences due to the proliferation of attained knowledge, the creation of new meaning, and the other ecological, reproductive development, environmental, social, and cultural changes that time would have allowed to occur for our benefit. Our conflict resolution will be different given the above circumstances.

If you agree that tension, stress, fear, and denial are emotions whose thought pathways drive attitude cues from the brain's basal, instinctive and limbic behavior systems through its executive prefrontal complex to process behaviors, then we are them and they are us. Stress, tension, and fear are attitude cues. Their proof comes from the brain's interpretation of environmental stimuli that serves as triggers to defense mechanisms, such as denial. Denial is known to us as a psychological <u>tool</u> of behavior as a defense mechanism, with overtones of emotion. Denial is activated from many sources; from situations involving other people, only the individual as a function or situation of self, or from outside environmental cues that create the resultant emotion and behavior decision. Our ancestors continuously encountered these scenarios throughout their lives; they also possessed this tool even before the changes of the Neolithic social Revolutions. Because we live in such a culture, this explanation is congruent with what our ancient elders experienced.

Even after commencement of those changes from the Paleolithic life of hunter gatherers, the Neolithic cultures maintained their mnemonic intelligence of nature's power and control over them as known by their ancestors. But now, a new dimension of power structures has come into practice. These structures were created by other human beings. The powers of nature were always reasoned to be overwhelming to the indigenous, but now an additional, formidable and overwhelming but now human administrator of social power and control eventually began to assert itself as expressed in the semiotics of primeval cultures.

For both animal and human power competitors, the animals were still the most formidable in the early times. A cult of social cooperation aligned with the human adversary in the early Revolutions to gradually wrestle power and control away from the agrios, assisted by increasing knowledge intelligences of technological, historical, labor, and social matters. A new, more totalitarian social culture slowly developed from these changes in the dynamics of growing tribal size, acclimation into structured communities that offered more opportunities to acquire and demonstrate power and control authority over others and their environments. These changes fertilized a new era of stress, tension, fear, and denial.

Extraterrestrial intelligence is contemporarily studied from polarizing lenses of inquiry. Popular culture is entertained by and expresses all these emotional sets, sometimes to an extreme by some members who maintain a cultist religiosity of the subject. Philosophers and normative thinkers reflect upon the acknowledged existence. The descriptive thinkers of the science communities seek data. Governmental authorities, who fiscally control the preceding two communities and try to dissuade the public, envision power and control opportunities and requisites for social engineering policy. Theology, as the oldest argued cohort to a documented interface with ET on any level, has been placed into a classification of the supernatural or paranormal, but the only one that effectively considers an eschatology of the divine through the lens of the soul. The features that bind any analysis of these institutions are that they represent but a small parochial subset of humans and the cathartic potential to appease their anthropocentrism via stress, fear and denial reductions strategies that belie an undeniable hard-wired involvement of the human communities in the search for discovery and meaning in other life forms. Each of these events will be a Copernican Revolution in their own right.

Every person possesses all the cognitive features of the human brain meta system, including all that you have presently studied. The quest for ultimate truth is ubiquitously challenged by an adversarial eventuality of personal bias into any discussion, especially one as emotionally charged as the imagineering of other intelligent life. This circumstance is always real irrespective of the level of training to the contrary.

Imagine a dartboard. When a dart, here known as a research statement, hypothesis or theory, is thrown, it lands somewhere around a bullseye. When more darts are thrown by others, ultimate truth of the argument is neared, but always knowing that a better bullseye can and will be thrown. This has been the human condition and our accumulation of knowledge since prehistoric times. So, it takes time to achieve an ultimate truth about a matter under discussion. We all possess the same physiological and psychological mechanisms that influence this journey. When reflecting upon the weighted argument of intelligent life from outside Earth, professional, situational, and emotional biases will factor into the discussion. Our sociology and psychology are the ultimate core essences of our attitude and behavioral minds as individuals. Our type, level and skill set of educational or professional training is just one influential commingled element of the larger analytic superstructure, as are the situational circumstances.

Emotional biases are inherently involved in an ETI situation, and consist of the aforementioned stress, tension, fear, and denial cues and defense mechanisms. Consider this experiment. We know that if power and control were prevented or taken from us in a scenario, our minds would compel attitude cues of stress, tension, and fear that drive a situational response. Common reaction to this scenario involving extraterrestrials is ubiquitously energetic and maybe not hyperbolic.

Some humans respond vulnerably to their stresses, tensions, and fears. This characteristic has driven a wide range of emotional responses about ET from unequivocal acknowledgment to irrational denial, perhaps a revealing diagnosis to the importance of the topic on our minds. ET represents an unknown quantity in many dimensions. For one, the unknown aspect itself results in a stress-inducing mindset. Other life forms contain an unpredictable nature to their actions and activities that make interpretation, analysis, strategy, and response mechanisms harder to establish in our minds. Other intelligent life forms possess the capacity for independent thought and can control their movements, activities, and often the immediate environment to guide their actions in a variety of ways. A wide range of attitudes, intentions, and behaviors await development of a decision tree by the human observer.

Not everyone yet acknowledges a reality that ET may have interacted with our ancestors. Earlier I suggested that ET could have been a form of superpower that they rationalized through a cult of spiritual ethnocentricity. I maintain that the creation of religiosity was influenced by this process and was itself so pervasive to our mind's psyche that it transformed our human nature. The diverse range of reactions we, as individuals and groups, impose upon resolution of the argument are activated by all these cues and mechanisms.

This landscape is different from describing an observational activity of an object in nature without the intelligent intervention of life forms. Say, for example, watching a large rock fall from a high ridge down toward you with no influence from another life form. The range of physical outcomes in this scenario then is limited primarily by the effects of gravity and weather phenomena. There is less uncertainty and, hence, less stress and tension toward potential negative consequences for you. Consequently, you would develop a less stressful strategy to interface with the situation given the conditions and information than if it were a living being coming toward you either carrying a rock or influencing its trajectory. The stress, tension and fear are higher because of the uncertainty of what that intelligent life form is going to do. The being's ability to use their intelligence to influence the situation is an abstract x-factor that would drive a more complex and difficult response process. Control is of importance here, or the incapacity by the human observer to resolve stress, tension and fear. The attitude cues, and resultant cognitive behaviors are more problematic to conflict resolution of stress, tension, and fear reduction.

For others, maybe a jocular reaction to ET stories by some in popular culture is a catharsis to a deeper fear of a suspected or speculative malevolent reality that ET may represent in our minds. There may be a level of peripheral operant conditioning going on with the exposure of a seemingly omnipresent motif of non-seriousness presented from all the mass media one is exposed to continuously in this digital age of uncommon immediacy. I should point out that there will not be one single symptom, diagnosis and treatment pathway available to reconcile this situation, for all of us are afflicted, affected and react in different ways. A most beneficial way to proceed is for me to provide information and data in an advisory capacity and inspect the inputs and throughputs from different positions. It is not about who is or of being right or wrong-it's about what is real. Adopting and adapting to changes that make our civilization better.

* * *

Does the public think of ETI as an apex predator? Is our mind motivated and conditioned by what we have and have not seen or talked about the subject?

Contemporary dissenters of non-terrestrial intelligence rely predominately on an *inference by analogy*. Our ancestral kin would have presumed

ETI to be godlike when they were encountered. Indeed, much illustrated symbolism from cave art, glyphs, and other external material objects serve as references that depict life forms which are not entirely human in form, substance and/or style. Their functionality would have compelled creation of a magical spirits cult within a meta structure of a mythology-based human condition.

All expressions of the cosmic superstructure mindset are reasoned away by those dissenters as shamanistic and entoptic episodes consisting primarily of opinion-based rhetoric. The set of resolutions is incomplete without consideration of the following. For one, the mythological element of human nature involved proliferation of the power and control strategy implemented by totalitarian authorities of the time, as you have learned. Secondly, there is the consideration of another option with potential explanatory appeal, some of which is ETI. Then, if some reference targets contain evidence-based attributes to a known ritual activity, two questions can be asked of the investigation.

The first question, is the evidence being interpreted correctly? Second, if some examples of illustrated evidence can be correctly traced to such practices, is it correct, valid, and credible to autocratically infer this argument to all illustrated examples? Those who wish to structure their conclusions using this analogistic argument of behavior manifestation cannot dismiss any of the other correlations of attitude, behavior, perception, cognition, character traits, and all other psychologies of the individual and of social cultures through our species' history.

There was undoubtedly a profound preoccupation with superpowers whose manifestations were entirely uncontrollable by ancient traditions. The first three conflict resolution strategies of stress, tension, and fear reduction were among the most monumental intellectual achievements for them. The 'supernatural' was its own field of study and practice that dealt with the *magic of life*. The newly adorned power elite cult assumed responsibility for dealing with this anthropic force of nature, and given the existing foundational cultural framework, was naturally selected to develop in the way it did.

When considering ET today, the methodologies of the science and investigative institutions clash with the public community. The methodology of empiricism, an indispensable institution of human thought, demands a physical capability for observation, experimentation, and physical testability. This system of practice did not formally exist 12,000 years ago. Empirical inquiry of this type, beyond the intuition-based proto-empiricism, is constrained by the three-dimensional constraint to nature. Its practice can support the existence of a particular phenomenon, but it cannot argue its absence with true certainty. Practitioners are financially compensated according to these directives - typically from government fiscal sources.

Inherent within this environment is the forced adherence to policy governance by the compensating authority. Practically speaking, if a researcher cannot gain a reasonable compensatory outcome for his or her time and effort, he will not officially pursue the research matter at all. The opinions one hears from those who comment are not from reasoned inquiries and investigations but serve often to prevent a 'professional suicide' amongst their peers and institutions. Additionally, if the practitioner is compelled by a compensatory authority to not pursue that research thread, the authority will ensure that their demands are met.

Some disciplines, such as astronomy, can only see and mindfully deduce, from other known physical laws, reasons for the existence of cosmic phenomena. We still cannot touch much of the sky world. When new discoveries are made that knowledge replaces older versions; and the new ones are soon replaced by newer ones. This book of knowledge will be rewritten uncountable times in the future. This is true of the cosmic professions as well as all human institutions of thought. We understand little about the Universe. The research and popular literature are filled with paid publications full of incomplete inquiry, wonder, opinion, and inference. But, in these ways, if astronomers can only see and reason new knowledge in abstract ways, why cannot ET study contain the same parameters and potentials for study, learning and knowledge.

What can be learned from a review and shift in thinking about these methodologies? If acceptable study prerequisites include observation, experimentation, and physical testability criteria, the observation qualification of the ET phenomenon has already been met by the cataloged reports from millions of such witnesses through recorded history and before. This form of methodology has been vetted and is valid and credible - vital prerequisites of inquiry and study in practice from other disciplines of knowledge and study.

Considering the experimentation criteria, one must tread carefully in trying to comingle observation and experimentation activities in situations such as this. Coaxing another intelligent non-earth being into observation or experimentation cannot be forced by making them appear as opposed to performing a hands-on experiment such as mixing chemicals in a laboratory and witnessing the mixture's reaction or testing an otherwise accessible object for such consideration. In proving existence and appearance, the testability requirement must always accommodate visual observation, measured data, and their analysis and comparison with other data sets. This is how all hypotheses and theories about nature are validated. The data is collected from experiments and observations, then analyzed, compared, and inferences made from this experimentation and analysis. Observation of a being is data, as is the measurement and comparison of artifact data in an analysis.

Because of this point, the physical testability qualification of ETI investigation has also been logically and definitively met by a similarly large sample set of reported physical trace materials, measured data and experience. For some, physically touching an alien cannot be quantitively tested; its proof relies on either visual and/or peripheral artifact data, such as fingerprints left on the witness, measurements of abnormal radioactive residue, or other chemical, metallurgic, and physical matter artifacts left at the scene of the encounter.

Fiscal dimensions must also be considered in these discussions. If a researcher is not "paid to play" his community's politics may provide additional barriers to entry for them. Financial awards are the single most motivational attitude cue in most of the human endeavor intelligence. Concerning financial incentives for research activities, it's also up to the authority to either encourage or discourage motivation to an undertaking of such projects. This attitude cue set is a major influence on the behavior dimension in the ETI area of research for many practitioners in the science communities.

For example, the governmental strategy and behavior of discouraging researchers and witnesses is imposed on those with UAP sightings or encounters. It is the equivalent process in matters of espionage, military, surveillance, or those in the political interest. This should come as no surprise that the social engineering doctrine is in full force and effect in all areas. UFOs and UAPs are public attitude cues taken from the governments' actions or inactions, whose behaviors are another universal characteristic between our elders and ourselves.

Power and control with an ET interface are universally observed within an attitude-behavior theme of stress, fear, uncertainty, temporary inferiority, a social rallying motivation, and pure entertainment, among others. These mechanisms are ignited and solicited as such by all commercial and profit-motivated institutions, not limited to any form of media, and any governmental authority. Scripts written for any of these commercial scenarios wish to have humans portrayed as being victorious as an endpoint - a crescendo peak after progressing a storyline challenge of profound stress, fear, uncertainty, and inferiority.

An institutional authority embodies a more complex behavioral dynamic. Their behavior takes on a character that borrows from the "fight or flight" concept experienced by an individual. This identifies as a situation whereas stress, tension, and fear are present, and can exist for an individual or in a group setting. If this attitude cue is present, a "fight or flight" attitude and behavior strategy is undertaken.

I propose, however, that another dimension to this well-known trait exists. In an "ignore" or "hide" dimension, this concept would now read, "fight, flight or ignore/hide." All people individually practice this behavior in their lives, typically, in medical health situations. In the context of both individual or group processes, if one cannot, or does not wish to fight, then he can either "flight", or if this option is not available, ignore or hide from the situation. In the context of government or other communal level involvements, hiding reality from others is a well-adopted reality of group human behavior, as a maintenance of a power and control regime, as a strategy to prevent other governments from obtaining dangerous technologies of a similar nature, as well as for other reasons.

In the UAP/ET realm, the authority's power and control politic is behaviorally driven like a similar regime from ancient societies, regarding this ignore or hide dimension. So as not to lose a significant measure of power and control, the authority can choose to enact policies that encourage ignoring or hiding (read 'covering up' in today's popular culture) realities from its' governing public. There can exist a deleterious tipping point away from total control if the unknown and fear-driving attitude cues of such denial and ignoring policies continue unabated or without resolution of those concerning behaviors. A popular explanation for a sociopolitical authority not pursuing a particular matter of national importance is, to paraphrase, "because it (the scenario) does not pose a threat to national security".

What incentives would the government have in the concealment of information and knowledge to the presence of extraterrestrial beings on planet Earth? One incentive could be maintenance of the power and control authority that they possess over society. There are other incentives to consider. World governments have a lengthy track record of explanations that conclude society could not psychologically handle or accommodate acknowledgment that other intelligent life forms exist, relying on the *fear factor* as support for their conclusion. This plays into the human psyche of fear and the unknown that is hard-wired into our nature. This thought experiment could be transposed into an inspection of the authority to hypothesize that they also cannot provide a satisfactory explanation to this situation as a reason for their behaviors.

In the future, as presumably occurred in the present and recent past, governments will participate in self-designed experiments to test societies' reactions to anomalous phenomenon of potentially similar natures that could and do test their collective psyche over such matters. Alternatively, this fear factor rests within the psyche of the authoritative body. The authority, in this situation, perceives itself as powerless and cannot be in control of the activities of the 'adversary' that is the ETI.

Another possible incentive supports a speculation that governmental authority has already established a relationship with an ETI. Perhaps human authority has been compelled by an outside force to employ a concealment strategy from society. In this case, the ETI has instructed the government to keep this relationship a secret.

Attempts at an explanation in these matters by a defense of authority strategy have persisted for a long time. Another popular use of inference by analogy opinion has been to accuse a government of 'not being capable of concealing information or keeping secrets and cite examples, usually of a social gossip rhetorical nature. All these strategies are logically flawed but whose indictment comes from the fact that we are all human and whose characteristic traits are universal in our nature and human conditions. We all share the biological propensity to use the denial defense mechanism when we judge it to be a 'best fit' strategy.

This said, we come to the fourth dimension of conflict resolution; the strategy of a denial defense mechanism. I infer that denial is another universal behavior in both individual and social group environments. Typically, what the initiator hopes to gain from a position of denial is that the recipient follows another attitude-behavior pathway leading to an end to the situation.

Initiators of a denial position, however, ignore their myopic tendencies in the ETI matter and fail to recognize the entanglement into which their positions are cast. The situational landscape of the ETI subject is too large, dynamic, active, persistent, full of unknowns and uncertainties, and contains too large a universe of evidence, inquiry and study for denial to work in the long term. However, some institutions were compelled to initiate or adapt to a platform of denial as their defense mechanism of choice.

Another strategy of human thought whose usage influences arguments over a topic of an esoteric epistemology is embodied within a 'pseudo' context. The ruling authority, often professional institutions, its peers and cohorts, will initially reject and deny a new theory as false, fake, or of trying to be - a pseudo theory. Studies of the psychology of group behavior in professional communities extensively support this conclusion to the following points. The twentieth century philosopher Thomas Kuhn wrote that "anomalies are observations that do not fit the existing paradigm and can eventually lead to a crisis and a scientific revolution" (Kuhn 1962). A community operates within a paradigm of 'status quo' until a theory of a revolutionary nature is proposed. The community will initially reject the theory, sometimes for many years. Often and eventually, though, the new theory is accepted, and the paradigm of the community settles back into a new paradigm routine.

Consider these historical statements and conclusions about natural phenomena defended as pseudo-science by the collective minds of their day. "The Earth is flat", "The Earth is the center of the Universe; all other planets and the Sun circled the Earth", "Man will never fly", "Man could not go to the Moon", "Natural selection cannot exist", "Life traits are not passed through gene transmission to offspring", "Craters could not have been caused by meteors", "The Earth's land masses do not move", "No other star systems contain orbiting planetary bodies." The cultural classification assigned to efforts that motivated the dissenting arguments was that of 'pseudo-science'. It took many generations of argument and a paradigm upheaval within the respective thought communities for each of these original hypotheses to become true and lawfully recognized, and to be unequivocally accepted by our civilization. But they all eventually attained a resolution of legitimacy.

Another behavioral dimension involving the denial of new and controversial ideas that are not part of the mainstream paradigm of community group think is the susceptibility of its adversaries to engage in prolific debates, often to the extent of personal degradation and harm. In his 1998 book, *Great Feuds in Science: Ten of the Liveliest Disputes Ever,* author Hal Hellman demonstrates that the ongoing nature of human competition over new ideas and their paradigm shifting potentials is as frequent in the professional communities as society at-large and can be viciously administered. Among the indicted include Galileo, Newton, Voltaire, Darwin, Alfred Wegener

(Continental Drift), Lord Kelvin, and Margaret Mead. All professional communities of their time behaved in the same way that we observe today in association with the ET debate.

Those, in summary, who are insistent on denying the existence of extraterrestrial intelligent life are exercising an internal power and control behavior response mechanism. The overarching belief that indulges all these behavioral traits in humans is identified as *anthropocentrism,* defined as, "The consideration of human beings as the most significant entity of the universe" (Merriam-Webster n.d.). This belief may originate from the Revolutions when the wholesale transfer of power and control was wrestled from the agrios of long ago.

The observed dimensions typically come from three anthropic sources; *perceptual, descriptive, and normative.* The perceptual dimension is abstract and contains numerous examples that you have studied in this book. Anyone would like to think that he can do anything to answer any question, solve any problem, or show that they know all the answers. Their intention of overall control is the attitude-behavior directive. An ET existence would mean they cannot, that a power greater than them exists (ET) that possibly possesses more power and can, thus, control more of the situation.

The descriptive dimension embodies the real-world as the incidents that we experience with our own senses in our own time. The normative dimension reflects upon the philosophy that humans should be and therefore "are" superior. Patronization has existed on a human-vs-human anthropocentric behavior dimension when the civilizations of the Revolutions permanently expelled an egalitarian ethos in favor of the new developmental forms of sociocultural behavior.

Many anthropocentric challenges exist in the realm of the extraterrestrial life controversy that stifle a critical thinking process within a descriptive, holistic perspective and an efficacious resolution in an open-minded, unprejudiced cognitive protocol. If how society's groups today react to an emergency can serve as a proxy for an ET reaction, then maybe our society needs help. The mass media over-editorializes, social "media" errs in fundamental accuracy and reality, and an environment of panic often prevails as manifested by these characteristics and the noted conflicts with knowledge and truth as involving authoritative decision-making oversight. These scenarios are hardly unique to our modern society, but their frequency of occurrence makes them feel unprecedented. The protocol may behave as a statistical function of increased population and advanced communication technologies.

One journey through this pathway considers a strategy influenced by benign ramifications to the admission and acknowledgment of any new life forms outside Earth. The psyche of our anthropocentric personality will be least damaged if we discover and acknowledge the existence of microbial life forms. These will (probably) not be a threat to our cognitive intelligence and authority so long as we take precautions toward their study and exposure, as we are aware of the consequences that organic microbes can exert on our lives. Our ancestors, for one reason, did not possess power and control in this context because they were not aware of this knowledge. For this example, the power and control dimension dominate our thought processes.

A second journey encounters many barriers to acceptance and missed opportunities in our quest for new life. The perceived rigidity of pre-requisites for life to exist both effectively and conveniently eliminates many opportunities to find and acknowledge new life and satisfies our inner anthropocentric psyche. The human behavior of *acceptance by analog* pervades this environment. Our only known reality is that life needs oxygen, water, and food to survive. This perception is not knowledge-based but a spurious reality that may be contaminated by inadequate training and, among other factors, constrained by the fiscal limitations of research communities. Do we know enough about life so as not to face the need for expanding our critical thinking to new horizons of observation, analysis, and inference?

Extraterrestrial acknowledgment is not a universal aspect of the human condition as a third challenge and will not become a universal belief for everyone alive today. Some people refuse to accept this reality. As is the case when examining many other situations within the cultural or professional landscape, the sphere of anthropocentrism, whether perceptual, descriptive, or normative, typically appears in the context of a defense mechanism. Other psychological characteristics can be cohorts in this constraint, such as the desire for attention; i.e., the "flat Earth" proponents who cling to their beliefs despite overwhelming contra-indications. This is another proof to the historical existence of the human condition which says that life experiences, educational, professional training, reproductive development, and ecological influences for the self and from the community condition and frame all attitudes and perceptual behaviors. Our ancestral traditions paved these roads for our adoption and practice.

A characteristic shared with the meta nature of the anthropocentrism phenomenon in the ETI realm, that of authoritative involvement, as either a contractual or coercive mechanism, is often used to compel an agent of authority to participate in a policy of dissuasion as a fourth challenge. Debunkers are either hired or pressured by the authority to argue a policy of dissention toward society. These dissenters employ a variety of social behavioral strategies in their argument, the truthfulness or rationality to which is not explored here.

Dissention arguments employ an attitude and behavior cognition to dissuade less-informed members against the argument. Some debunkers, alternatively, are not influenced by the various processes of authoritative involvement, but are influenced by a fiscal one, whereby compensatory benefits become a reality as a rationale for their participation. I introduce the point because the results of this strategy complex are often significant to its intended recipients and have been used as a viable human strategy throughout history and prehistory.

Professional constraints to the extraterrestrial intelligence argument, as a fifth challenge, are not immune to this longevity of human behavior. A member of any such labor body, for as long as their work communities have existed, faces a unique and often complex social behavioral paradigm. I have noted the ubiquitous existence of this social psychology often throughout our discussions. Often undertaken as instruction sets for its constituents, the professional derives his or her beliefs and behaviors from an institutional overseer, and to which I acknowledge that some are allowed or otherwise have taken upon themselves to offer both professional personal opinions in these matters. The professions of academia, the sciences, law, arts and humanities, economics, and the social and sociopolitical communities are constrained by their unique internal political and physical operating paradigms. The behavioral ties that bind this population of decision-making choices are typically fiscally driven.

Another challenge exists to create a universal adaptation to a human, and not just a fractured sociopolitical or other skewed parochial ideology, toward an ETI consciousness. No mindful sentience exists, on a normative philosophical level, to deal with features of what form, substance, and style ETI could take. Empirical justifications to if and what ETI is and could be, therefore, will not be offered by many practitioners until our conscious human nature, beyond popular culture dynamics, is willing and able to acknowledge and accept a logistic pathway for what is desired to learn and know about them. Denying the existence of empirical evidence is also wrong as much as hiding evidence. The monumental importance that integrating a normative and descriptive ETI consciousness into our ethnocentricity and psychology will be a Revolution on the order of what Plato, Aristotle, Buddah, Confucius, Jesus Christ, Mohammed, Copernicus, Galileo, Einstein, Tesla, and Nam and Muh accomplished.

The last journey I will introduce you to is the one that addresses the shortcomings of all the other journeys into the most beneficial blueprint moving forward. A multidisciplinary plan for "the future ET world" addresses all the constraints and barriers to enduring global acknowledgment (EGA) and enduring global relationships (EGR) with those intelligent lives that were, are and will be part of our future. My 2022 title, *The Humaniverse Guide ®: Will ET Talk With Us?* offers a detailed analysis and provides feasibility and proof of concept to the matter of a multidisciplinary plan for ETI discovery, acknowledgment and relationships; the EGA and EGR of our future. Those discussions are synergistic, more detailed, and supportive of this thesis. What I present here is a summary of that detail.

## EXTRATERRESTRIAL

\* \* \*

The Revolutions were a competitive entry point for the Neolithic mind into a new era of complex entanglement. Our adversaries, after the preliminary round against animal and environmental agrios, primarily became ourselves; the Revolution of human thought, as I have proposed. We became comfortable with our statuses and relationships with our animal cohorts, and we learned quickly to adapt and adopt new interfaces with weather, climate, and ecology. The social Revolutions created new challenges of stress, tension, and fear. A complex entanglement of what Hodder (2018) describes as "humans and things" was created, out of necessity, for us to be able to cope with the challenges and drive success of an urbanized existence, labor, external material, and spiritual ideologies. I did not include cosmic ideologies here. This will be addressed next.

"Things" are those material inventions, instruments, devices, social ideologies, institutions, and cults designed to help us better coexist. The development of mindful complex entanglement occurred alongside an expansive universal adoption of symbolism within these external material cultures.

This regime was enabled after the nomadic civilizations of the hunter-gatherer transformed to the sedentary habituation of post-Revolutions living. The path to a complex entanglement of things was laid after potential for the accumulation of material wealth dramatically increased. The growth of these external material cultures partnered with the system of symbolic representation to soon create the abstract metaphorical mind; one where often each of these material cults took on more than one, sometimes many contextual meanings. The appeal of these two cohorts to adopting human cognitive intelligence happened when, as Colin Renfrew suggested, "Human culture became more substantive, more material" (Renfrew 2001, 128). I am proposing that, as we are them and they are us, we can learn a lot from this in charting our future.

Pictured like many contemporary examples in the creation and shelf life of an invention, when a thing is put to widespread use, new challenges, constraints, filters, and questions arise that need to be addressed regarding the productive efficacy of the new thing - both in the short and long-term. New things are created as answers to the old things' questions. A pattern is created where, according to Hodder, "Humans depend on things that are entangled in consequences that draw humans into greater dependence on things" (2018). This web of entanglement expands like a balloon each time more entanglement air enters. The invention may create new efficiency but is negated by new challenges that fail to consider potential constraints and counter productivity that hinders those efficiencies going forward.

In summary, the many ramifications of a thing's life trajectory: good, bad, short-term and long-term, are not mindfully considered in their time of adoption. These results often necessitate the invention of newer things to combat the problems with the older ones, or the fiscally motivated reiteration of a "new and better" thing. This is the homeostasis of a complex inflated balloon entanglement.

Now to address the cosmic ideologies, the cosmic necessity of our human condition. In a classic view, advancement of our human condition is perceived to be a series of iterative material advancements toward an imagined ideal civilization, a relatively ordered universe. Another is thought of as one where it is natural selection that determines the progress of our human condition, a directionless one that exists within an uncontrollable chaotic realm. Whatever position you may take on these viewpoints from recent debate history - order vs. chaos, or the web of entanglement, is present in both. So, the metaphoric balloon itself is a closed system that can grow more volumetric and entangled as more air is introduced into its system. Conversely, it can be made to shrink in comparative complexity by releasing air. Our intelligence: attitude, perception, and cognitive behaviors drive this process.

As society accepted, through time, an exponential growth in the invention of new "things." the natural infiltration of this similarly exponential growth of complexities and entanglements into society have caused a condition of myopia and undue reliance upon these things. Our material exploitation of these things is our contemporary perception of progress. Our inability, or unwillingness, to accept responsibility for not proactively addressing the constraints of these new things to make them more holistically beneficial and practically useful for us, in favor of fiscal potentials is a direct cause of these complexities. Each invention's baggage of undeniable constraints to progress causes a volumetric increase in the size of the entanglement balloon.

If we are to better develop our future human condition in any positive constructive way, we must be able to recognize and plan for dealing with a cosmic entanglement to our existence, that is ETI. ET, and all extraterrestrial life, comes from and is part of the cosmos above and out there. Therefore, by logical extension it is tethered to our existence. It cannot be detached or opined away and must be a de facto part of the discussion.

Our ignorance of the Universe, our lack of knowledge, our stressful, fearful and tense reactions to its encounters and manifestations, and our denial of its existences due to power and control insecurities and strategies both within and between us, presents to us a new level of complexity entanglement. In front of us is situated a great cosmic filter that we first need to acknowledge and then learn how to interact and reconcile this myopic progression of entanglement. Hiding or denying foundational knowledge, in the form of ETI information, makes this development process that much harder. If this strategy remains the case, all segments of humankind will suffer the need to create even more complex coping entanglements, or they will implode. A breakaway society would also succumb to this entangled balloon implosion.

Adapting and adopting to a coexistence with any ET life forms, either directly or from a distance, is a necessary strategy that cannot be argued or ignored. If an ETI is adversarial in nature, and I believe beings in both adversarial and benevolent realms exist, then suppression of or ignorance of knowledge that enlightens us to this reality is among the most fatal mistakes we can make as a life form. An inspection of this current landscape, through the myopic lens of collective parochial power and control group think, is not an answer for this example of evolutionary complexity. As learning about the cosmos is perhaps the most meaningful learning experience humans will ever encounter, we are reminded that this fully qualifies as one of Robin Hanson's Great Filters.

The implications of an EGA or EGR from beyond Earth will be far reaching. Humankind currently possesses no globally conscious cosmic awareness that allows for a social/cultural development to where ETI does exist, at least in situ. Awareness has been at least hinted at us in the entertainment realm through the lenses of the protagonists and antagonists, but not as a meaningful motif included in the script that pertains to the inhabitant's day-to-day lives. The consumers of this entertainment, therefore, do not engage with any level of awareness as it is not scripted into the story and because there is no existing anchor of an awareness form and substance within the viewer.

A 2014 study conducted by experimental neuropsychologist Gabriel De La Torre identified space, time, and technology as physical factors, and psycho social and physiological factors that affect this awareness to cosmic consciousness. The study concluded that many factors contribute to this lack of awareness. These include a deficiency in space-related knowledge, different levels of self and global consciousness, religious beliefs and the "current modus vivendi" in our society today (De La Torre 2014, 582). Today's complex entanglement of a 'things' landscape is that reality. This quote from Alan Lightman supports my thesis on cosmic awareness, "Science has vastly expanded the scale of our cosmos, but our emotional reality is still limited by what we can <u>touch with our bodies</u> in the time span of our lives" ( 2013). This acutely correlates with our ancestor's creation of a mythological ritual culture as a direct response to their "inability to touch the sky" as I have noted.

I assert that space exploration is currently envisioned and busied to exploit dominions such as ownership and economic gain from space bodies and resources. This fantasy has been driven (flown?) from pseudoscience to a horizontal reality by imaginative thinkers and decision-makers who possess the financial accouterments to entertain this conversation. For more insight into this matter, I refer to the 1960 NASA publication *Proposed Studies on the Implications of Peaceful Space Activities for Human Affairs*; a.k.a. *The Brookings*

*Report* (1961). Contemporary thought has been shaped from this seminal publication. But still no plan of coordinated plan or action is yet known to exist.

What will ET say about what they see in the behaviors of some money-driven human beings in this situation from their perspective? A multidisciplinary focus will address this contingency by accepting consideration of expert knowledge from the many perspectives of human communities without interfering with bias or unbalanced influence from special interest or otherwise parochial group factions, in this example the monetary influences.

Would an ET announcement propel public opinion into a frenzy of wanting to ignore government directives and move in their own way? This is one possibility of what I call enduring global acknowledgment (EGA). An EGA could happen in several scenarios. ET could come down and directly introduce themselves. Another is in an enduring resolution to the ongoing disclosure controversy that exists between governments and society. A united governmental representation or a subset thereof could enlighten our society in many ways. I will elaborate on this enlightenment proposal later. Or is it possible that governmental authorities fear a usurping of power and control over its constituency?

Alternatively, perhaps another non-governmental body, such as a religious authority makes the announcement. Maybe the cumulative body of evidence propels the public away from governmental directives and into thinking into a ubiquitous acceptance and bypassing the other considered opinions. This option could help to explain the continued existence of the many UAP/ET public research communities. I have spoken of a "water drip effect" theory that may or may not be a conscious strategy by authorities to desensitize society to this acknowledgment in a gradual process. Because water drips have been continuously added to this "pool" for the better part of a century now, it is now full. A logical implication would be that the acknowledgment of ETI has already taken place for most people (Seland 2019; 2020).

The preceding reasons only consider announcement scenarios and do not address my relationships of an enduring nature (EGR). A conclusive determination to these manifestations of frenzy has not attained universal acceptance. To drive this ubiquitous state of acceptance requires more data, experimentation, and analysis. The wealth of the modern record and more ancient discoveries oblige this progress by documenting and figuratively "pouring new water into the pool of acknowledgment". My proposal suggests a call for further study in this area. Dissemination of a multidisciplinary plan protocol would significantly assist in defusing stress, tension, fear, and slow the torrent of societal denial that has combusted to the detriment of the world in which we live.

Another contingency addresses the doomsday scenario cult, its' lack of contributory reliable knowledge, and to which I extend this call for additional data collection, study, and analysis. Will the occurrence of an existential collective threat be the only possible motivation for us to unite and to protect ourselves both from that threat and each other? If this doomsday initiative was not threatening, but instead contained a benign or benevolent purpose, could and should we plan for proactive recognition of and/or for response contingencies?

Has our society already been preconditioned to accept the arrival of ET as a declaration of war? Many groups and institutions can be indicted for adoption of this ideology. Contributors include entertainment and mass media, government, military, academia, and their cohorts making the claim that ET does not exist. The ET portfolio mostly contains commentary to their overwhelmingly advanced intellect that is manifested in the presumption that they would destroy us, and because we are still here, that they do not exist. This anecdote is a fallacious strategy created by a less than rational reasoning. This confirmation bias is a ritual exercise of redundancy on an institutional level and often does not reflect a truthful reality. A multidisciplinary plan would help untangle this web of entanglement. Is the mental frequency all about conquering space or to immerse within it, a competition of perceived adversaries vs. coexistence and amity?

Does our modern perspective view of the cosmos compare, on any significant level, with that of our Neolithic ancestors? Is there any validity to comparing the cosmos as our modern agrios that included extraterrestrial intelligence to our ancestors' agrios of the animal world of the Neolithic?

The possibility for communication barriers to occur in any contact scenario with "the other" provides a real challenge to acknowledgment and understanding. This language conundrum has been a popular theme in the entertainment industry. As is often the case, inspiration for the invention of new technological "things" and chosen career paths comes from people's insights while watching their favorite science fiction installments as children. The 2016 movie *Arrival* is a good example to where many different story lines, besides the inability to talk with each other, and one that could be present within a real contact scenario, are addressed. Among these lines include the omnipresent sociopolitical, military and emotional human-interest subplots. There has been no difference in creative representation of human frailties and societal faults in the movie industry since the modern age of ET began in the 1940's. The 1951 classic movie *The Day The Earth Stood Still* offers a good case in point.

We may find it difficult to understand an ET intelligence that does not use thought mechanisms of pattern search and/or cycles, and syntactic meaning in a manner like we do. An in-situ search for common means of communication would be counterproductive and present a real possibility for misunderstandings that could escalate into a combative interaction. A pre-established plan derived from simulation analysis and foundational knowledge could effectively and proactively integrate much expertise and insight into a real-time situation and potentially defuse an otherwise apocalyptic scenario. Perhaps inspiration and this foundational knowledge could be learned from a dedicated study to more effectively comprehend and utilize a communication process with our animal cohorts. The strategy would embody a parallel study approach in that, if we were dealing with and learning from a more intelligent ET, then our learned knowledge from a less intelligent animal kingdom would be an initiative offered from a great new perspective. The learning could be transformational for both us and the "other," i.e., animals as well as ETI, as all of us would become new cohorts in life and our natures.

Could we do better to study "the other" by effectively utilizing a purely exploratory, open-minded, accepting, unbiased, unprejudiced, decompartmentalized intelligence model? To summarize, a multidisciplinary approach to planning for a future with alien intelligence effectively maneuvers through this 'great filter' for the advancement of our species. By reconciling any challenges with the anthropocentric and parochial ideologies inherent within any claim made from a less than rational logic by extracting each's best features and melding them into a new comprehensive methodology, you get the best of all worlds. This new methodology considers situational characteristics that recognize the influences of the physical, social/biological, and abstract nature on the scenario. It is both the physical environment and the thoughts, attitudes, cues, behaviors, and cognitive intelligence of the sentient thinking actors in the story that drives both its existence and the story's resolution.

These realities mandate the creation of a plan whose contributions of intelligence from all the disciplines of human thought will guide us into a more holistic, benevolent, responsive eco-centric reality. A multidisciplinary approach addresses the shortcomings inherent within the narrowly focused tendencies of some research communities. A more comprehensive and collective approach can offer an open-minded opportunity to examine hidden and ignored knowledge, perceive, reason, assess, and reflect on alternative possibilities from these inclusions. Our limited intelligence about what can constitute life currently offers a spurious thesis through use of an excessively stringent definition. This rigid position is prone to harboring the oversight of other potentials. Rejection of known evidence and ignorance to unknown evidence suggest that one of Robin Hanson's existential filters may exist within us.

My prior title in *The Humaniverse Guide ®* series, *Will ET Talk With Us?* contains prolonged and in-depth discussion of these topics and addresses the underlying premises of a 'proof of concept' thesis that a comprehensive plan of action for a future with ET be designed and undertaken immediately. This reference will enhance your understanding of the history, rationale, feasibility, and factors that populate this proof of concept.

The ETI thesis is far more expansive than allowing for parochial agendas of categorical denial as suggested by Carl Sagan, "absence of evidence is not evidence of absence"(1995). The Brookings Institution Report of 1961 seems to agree that leadership could stand to benefit by rejecting this agenda in many ways:

The degree of political or social repercussion would probably depend on leadership's interpretation of its own role, threats to that role, and opportunities to take advantage of the disruption or reinforcement of the attitudes and values of others. It would be most advantageous (for leadership) to have more to go on than personal opinions about the opinions of the public (Brookings Institution 1961, 103).

J. Allen Hynek, professor of astronomy and lead researcher of Air Force Project Blue Book in the 1950s and 60s, himself a converted skeptic, refutes those spokespeople that use ridicule and rebuff in their denial arguments:

Ridicule is not part of the scientific method, and people should not be taught that is. The steady flow of reports (ETI), often made in concert by reliable observers, raises questions of scientific obligation and responsibility. Is there *any* residue that is worthy of scientific attention? Or if there isn't, does not an obligation exist to say so to the public-not in words of open ridicule but seriously, to keep faith with the trust the public places in science and scientists (Clarke 1998, 305).

A researcher for the Search For Extraterrestrial Intelligence (SETI) and science professor, the late Allen Tough, compiled a lengthy catalogue of "What We Can Do Now" strategies and simulations. His design was purposed to support beneficial endpoints from contact, interaction and relationships with ETI through a comprehensive and rigorous academic curriculum for undergraduate and graduate study using a multidisciplinary approach. Academic oversight and dedicated research facilities, all of which will require continuing fiscal capability and effectiveness, would come from the creation of an academic professional association (Tough 1986).

A multidisciplinary involvement will also erode the anthropocentric ideologies that permeate human thought, attitude, and behavior. How will it exist post-I EGA/EGR? When new discoveries are made, they chip away at the armor that is our anthropocentrism, as they did with Einstein, Tesla, Galileo, and Copernicus. These are the revolutions philosopher Thomas Kuhn was referring to the paradigms of science communities (Kuhn 1962). If one makes an honest, rigorous examination of all social community behavior sets, this condition of anthropocentrism, as well as the politics of the power and control mechanism will be identifiable and probably predominant. Instead of falling into this web of entanglement, might it be better to view any changes to the anthropocentrism behavior intelligence as a re calibration instead of a feared and predicted destruction? Authors Jack Cohen and Ian Stewart point out that because of our present mindset; we cannot currently make predictions about ETI behavior. This anthropocentric frame of reference limits our capability to analyze other advanced civilizations, especially those more advanced than us:

First contact could happen any time…Don't hold your breath, though. The aliens will have evolved somewhere incredibly unpleasant to us, will resemble nothing we have yet conceived, will behave in incomprehensible ways, will use technology we don't understand, and will communicate in a manner that we've never thought of, and which we can't even recognize as communication. They will be here for reasons that make no sense to us, and they probably won't find humans the least bit interesting. We will find it almost impossible to understand them.(Cohen and Stewart 2002).

More detailed analysis of Allen Tough's, Jack Cohen's and Ian Stewart's models is referenced in my title *The Humaniverse Guide to First Contact With ET.*

\* \* \*

I've offered, for your contemplation, pragmatic looks at how the human condition for Nam and Muh were shaped by practical applications of intellectual and external material advancements to their culture and their environments of the lower world, living world and upper world. These three ancient cardinal directions of existence provided a basis for their creation and application of The Great Chain of Being. All were alive, vibrant, interconnected, and devotional. What their minds and thoughts reasoned to accomplish from this nature was a lasting life in the place they called home. Many factors influenced this path of accomplishment and failure, as variables present in My Algorithm of Humankind. As mathematical inquiry dictates, a change in any one variable changes the equation's result. The results of $\Sigma T$; the sum of the algorithm, would have been different if the value of $T_1$; who we were, turned out different.

We know that they were devoted to maintaining an equilibrium among all three vertical directions of existence. The functionality of Nam and Muh's human condition was also expressed as the four geophysical cardinal directions of north, east, south, and west. To many, the cycle of birth and death were mirror reflections of the lower world and upper world and governed respectively, in large part by their actions in the living world. This was their mind's version of mathematics and destiny.

What Nam and Muh observed coming from both vertical worlds were many life forms that did not look or act like them and meaningfully affected the course of their lives. We benefit today from this by communicating to us their observations, interactions, and their far-reaching interpretations.

The attitude, intention of and behavioral response to many of these interfaces, including super powerful beings from the extraterrestrial realm, held the power to do things for them they could otherwise not accomplish. These keys to life were encouraged and celebrated by their people through socialized strategies of repetitive and rigidly enacted ritual cults for relief from stress, tension and fear and as human power and control tactics. They were response tools of strategy expressed through the ritual cult, that competed against and reasoned with the cataclysm of the day. These activities were manifested through a mythological creation of being that gave form, substance, and style to their otherwise untouchable adversaries. For activities that included ETI, such a cognitive pathway was not necessary as there existed a real potential to "touch" or be in physical proximity of them. A paradox to consider here embodies a process where we will uncover irrefutable evidence that some of the ETs that interacted with Nam and Muh's people were really humans from our future.

While Nam and Muh won the competition against the wild animal natural environmental agrios, their newly adopted urbanized world simultaneously became faced with waging a new one; between themselves. And there were still many competitive existences they could not control, including those with mother nature and those that involved other beings and superpowers. Resolution to the dilemma these super powerful beings posed, consequently, became predominately an intellectual challenge that was dealt with by engaging in a competition that included utilization of mindful abstractions rather than just spear tips.

The story about our ancients is still being written. A most exciting feature of the nature of any investigation like this is being able to consider that we still have much to discover and learn. First, though, we must thank Nam and Muh for giving us the means to obtain what we have thus far and will obtain further down this road. However, much more of what was told to us about their histories remains undiscovered and untranslated. It is partly because of this that I tell you only the film on the window to this hidden universe of understanding has been removed for us to even peek at what lies beyond. The underworld, the living world, and the upper world are still there teeming with life waiting for us to rediscover. Armed with more pragmatic understanding than Nam and Muh could see, touch, feel, and comprehend, the book of their future, our history, is there free for the instruction. You should throw open this window and place your signature stamp on the akashic record. *Akasha* is a Sanskrit word from Hindu cosmology that literally means "ether and sky" and is believed to exist in a fluid state outside the three-dimensional cosmic plane, inaccessible to empirical inspection, for now.

What will be the agents of change, the cause of a shift in our species' perspective that allows for acceptance of a reason, rational universal perspective on the existence of intelligent life or originating from outside Earth. Do they contain global initiatives? Should we compel ourselves to update our view of the world and how it operates to separate from a manifest of power, control, and runaway competition in its present form; a continual fight against our agrios, the wild of the environment and ourselves? Should we relocate our human condition to an empirical ethical recognition of harmony, equilibrium and balance that exists, in resolution to the dilemmas posed the behavior of natural matter in Edward Lorenz', *Theory of Chaos* or Lord Kelvin's, *Second Law of Thermodynamics*? Is there a higher level of cosmic equilibrium that exists but to which we are not aware of or can comprehend?

We know that the Octet Rule in chemistry applies to all atoms who naturally seek to fill their outer electron valence shell and cure their electronegative "chaos" and randomness, usually through molecular sharing to chase a preferred state of equilibrium and harmony. Another refers to the seemingly natural economic behavior of supply and demand for "things." Applying this view of nature in a thought experiment, does chaos and randomness ubiquitously move toward equilibrium? Does this theory contain lasting potential for our future? Data samples for analysis in this experiment include the reality of say, the act of competing with the actions of others on the road, at work, or in most of any human community. Group politics are present in any social setting as defined by our psychological constitution. We seem to embrace the agrios today as a tool of observational surveillance of other people's wild attitude-behavior mindsets in their daily lives with which we compete in exercises of power and control cycles.

Does ETI already possess this understanding, many having matured through the Great Filters, being older and wiser than us? We may not be ready yet for ETI to extend an invitation to join their galactic club because we don't recognize our global similarities as a species. We view our other human communities as enemies to be conquered, adversaries to out compete, or just trade partners to be commoditized and exploited ($$$). Like the tree that manufactures oxygen for us to breathe, The Great Chain of Being includes the capacity for humans, no matter their origin, phenotype, or perceptual critique of their fellow humans, to cure, heal and save the lives of their brethren through biological intervention like the sharing of blood, organs, etc. Yet, we do not reflect upon either protocol in these life ways but more like a commodity of utilitarian pursuit. If you subscribe to the notion that the "others" are observing us, you may suspect they already are aware of our actions in this area of social behavior. The evidence, the validity of which extends far beyond anecdotal, shows that there have been uncounted reports, by a large population of credible, trained professional witnesses from every human community, of a keen interest in our nuclear things since the Hiroshima and Nagasaki human communities were obliterated in 1945.

I restate this state of behavior in another way. Here is a large reason the world government, civic, and religious communities should disclose all their knowledge about ET to help motivate and bring together all of humankind. Our species has not yet seen a time when all humankind was one collective. Instead, we have continued to war and compete on all levels, thus being unable to recognize and promote our species as one. Maybe this has been because our behaviors prevent us from being aware or denying a larger life landscape environment than the little planet Earth. Access to this knowledge about intelligent beings from outside Earth is the catalyst required for us to begin thinking of ourselves as a species instead of just hundreds of fractured, segmented and segregated sociopolitical factions that promote the malevolence agenda.

Perhaps inspiration will come from what is written in the akashic record about a core nature and purpose to life, to which we don't even realize but may yet discover already exists in our minds. Please accept this quote from French archaeologist and paleontologist André Leroi-Gourhan as your own:

The point is that, for a good billion years or so, certain living beings have been engaged in a search for conscious contact. The whole of evolution boils down to this search. All spirituality and all philosophical and scientific exploration are the end goal of the same search for contact, which is governed by the mind. At all levels such contact is achieved through the two coordinated structures of the body and the nervous system. (Leroi-Gourhan 1993, 59)

Perhaps we could reflect on the quote from Nikola Tesla and choose to make this our own, too.

*We are all one. Only egos, beliefs, and fears separate us.*

Our divisions are illusions. We are all connected - Nam, Muh, us, the extraterrestrial. This idea could lead to a more harmonious understanding of the three worlds - the lower, living and upper worlds.

The story so far to this world...

...opens finding you and I tasked in our day with many stresses and hopes on our minds; a never-ending roller coaster of travail, tension, and optimism in the search for food, adapting to this rapidly changing eco-world, and experiencing a new mindset of social urbanization.

The end?

Or the beginning.

*References*

Brookings Institution. 1961. *Proposed Studies on the Implications of Peaceful Space Activities for Human Affairs.* RRO.org (Beau, Jerome). Retrieved December 2, 2024.

Clarke, Jerome. 1998. "What Is Science?" In *The UFO Book: Encyclopedia of the Extraterrestrial*, Detroit, MI: Visible Ink Press. ISBN 1-57859-029-9.

Cohen, J. and I. Stewart. 2002. *Evolving the Alien: The Science of Extraterrestrial Life.* United Kingdom: Ebury Press.

De La Torre, Gabriel. 2014. "Toward a New Cosmic Consciousness: Psycho educational Aspects of Contact with Extraterrestrial Civilizations." *Acta Astronautica* 94 (2): 577–583.

Leroi-Gourhan, André. 1993. *Gesture and Speech.* Boston, MA: Massachusetts Institute of Technology.

Hellman, Hal. 1998. *Great Feuds in Science: Ten of the Liveliest Disputes Ever.* New York: Wiley.

Hodder, Ian. 2018. *Where Are We Heading? The Evolution of Humans and Things.* New Haven, CT: Yale University Press.

Kuhn, Thomas. 1962. *The Structure of Scientific Revolutions.* Chicago, Il.:

University of Chicago Press.

Lightman, Alan. 2013. *The Accidental Universe: The World You Thought You Knew*. New York: Pantheon Books.

Merriam-Webster, n.d. "Anthropocentrism," Merriam-Webster.com Dictionary. Accessed January 3, 2025, *https://www.merriam-webster.com/dictionary/anthropocentrism*.

Renfrew, Colin. 2001. "Symbol before Concept: Material Engagement and the Early Development of Society." In *Archaeological Theory Today*, edited by Ian Hodder, 122–40. Malden, MA: Blackwell.

Sagan, Carl. 1995. *The Demon-Haunted World: Science as a Candle in the Dark*. New York: Random House.

Seland, Keith A. 2019. *The Humaniverse Guide to Better Reasoning and Decision Making*. New Jersey: Newman Springs Publishing.

Seland, Keith A. 2020. *The Humaniverse Guide to First Contact With ET*. New Jersey: Newman Springs Publishing.

Tough, Allen. 1986. What Role Will Extraterrestrials Play in Humanity's Future? *Journal of the British Interplanetary Society* 39: 491-498.

# About the Author

This title is part of an ongoing series within The Humaniverse Guide ® platform. These titles include: The Humaniverse Guide To Better Reasoning and Decision Making, The Humaniverse Guide to First Contact With ET, and The Humaniverse Guide: Will ET Talk With Us?

Keith A. Seland is an international research anthropologist, futurist and Ufologist. He is also the publisher of the education platform known as 'The Humaniverse Guide'. 'The Humaniverse Guide' is a registered trademark owned by Keith A. Seland and THG Authors Incorporated.

All titles, as well as future title updates in The Humaniverse Guide series, will be available on Keith's, The Humaniverse education platform. All of Keith's works on this platform universe can be accessed from searching the digital keyword, 'The Humaniverse'. This includes Keith's website and all media.

You can enjoy and learn on any of Keith's other platforms, including his YouTube channel, Keith Seland The Humaniverse - YouTube , social media, and his frequent public speaking engagements. Please refer to these platforms for updated information on his speaking schedules.

Enjoy!

**You can connect with me on:**

🌐 https://thehumaniverse.org
📘 https://www.facebook.com/keith.allan.565681

**Subscribe to my newsletter:**

✉ https://thehumaniverse.org

www.ingramcontent.com/pod-product-compliance
Lightning Source LLC
Chambersburg PA
CBHW020455030426
42337CB00011B/123